Amylou

Amylou

ROBERT MEYER

Library of Congress Control Number: 2025905438

ISBN: 979-8-89228-530-8   (Paperback)
ISBN: 979-8-89228-532-2   (Hardcover)
ISBN: 979-8-89228-531-5   (eBook)

Printed in the United States of America

Contents

*A*ll right, fellas! "All right, fellas! That's a wrap. Bring it on in!" Bob shouted to his young charges. "Good practice, guys," he asserted, clapping his hands. "We're ready for M.V. tomorrow. Bring your jacket, K.B. We'll roll at five o'clock."

As they filed past him toward their individual cars, Bob smiled, grateful to be standing so near those former members of his Little League team—the ones who'd brought him so much joy six years earlier. The ones he'd stayed in contact with throughout his miserable tenure in Thurman. How many times, he wondered, had they woken him from his anguish there, knocking upon the lid of that veritable coffin, beckoning him up off the puke-green couch? Inviting him, as it were, to convene with both his past and future by drawing his beaten self nearer to the likes of "Crazy Rusty," "Cralt," blue bandanas, backward baseball caps, tobacco spit, Budweiser bottles. His "boys," these careless, shortsighted ones who'd never allow him to die alone. If it weren't for them, man...

He bent to remove the bases from their inserts, nearly toppling over headfirst at the sound of a blaring horn an instant later. He turned and smiled at the sight of the '98 Topaz approaching him, unaware of the detachment that mirrored his gaze, affixed as his senses were to the gorgeous yellow curls, the fathomless blue eyes.

"Amy Lou!" he shouted as she braked the car to a stop.

He stood motionless as she opened the car door, shuddered as she set first one, then the other bronzed leg upon the ground—then felt his own feet in motion at the sight of her rising from that station.

"Damn," he whispered aloud. "Somebody pinch me."

He forgot about the sweat clinging to his forehead and chest and embraced her, pressing his fingers firmly into the small of her tensing back, finding her lips with his own.

"Get a room," Rusty shouted amid the sound of whistles and laughter.

He felt her slip from his grasp, heard her playful plea: "Please go take a shower."

He heard his own breathless reply: "Only if you'll join me."

Man, it just seemed different somehow today, he observed, winding his fingers around hers as they walked off—so natural, this union of him, her, and the Andrews baseball team.

"Hell," he asked himself as his feet stepped upon home plate, "who needed anything else?"

She had come to him months earlier in a manner that might have occurred only in a dream. Years after that last unplanned meeting at the Tap, his less-than-halfhearted application to the Indiana Department of Human Services became the medium that reunited the talented twenty-six-year-old administrator and the underachieving thirty-two-year-old miserable waiter.

Yes, he waited glumly on that most unlikely morning, wearing his frayed Dockers, scuffed Payless shoes, and mismatched sweater, for the opportunity to find a job in an unrewarding, low-paying, "babysitting" position. He was already envisioning some rude twenty-something girl ordering him around when he felt someone approaching him.

"What the hell?" his mind had called out, focusing on the perfect figure approaching him.

"It can't be," they told his eyes. *"You're tripping, dude—look again, square this up, homes."*

"Hi, I'm Amy," he heard as the hand before him reached for him, taunting him.

"I know!" he shouted as the angelic face before him was replaced by a perplexed look, visited by a fleeting trace of recognition, hidden by either fear or confusion.

He followed her without hesitation, let her lead him on, eyes fixed upon her—talking to those enticing hips, as it were.

"Remember when you and Jenny lived in Holmgren your freshman year? You sent me those roses the day after we met," he chuckled. "Valentine's Day. Man, that's one holiday that'll never be the same for me. Best times of my life, best weekend I'll ever have, tremendous memories. f it weren't for you…"

She held the door open for him, temporarily ending his speech.

"Thank you," he said, looking through the glass at the nameplate on her desk.

He did not pause to reflect on the memories of that long-ago liaison, did not make obvious the fact that he'd come to equate her image with bitterness and regret as he looked upon her breasts.

"I've never forgotten you. Lot of nights here when I couldn't sleep, flooded my consciousness with visions of you, letting all the rest of the B.S. fade. Damn, I'd be asleep in minutes, dreaming of magical, sparkling lakes, golden sunsets…"

He'd never told anyone this; only his personal God was awestruck at the galvanic effect she had on him now.

He could feel himself swaying beneath the weight of the same turbulent waves of the aforementioned lakes in his slumber, watching her silent, shocked face stare through the papers in her hands.

"I remember you now," he'd heard her whisper—but could vividly relive the inflection of the same.

The labored interview questions she immediately launched into would have no impact, could not reach his mind deep within UNEI's 302 Holmgren.

"What the hell is this?" Amy asked herself as she recited Question #19 to the blank, placid face, her pencil having listlessly recorded his vague, distant answers. The painful alienation revisited her, this friggin' gaping chasm she could not fill up... How did this come back and find her? She sighed silently after asking the final question.

"Yeah, I really don't know what I would do," was his answer.

I believe that you wouldn't, she thought to herself. Aloud, she stated, "Okay, well, that's all the questions I have, Bob. Do you have any questions for me?"

"No, I just wanna say how damn good it is to see you again. Man...."

She smiled wanly and walked to the door, excusing herself as she stepped out. "Take care of yourself. Thanks for coming in."

He sat in the chair until he was certain the feeling had returned to his legs. The twenty minutes of excitedly pressing his toes into the floor had numbed them, the static contraction of his calves making movement difficult now. He slowly rose to his feet and hobbled out in blissful disbelief, her mere presence awakening long-dormant hope inside him.

"How could I have dared to believe any of this?" he asked himself when he finally reached his car. "Look what followed me home," he sang softly.

Man, this will be different, he thought after quickly surveying the most significant categories of his life, assessing how her nearness would impact each.

"She's probably living with someone," he muttered, his exhilaration temporarily waning when he reached the mental file he'd labeled "social." He began to curse the whirlwind of fate that had placed her in his backyard. Like a UFO landing. "It's just so damn unbelievable."

Upon catching a glimpse of his confused face in the rearview, he flashed himself a silver-capped smile.

"C'mon, boy," he chided himself. "Let's go."

He placed the car in reverse and backed out of the drive. Pressing his fingers to his lips after shifting into D, he sent Amy an imaginary kiss.

"Lord, she has to understand that it will be too tempting for me to have her so near. I'll have to call. She's got to know I'll pay any price to sustain even the weakest bonds," he assured himself, his mind now drifting to the video wherein the old guy is wandering through the town where he'd met his boyhood love.

"Has anybody seen Amy?" the youthful singers inquire in the background.

"Why, yes, I have!" Bob replied. "Yes, I have."

Page 449—*Alcohclics Anonymous*, about acceptance— he reminded himself as he signaled to enter the mall parking lot. Destiny. No fluke. No way. Take your medicine, punk.

His stomach stirred as he pulled into the parking space, his mind now whirring amidst the barrage of golden and blue colors shining. He whisked himself quickly toward Taco Bell.

"Can I help you?" the fair-haired teen inquired.

"Yeah, a combo platter and a medium Coke, please," he responded, shifting his weight from one foot to the other. "Gotta put out the fire," he whispered. Regain my bearings.

Something is going down that I can't quite decipher.

Wow...

It would have been the first place she'd have hurried to on this Friday, she thought; she needed such a venue to resuscitate her waning spirits. That Ron had called for her to meet him there made such a destination even more viable. The urgency in his voice was so compelling, so urging, she cursed—4.0 GPA, the honor grad for the whole department. Attained all society expected of an Indiana girl and then some, studying amidst a barrage of phone calls from farm boys begging her to give 'em a chance and go out with them.

Challenges met, obligations fulfilled—wasn't that what life was supposed to be about?

Then why this empty despair, mirroring her every step? This was not right, not fair.

Oh well, being with Ron should stimulate me, she surmised, envisioning the tall, hulking figure behind the bar at Matt's, her pace increasing now with each step.

Twenty feet from the door, she nearly stopped abruptly, the sight of the man she'd interviewed earlier disturbing her.

"God," she whispered. "Hope he doesn't see me. Look at that goofy smile," she implored herself, cap pulled low over his eyes, that exaggerated swagger. "As if he'd known me his entire life, took liberties with me, bludgeoning me with memories of wrongdoings made by a heinous teenager in a strange place. Well, forget you, baldy! I'm all grown up now."

"Amy!" she heard his cry ring out.

She felt her fists clench and unclench and envisioned herself giving him hell—smiling at him in the process. "What're you up to?"

She forced herself to remain locked on his face with her squinting eyes. *Be professional, poised,* she reminded herself.

"I'm meeting a friend at Matt's. Would you like to join us?"

"Yeah, uh, yes, I would. Let me throw this food in the car, okay?" she heard him respond.

She nodded silently, without effort.

He walked casually by his own assessment. What he wanted to do was break out in a full sprint in either direction. Opportunity in the form of that pretty thing behind was knocking so damn loud he couldn't think clearly.

"Amy Lou, how do you do?" he asked—a ridiculous monologue, engaged in by a man gasping for air.

"I need to lay down," he thought when he opened the far door. "She'll be there when I get back. Yeah, that's the idea."

In a moment, he was jogging ridiculously back toward the mall. He stopped to let a car pass before him. *Calm your hormones, boy. Ain't that what she'd ordered him to do in Holmgren? Yeah, I see you, little Amy, showing me your back. Uh-huh, you ain't getting away. Not this time,* he whispered as his hand met the door.

He walked right up behind her, placed his hands upon her waist, nearly stumbling in the process. "You ready?"

"Yes," she replied, turning sharply on her heel.

He followed her into the darkness of the bar, feeling an eerie sense of rebirth within the haze and neon.

"Something about her, man," he mouthed to the unresponsive patrons at the trough.

He pulled out her chair when she set her purse upon the corner table, again finding "Crazy Lou" within his actions, helping Cherry Holmes into her coat.

Focus, dummy! You've got another chance, a blown two-strike call by the ump. Don't 'K' this time, he demanded of the walls.

"Hi, welcome to Matt's," the waitress announced as she placed the coasters on the table. "What can I get you?"

Bob thought to himself, *You can get me out of here,* as he reached for his wallet. His voice instead uttered, "Coke for me."

"Bud Light, please," his "date" countered, scanning the room, her eyes narrowed as she peered—hatred spilling over from the top of the pretty vessel.

Suddenly at ease, he began to speak, attempting to hide his shame at being placed in such an awkward predicament by a female adversary.

"What've you been up to since leaving Younkers?"

"I was working at Queens right after graduation at an emergency shelter before I came here."

"What made you come up here?"

"It was a better opportunity—more freedom and benefits."

"Do you miss home?"

"A little. I miss seeing my family every day. What about you? What do you do, other than work around here?"

"Not much. It sucks. If it weren't for these kids I used to coach..."

"Do you have a girlfriend? Do you have any prospects?" She grinned.

Bob sighed. "Nah, nothing's going on there. How about you?"

"I was engaged, but..."

"I'm sorry."

"It's all right. I broke it off. We're still friends."

"What's he say to you?"

"We don't talk much when we're together," she said, smiling.

"I hear ya. I remember when I first laid these eyes on you at Sir John's. That dress you were wearing. Man! I had to talk to you, didn't give a damn what you'd say. Then when you got closer... wow! I wanted to play it safe not get my hopes up, especially with all those rich dudes surrounding you—all those guys literally hitting you up to get your phone number." He chuckled. "Why the hell did you ask for mine?"

Amy shrugged.

"Even after I gave it to ya, I wouldn't let myself believe you'd call. No way I'd have dreamt the next day I'd be walking hand in hand with you at the mall, all those jealous punks staring, thinking it should have been them instead.

"Back then, though, trouble was I felt overmatched. Especially the next day—Valentine's Day—when you sent me the roses. Dang! It was too late. And then in your room later that night..."

"This ain't 1989," she angrily interjected. "I wouldn't touch you on a dare now. Some of us have a future. You really need to get a life!"

"Yeah," he countered, emboldened somehow at eliciting such passion within the seething Dutch girl. "Well, big deal. I got hung up on your little bony ass. I told you I was screwed up the day we met, warned you off. You should've paid attention to what I was telling you. I gave you an out, but you didn't take it. Now you're on my mind every damn day. Years after I touched you, saw you, talked with you. I'm a train wreck. No one or nothing else now measures up to *my* Amy. And I've been trying to get a life. My stupid job ain't going to get it done. Serving eggs... what a bunch of crap! I've seen hundreds of women like you, but could no more shake your memory than I could get away with drinking that beer you have in your hands."

Amy watched the veins throb in his temple, heard the voice strain, face pale, and opted to throw him off stride, summoning the will to resist lashing out.

"I understand, I do," she began in a somber tone. "It's all I can do to drag myself into work each day. I just can't seem to believe in anything, anyone, anymore."

She lifted her drink to her lips, scanned his easing expression, then proceeded to seize the momentum.

"You see," she spoke into his attentive brown eyes, "I've been in a position where I've had the opportunity to view the steady, slow ascent of dozens of young people. Most of them have had a rough start at life, yet they have valiantly scaled the wall to the top, so to speak, finding happiness, affixing themselves against the hard, jagged cliff, never looking down. Smiling even now."

She reached again for her drink, the long, languishing pull she took from the bottle mocking his helplessness, his inability.

No, he'd not be allowed to duplicate the feat, nor could he become the bottle, and he would never taste her lips in such an inspiring fashion, she mused. *Ain't that a shame.*

"Then these same climbers would abandon the chase in their haste to convene with the siren calling to them from the flat wasteland below. There they'd be exploited, stored like produce, waiting to be devoured—decaying corpses stacked up before their captors, catching bullets not designed for them. Beaten from conception, surrounded by those who don't care, what choice do they have?

"Of course, they align themselves with this certain unfortunate destiny. They try hard, against this background, to impede the perpetuation of the same—through rubbers, pills to ensure they don't sentence another to a similar hell, fighting intimacy. Love. The worst type of back-alley mugging for 'em, an ambush leaving 'em immobilized in a heap, gasping for air."

Again, she paused, ensuring her words had disarmed him, reduced his anger to rubble, emasculating him. He seemed to be in a trance-like state, eyes looking past the tears on her cheek to the neon glow of the Bud sign.

"Gotcha," Amy whispered into the bottle.

In truth, the tears had taken away his edge, destroying his passion for the present, locking him back within Holmgren with the ghost of an adolescent, flaxen-haired blonde, blotching the letter addressed to him. That message was embellished with a photo of a solitary, inquisitive feline, conveying to him her anger at the aloof fashion in which he'd initially responded to her.

There was pain, she'd told him, in being surrounded by those who give love but don't love *me*—loneliness and a truth that hurts, the residue of opportunities slipping through her fingers. *All she wanted, gosh damn it, was for someone to say that they cared.*

Oh man, that note had messed him up. He could still see the words, elegantly written phrases not slammed shut by a period but rather slowed by often-presented three dots... thus ensuring the words would drift deep into his consciousness, forever attacking him.

What was her angle, he wondered now? What penalty did she want to throw upon him then?

The guilt did get to him—her inquiry as to how he could have just turned from her, never looking back as she reached out, calling his name, making him feel terrible then. That latter phrase was nothing, however, compared to her assertion that her friendship was *"not something that he could turn from and leave behind."*

Cruel, prescient irony, reducing him to nothing.

A friend is a forever thing, she'd inscribed above the kitten, the statement kicking him in the groin, time and again, as he reflected within the box of skepticism upon the "pitch" he'd just missed on that day.

Habit, that's what prevailed upon him, he thought. *Behind in the count, his whole damn life, never getting his pitch, always flailing defensively at the 0-2, the 1-2.* How the hell was he to react to the hanging curve represented by *Ms. Amy, age eighteen, gorgeous and lonely?*

Of course, he couldn't pull the trigger—that is, until it was too damn late. The feeble "fly ball" his hesitant efforts produced became his metaphorical gift to his world.

A wasted at-bat, he thought to himself as he stretched his arms above his head, waking from his slumber in time to hear her address the event that had forever absolved her of wrongdoing.

He reached reflexively for her hand, guided her gently up and out of her chair.

"I'm sorry," she whispered repeatedly as they made their trek from the bar to the parking lot.

"It's all right," he assured her as he caressed her hand with his, slightly ashamed, even, at the arousal the reunion produced within him.

"Where's your car, buddy?" he asked as he held the mall door open with one hand, the other pressing gently against her back.

He retained this stance as she led him to her car, held fast even as he turned the key in the lock.

There was something within the vulnerability that fired him up, made him want to once again palm that seductive body, to pull her atop him.

He was almost relieved to see that the tears had dried and her professional demeanor had been regained.

Still, he was compelled to ensure he'd not lose sight of her again or get caught up in that parade of unanswered phone calls, saying *"Sorry, wrong number"* to her rich boyfriends, or—every time some pretty, blonde country girl turned his head—to ask, *"Can I spend tonight with you?"*

He offered weakly, "Damn it," then chastised himself aloud.

As she opened the door, she thought about his question, feeling herself weakened—seeing the soft snow falling outside Holmgren, a stranger's hands brushing the tresses from her tears, sincere, reassuring prose filling her ears.

To hell with that, she countered, as the image rapidly faded. That was years ago.

"We're not sleeping together, Bob."

"That's cool," he said, biting his lip. "I just don't want to let you get away."

At that moment, his soul whispered, *I love you*, as his mind shrieked, *Oh no!*

"C'mon then," she said.

He slid haltingly beside her, felt his mind drift as the key in the lock unleashed the soft voice of Sade from the stereo.

Lost in *Sweetest Taboo*, he reclined, eyes closed.

"If I tell you... if I tell you how I feel... will you keep on lovin' me," he felt himself singing along.

He felt her press a slender finger atop his lips.

"Shhh," she whispered.

He closed his eyes again, allowed Sade to interpret what he was experiencing—to crush his denial.

Never felt this good before, this quiet storm, never felt this hot before... Giving me something...

"We're here," she suddenly shouted as she pulled up to the curb.

"Poltergeist!" he laughed, envisioning the blonde, brave, blue-eyed little girl locked in the television, as objects swirled about inexplicably.

Here indeed, he thought as he opened the door and stood up, his movements inadvertently intercepting her path from the front of the car to her house.

He reached out in the darkness for her hand, weaving in the dusk.

She left him whirling, spinning deftly from his grasp in her haste to enter the house, the curt separation somehow recalling the memory of a summer evening years earlier in the desert.

Shy-ass Maxine.

He could see her now, throwing his beer-drinking arm off her shoulder, leaving him to wind his own drunken path back to their barracks. She, like Amy, had done so without comment, without breaking stride, without pissing him off. Hell, she'd merely canceled his sodden request in the same fashion she coolly denied undeserving customers their requests for helicopter parts during the day.

Never shoved it back at him, even when goaded on by his own laughing roommate. Never acknowledged his misstep.

Maxine—that's who this little white girl resembled in comparison today.

Straight up pardoning him for yielding to his grasp onto that which was capable of being at once both comforting and prolific.

As he followed her up the steps, he could hear himself playfully declaring that he'd *"never even held the hand"* of the one they'd accused him of impregnating.

This fleeting touch tonight transcended any sensual impulse he'd felt before.

No, this was better—the area affected far above.

There would, he feared, be no predictable ebb to this type of surge.

The door opened onto a sparkling white carpet, and he thought he had better remove his boots.

"The place is so friggin' clean and orderly," he whistled softly, his eyes focused on the cards bearing messages of *love* and *congratulations* standing on her well-polished buffet.

A Bible stood nobly on a bookshelf next to a photo of her being presented a certificate by Governor Dempsey.

Only the thinnest smile was etched upon her face by the camera at what must have been a momentous occasion.

On an adjacent corner stood a pristine UNEI diploma, its royal purple and dazzling red exterior unblemished. Inserted into the corner of the document was a picture of Amy and a female classmate at their high school graduation.

The sight of the beaming eighteen-year-old face made his hands tremble.

It's those eyes, he thought to himself, summoning the will to look at the glowing orbs.

Her place, he concluded—smiling at the plaque bearing the phrase Lead, *Follow, or Get the Hell Out of the Way*—was a shrine to determination and faith.

He called to mind the disheveled state of his apartment, his own dusty diploma lying askew atop the television, displayed as bitter testimony to his disillusionment.

"This place looks great," he said as she opened the bedroom door.

She disappeared behind.

His eyes locked onto the stretch of thigh revealed beneath the pink shorts she wore beneath the matching button top.

"Hey, I appreciate you bringing me here tonight," he said. "You've got class."

She shrugged as she tossed him the remote control.

"Make yourself at home. I'm going to clean up."

She disappeared behind the bathroom door as he whispered, "Thanks."

His gaze fell upon the waterbed beyond the open bedroom door as he heard the spray of water splash against porcelain.

He imagined himself pressing her firmly against the frame—her moaning, writhing frame twisting beneath him, enveloping him further—the sweat matting the soft curls to her forehead as his tongue pierced her lips, the roar of the waves serenading him, goading him until...

"May as well go sleep with myself," he sighed as he hobbled to the couch. "I don't stand a chance in there."

He pulled himself deeply beneath the thick purple afghan draped over the firm back of the couch, pausing to place the throw pillows beneath his head with one hand, engaging the remote with the other.

He looked above him, listening to her bathe, melding with the coinciding print of a mountain towering over an icy lake, hearing the water splash against the rocks as he reclined in the soft grass—fighting sleep, waiting, giddily, for her naked frame to swim near him.

"Yeah, I love you, girl," he whispered to the young singer on the TV screen as he faded.

CLICK!

He woke with a start at the sound of the bathroom door being locked.

"What the hell?" he asked of the young woman before him.

"I ain't gonna try to jump ya, Amy," he said silently, shuddering at the memory of Marley repelling his foray as he squeezed her breasts, twisting from him, repeatedly pleading, *No, no, no...*

"Yes, yes, yes," he'd responded to her rapidly cooling, trembling body, pressing hard against her silky skin—all too angrily.

Too late, too damn bad, he heard his young voice assert.

What are you doing to me?

He shook his head at the unusual thought, grateful he'd not been prosecuted.

Marley knew better, though, he assured himself. She just wasn't thinking.

Amy was, though.

The little fox told him he couldn't get any loving.

So what?

At least he wouldn't waste all night worrying about it.

Wouldn't feel like less of a man for not trying.

His eyes closed for a full second before reopening—this most unlikely day drawing to a rapid, unspectacular close.

"Beats being alone," he assured himself as he dozed off.

What seemed like hours later, he became overwhelmed with the sensation of her lying near—met by the smell and taste of sweet, soft, blonde curls upon his chest.

He felt her hand clutching his, felt the warmth generated by the slender legs wrapped around his.

Was she asleep?

Hell, for that matter, was he?

He tried to hold still, to assess, but his body moved of its own accord, sabotaging him.

"I blew it," he whispered aloud. "Couldn't keep my hormones in check."

He mumbled as he felt along her soft yet tense back, pressing apart her legs with his needs as he did so.

"Shut up," he heard her reply as she pulled him closer.

"What's up with this?" he asked in disbelief, as his clumsy motions became lost within their elegant wake, transforming him—broadening his chest, adding thickness to his arms, hair to his head—as he pushed and pulled into oblivion.

His breathing became more pronounced and stable with each passing moment, confidence surging, sp lling over, lapping away at his angst as he inhaled—self-esteem restored twofold with each exhalation.

"Damnnnn!" he exclaimed repeatedly in awe, until the bliss borne of his effort ended his evening.

It would be morning before he became conscious of her presence again—the sparkling sunlight filling the room in tandem with the sound of running water, placing him immediately at ease.

Man, she loves bein' clean.

He smiled as he turned his head into the pillow, basking in the fact that nothing lay before him but an easy Saturday.

He rose when she opened the bathroom door, still wrapped in the blankets, the sight of her pretty frame filling him with the urge to embrace her.

His breath left immediately at the presentation of her in the white robe, the clinging garment enhancing the bronze ankles, the red lips. He could make out the shape of her elegant breasts beneath the cloth.

He was transfixed by the picture of her standing so near, so still.

It seemed to him that she wanted him to speak and was willing to allow him to gaze upon her in exchange for hearing him talk.

But still, he lay—longing, hoping—until his attention was broken by the rustling of the bright blue towel she held in her slender fingers.

"Damn," he sighed as his gaze shifted to the icy, squinting blue eyes. "I could just take a bite out of you," he whispered.

She averted her gaze in response.

"I'll drop you off at your car when I get dressed. Then I have to go to work," she stated as she opened the bedroom door.

"Yeah, sure," he replied.

She untied the cloth belt and pulled the robe from her bare frame.

I hate to lie, she lamented as she examined her body in the glass on the closet, but she assured herself it was either that or have him follow her all over today.

Yes, he wanted this badly, she told the mirror as she pulled the panties snug upon her waist.

"Bite me," she hissed as she looked out toward the adjoining room.

"I don't think so."

She set her bra on the pillow, then laid back, pondering on the bed, uncertain as to why she'd allowed him to set foot here at all.

Sure, it would be consistent with her vindictive intent to break him down, drawing him nearer, making the rejection that much more damaging, but... still...

There was something that compelled her to watch over him, to take satisfaction in seeing him smile in his sleep as he turned lazily upon her couch.

"Damn it anyway," she swore as she snapped on her bra.

What am I doing stringing this jerk along? Should just go out there now and tell him to go away, or else... else... I'll call Ron and his buddies over, have 'em beat on him.

Yes, that's it—walk out there, naked, climb on top of him, rub myself all over him, then tell him.

That'd kill him.

She smiled as she readied for the door.

Hell, why not, she asked, staring at his head.

She reconsidered when he turned toward her and stepped gracefully out of view.

"No, not yet," she stated as she slipped on her blouse

This can all wait. I'll think it over this afternoon.

"Damn it, anyway," she cursed as she slipped on her slacks and walked out the door.

"All set, let's go," she ordered him.

He rapidly pulled up his own slacks and, rubbing his eyes, strode gingerly to the door.

"What's wrong with your leg?" she inquired.

"You."

"What? Oh, never mind," she said as she started down the steps. "Lock the door behind you."

He fumbled with the door for a minute as he slipped on his boots, finally discovering that he'd met the objective.

She was already in the car when his feet met the concrete, her eyes shrouded by the tortoise-finish sunglasses, face etched with a frown.

He smiled at the sight as he slid in beside her.

This has got to look good, he thought, imagining himself nibbling on the earlobes he was staring at now. *Hope one of my buddies sees me.*

"You're putting in overtime today, huh?" he asked giddily, toying with the tough-guy dialect he'd been rehearsing.

"Yes."

"They treating you okay? It's a good job, right?"

"It has its benefits."

"You're already in charge there, though?"

"Not really."

"You're young, though. You've got it made."

"Yes, I certainly do," she responded, her voice tinged with sarcasm.

"What do you have planned today?" She thought to herself that she wished he would just shut up. "Do you have to work Saturdays?"

"Not today," she heard him reply in a halting manner, his voice now regaining its natural tone. "They didn't ask me to, fortunately."

"Why do you say that?"

"Because this way I don't have to feel like I've blown an opportunity. I hate that," he sighed.

His rapid return to quietness surprised her. It would be the choice of communication for the duration of their journey.

His sagging, bent spirits whispered tales of disappointment into her ear as he looked out the window, holding his hand to his forehead.

She nodded silently in understanding.

"No regrets, you know," he said suddenly, without provocation, startling her as she entered the mall parking lot.

"There it is, my Amy," he said, sounding somewhat like Sylvester Stallone.

My Amy, she thought silently. *My ass...*

She saw him point to a burnt-orange, rust-marred vehicle, standing alone and beaten in a corner of the lot.

Drawing nearer, she became repulsed at the sight of the dirty vehicle with its hood slightly ajar and a black garbage sack protruding through a gaping rust-torn gap above the right rear tire.

The car seemed to be caving in.

A single disposable BIC razor lay inexplicably atop the dash.

"You must really be concerned about appearances," she smiled as she peered into the interior.

Silence met her mockery as she pulled to a stop.

She leaned back into the plush seat of her own sedan— the spotless, regal exterior gleaming in the sun.

Efficient. Economical. Modern.

Unlike that piece of crap seventy-something, polluting, *thing*—a malfunction waiting for something to happen.

Just like him.

"Guess who this S.O.B. is insured by in West Queens? Forty dollars a month for liability—which I pay to your rich homies so they can blow it on their little blonde-haired princesses like yourself. Taking advantage of the poor guy—that's how you got where you are. Remember that," he said, temples throbbing, chest heaving.

"Yeah, yeah... get out. At least I have something to lose."

He stepped out.

"Thank you so much, little Amy," he said, slamming the door.

"Certainly," he heard her reply.

He felt strangely light despite his outburst, amused at the sight of the parking ticket on the windshield, the food container on the front seat.

He turned to his left and watched her departure, following her until she was out of sight.

He pulled himself down behind the wheel and engaged the engine, twisting to the left in the process—just in time to see two Latinas winding their way to the mall.

"Dang," he said aloud, inadvertently pressing his elbow against the horn.

Both turned sharply, their pretty, dark features etched with disapproval.

He smiled broadly in response, despite their scorn, shrugging his shoulders as they turned back around.

He reflected on how many struggled with accepting the arrival of Hispanics into Rulgery.

He did not.

He liked the diverse opportunities their presence provided—different dining experiences, a different look.

Hell, he adored Hispanic women, ever since the Hernandez sisters showed up at his school fifteen years earlier.

He was ready to fight his own buddies back then for their attention, willing to discard years of friendship over imaginary transgressions.

"Women," he whispered.

"Gwims and D.C.," he smiled as he said the names and pulled out of the lot.

Friends are more important than girls, he could hear the cowboy professing on the hood.

"That's why I didn't respond."

Old Beck was right.

He knew this now, but he had not been enlightened as such when the bells of Mexico City rang through his adolescent head.

No way he could have done as Beck had then—merely sat back and let his friends prevail with the one he wanted to be with.

Hell, no.

He winced at the memory of snubbing Gwims—his best friend since second grade—at the senior prom, literally turning his back to him as he honked his horn.

"It wasn't right," he whispered.

Man, he'd done so much for me—letting me stay at his house for weeks at a time, teaching me about lying, drinking, trusting me with his deepest, darkest secrets.

Me? I was naïve and knew nothing about any of those things.

"Gwims," he uttered as he headed south.

Sober, honest, celibate Sellers—being pulled along in these forays to the teen clubs, learning the lingo, the walk, the heartbreak.

Beating the bushes, so to speak, in that Rookie League setup.

It was that jealousy that began at that time—that same B.S. he felt toward his brother—that ultimately ruined any positive possibilities for the duo, he concluded.

Gwims always winning, always trying, kicking ass while he watched from both the bench and the barstool.

When Gwims met his soon-to-be first wife, the split was complete.

Boy vs. man.

Living vs. dying.

D.C. brought Sellers into the fold after Bob had been beaten down by the eighth-grade classmates.

D.C. seized upon the opportunity to add to his small number of acquaintances, staying near, even as Bob and his crippled self-esteem hobbled rapidly away from the whole social scene.

Hanging in there even when Bob drunkenly banged up D.C.'s mom's car.

Tolerant son of a gun—that's what he was.

Could always count on him...

Until he met his "steady Betty" before his senior year.

Then he too was nowhere to be found.

Yes, it was certainly a surprise to Bob to see those boys stride in among him and his girls in Spanish class that first day—his long-lost pals' beaming faces dissolving his daydreams of marrying those exotic Spanish jewels.

Can't these greedy sons of guns see I'm working on something here? he'd asked himself then, watching the pair move closer to his former pals.

I've been making my moves, asking them how to say 'chair' and 'desk' where they come from. It's just a matter of time before they ask me out.

"Yeah, right," he said aloud as he stopped at the red light adjacent to the truck stop.

As powerful as those sisters had seemed, it was one of his own that had rendered him useless this a.m.

"Amy, what you gonna do?" he sang, wishing he had an answer.

He yawned, wishing he had a cup of coffee, as he watched the railroad cars pass before him.

The truck stop ensured he'd be set free from that want, but as the last of the cars passed by, his foot pressed automatically upon the accelerator, and he headed back toward Thurman.

"What are you doing?" he asked, mocking the phrase too many of his female accomplices had addressed to him in too few bedrooms.

"Oh well, I can go see what glorious news awaits me at the post office," he said sarcastically, envisioning yet another rejection letter from some apologetic social service agency cluttering his box.

Oh well, they make good scratch paper.

He couldn't help but feel strangely hopeful today, though—not after running up against her.

Good karma. A spark.

Who cared what the professional world thought of his prospects, he thought as he pulled into the lot.

At least I ain't the only one caught in the web. She's in there with me, whether she wants to be or not.

He turned the key in the lock and pulled out a letter addressed to him from his old school, Andrews High.

"Yeah, whatever, guys," he cursed, remembering the hope with which he'd responded to their advertisement expressing their desire to hire a coach/counselor.

"Who needs ya?" he muttered as he tore open the envelope.

Curious to see how they'd tell him to bug off, he pulled the letter up and out—his eyes catching a glimpse of the incongruent Congratulations!

What the hell?

He became spellbound as he read on.

We've decided upon you.

He was in!

He'd done it.

Attained a *REAL* job, right in his hometown.

Time to pack, baby! See ya!

He was thinking all this as he nodded his head defiantly.

"Hold up, son," his mind whispered as he swaggered toward the door.

"Got to be a trade-off somewhere. Are you sure you want to do this?"

"Heck, yes!" he answered himself loudly.

"Whoops, excuse me, Mrs. Smith," he said to the red-faced patron in his path.

"Time to burn some bridges," he whispered as he climbed into his car.

DAMN!

This surpassed even his highest expectations.

To reconnect with *THE* game—on the same fields where he had played as a kid and later as a coach.

This time, he wouldn't falter.

It would be a continuum of movement, wearing out the pages of Polk's book, looking for insight.

He'd be a man this time—sweating his ass off to confer a positive feeling onto his charges.

No more of that negative, head-hanging stuff.

The essence of life—that's what winning a baseball game was.

Stepping out of that cage, free, jubilant.

"Man, nothing was better," he asserted, his mind flashing to the scene of chipper tones racing around the bases—beaming, talking loudly throughout the journey, slapping the hands of both rookie teammates and middle-aged coaches.

Subsequent to hitting a game-finishing home run.

Oh, man.

And this very cohort—he heard himself telling them years ago—he'd "coach anytime, anywhere."

Cooperative. Humble.

That's what they were.

Their enthusiastic contributions producing a synergistic effect, surpassing.

No woman could substitute for this, he said, rubbing his groin.

No guilt afterward, no shame.

Just sheer pleasure.

Like—no way—like he'd just felt with *her*!

Implausible as it seemed, he had to admit to having experienced these same transcendent, sensational moments by merely drawing close to her.

Hell, for that matter, by merely looking upon her.

Adrenaline surging.

Sights, sounds, overwhelming.

Yes, that's exactly how he felt—if only for a moment.

An offset.

Compensation.

That's what she seemed to be—like the $25 MCI paid to "win back" former customers who'd strayed.

He shook his head, wishing to be free of the thought.

No time to think about telecommunications. It's time to celebrate!

With a Thurman breakfast, he decided as he drove.

Been waiting too long.

Carrying on the legacy—my legacy, he asserted as he stopped before the restaurant.

He walked in confidently, his aura seemingly startling the regulars who'd rarely seen him smile as of late.

"You finally get something?" Howard asked.

"Almost. I'm not sure," Bob replied as he slapped the older man on the back.

"You work today?" Deanna asked.

"Hmph," Marv responded. "He never works."

"I'm out, Dee!" Bob shouted.

"What are you talking about?" she asked as she handed him his coffee.

"Moving back to Andrews. Going to make twenty million."

"Who's going to pay you that much to stand around and drink coffee?" Marv asked.

Bob could only laugh, watching Marv sip his coffee, the omnipresent silly smirk partially concealed by the trembling hands securing the cup to his lips.

Joe appeared from the kitchen before Bob had the chance to inform Marv of his new position.

"No way you're going to be a cop, are you? First time you got shot at, you'd wet yourself!"

Bob smiled again, gulping down a triumphant drink of coffee.

"I'm out!" he shouted, emphasizing the point like a Major League umpire, thumb jabbing the smoky air.

"You weirdo." Joe said, rolling his eyes.

Within a week, he'd departed after saying goodbye to his colleagues at the restaurant.

"See ya, everybody!" he said as he walked out the door.

"Take care, Buffalo Bob!" John shouted.

"Don't come back," were the last words he was to hear—the line delivered by Joe.

"Kiss my ass, Joe," he replied when outside.

He drove slowly through town with his belongings, taking one last pass by the old house that had sheltered him for the last five years.

He dabbed at his eyes as the structure faded from view.

"C'mon, punk," he chastised himself. "Forget about that rat hole."

It had been like a Goodwill drop box—neighbors discarding couches, TVs, clothes, cookies...

Good people.

Damn good people.

But hell, he cursed as he left the city limits.

What had he secured on his arm here?

He'd gotten his ass kicked here, branded with a Big L for loser.

He, with his B.S. degree, unable to tolerate the onslaught—a nervous, angry, guilt-ridden, defeated man.

Backing down, insulated only by a hollow depression.

A fool's scheme.

Lucky he was still upright.

It was time to make a change.

Redemption, he surmised, lay just ahead.

In what seemed like moments, he found himself in his parents' drive, the April rain exploding onto his windshield, exacerbating his anxious state.

He stayed in the car, in no hurry to step inside.

"Twenty-five years," he muttered. "A quarter of a century. Shake it."

Two young boys—he could see it now as he closed his eyes and held his hand to his temples.

Could see the scissors in his hand.

Could feel it jerk forward as his mother screamed.

"God," he groaned, his trembling left hand reaching blindly for the door handle. "How in the hell could it have gotten so bad, so quickly?" he asked as he opened the door and stepped out.

He wasn't a violent person.

Thank God he'd missed.

Painful memories raced through his mind as he stepped onto the porch.

"Robert!" his mom called out, opening the door before he had the chance to knock.

"How's it going, Mom?"

"Good. What've you been up to?"

"Not much. Got a new job here at the school. Mind if I stay here?"

"Of course you can!" she said as they walked inside.

"Brody, leave him *alone*!" she shouted to the eldest of two boys grappling on the floor.

Bob winced at the sight, slumping into the chair.

"Have you had anything to eat?" his mother inquired without turning around.

"Yeah, I ate at the restaurant. I'm just so drained."

"You're all worn out, huh? What're you going to be doing at the school?"

"Coaching. Baseball. Counseling," he whispered.

"That's great, Bob! When do you start?"

"Tomorrow if I have my way. Wow, Mom, I think I need to go lay down."

"Sure. You know where the blankets are."

"Uh-huh. Thanks," he said as he rose.

Man, this hurt, he thought as he stepped lightly toward his father's room to secure the blankets.

He considered himself lucky, as he watched his father twist nervously in his slumber, to have lived alone for the past few years.

Good people, but within these walls, his fate had been sealed.

Certainly things have changed, he mused as he prepared his bed on the floor beneath the couch upon which his sister and her boyfriend lay.

Perpetuating the pain—*his* pain—she was, with the help of these fugitive young men, those who'd ultimately deprive her of the fifty percent of the freedom that was rightfully hers.

They sure knew how to *play hurt* here, he sighed in reflection, remembering how his father would drag himself to his unrewarding, physically demanding job six days a week, gratefully accepting the meager compensation into his now gnarled hands.

Yield, he would not, shielding all from his disappointment when he traveled deep into the woods of Kentucky, pockets empty, to comfort his whimpering, homesick eldest son.

He wasn't sure which hurt worse as he stared into the blackness—the behavior that had induced his father's sympathy then or the nocturnal collect calls, ten years hence, which must have all too often sullied the temporary picture of tranquility herein.

Those slurring words waking them, incomprehensibly, from a thousand miles away in the desert.

RING!

"Terri, it's Stan," his mother called out to his other sister, who lay in the bedroom behind him.

"It's eleven at night," Bob muttered aloud. "Why is he calling now?"

There would be no reply.

No one had a satisfactory explanation.

Stan—his former catcher—seemed to be unable to break free from the illusion of resurrecting the corpse that was his relationship with Terri, running past cute Amy lookalikes in his haste to convene with her, imprisoned by his denial.

He sighed as he watched his sister step reluctantly to the phone, feeling with certainty that his alienation from them all could not have been more complete.

He couldn't stay here, he decided.

This *was pain squared.*

Bob stood regally within the midst of the pocket in the hotel room in Rice, surrounded and feeling quite at ease in this new home.

Pell, Cralt, Rusty, Greg, Vale, and Eddy stood on either side of him in various stages of discomfit, along with their latest girlfriends.

Things just seem to appear out of nowhere, he mused.

Old flames, old jobs, players—it made no sense.

He felt as if he could not have been happier, even as he watched the minors consume heaping quantities of beer before him.

His initial fears, long ago calmed, allowed him to play at the role of bartender.

"Need another, Eddy?" he asked the twenty-year-old in the corner.

"What do you think?" Eddy replied as he threw his empty can at the adjacent wall.

"Catch this, then," Sellers said as he lobbed the can.

Eddy removed his arm from the shoulder of one of his female guests just in time to make the catch.

"Two hands," Bob admonished him.

"That's what she says to me," Eddy said, gesturing toward the girl he now resumed holding.

Heartened by the presence of his boys, Sellers joined in the merriment.

"Speaking of which," he said, climbing atop the coffee table, "for security purposes, I need all of you who are not of the male gender to line up single file in front of the bedroom door for a strip search."

He could feel himself blushing—the act infusing his boldness.

Thus, he began to laugh, hoping to impress upon them that the ruddiness of his face was inspired by the force of his amusement at his own joke.

Laughter mingled with his from both sides of the room.

"You wouldn't know how, would you?" one female challenged him.

"He'd probably have a dollar in his hand first," Rusty shouted.

"Good one, Rusty," Bob deadpanned as he stepped down.

He threw his arm around the first girl he encountered—*a thuggish-looking* blonde, some seventeen years his junior.

"What're you doing hanging out with this cowboy for?" he winked at Jack. "Wouldn't you like to be with a more experienced man? Oops," he smiled, "I guess that would still be you then, Jack," he laughed, releasing the girl and slapping Jack playfully on the back.

He winked at her as he did so, scanning her face for emotion—startled by the features.

The defiant, mocking look met his gaze, presented by the blue-eyed, petite blonde.

She seemed to him a vision of what Amy must have looked like at one time.

"Man," he whispered as he walked to the adjoining room. "I need to keep away from that girl," he said, looking back over his shoulder.

It was the first time that evening that he recalled proceeding with caution regarding his dealings with his guests.

No high as he was atop the hill on this night, he could feel himself being taken by the magic.

Yes, he was *the big train* tonight, mowing down imaginary batters from his perch, knocking them off the plate, K-ing them with the breaking ball on the subsequent pitch.

He went into an imaginary stretch position, holding Pell on the beer cooler as Cralt strode to the paper plate ying near his feet.

Bob stepped back, acting confused, shaking his head at an unseen catcher.

"You weirdo," Rusty shouted from behind them. "How are you supposed to throw a pitch if you don't stand on the rubber?"

Bob saw the condom flip off his shoulder.

"Thanks, Rusty. What's the shelf life on these things?"

"Five years. You better start asking around soon."

Bob chuckled as he headed toward the bathroom.

He turned the knob, felt the unyielding door remain in place.

"Go outside," he heard Vale shout within, as an adolescent girl laughed on Vale's side of the door.

Bob excused himself as he brushed by Jack, his eyes catching a glimpse of both his catcher's boots and his blonde companion's as he passed.

"Sellers, you're like the puppy we placed in a cage with the wolf cub back home," he heard Beck state in the blackness. "If it survived, we knew it would be worthy of taking on the hunt; if it didn't... oh well."

"Yeah, Beck, I'm out of the cage now," Bob muttered. "A little bit up, but still standing—a full-grown dog," he asserted as the vision of the cowboy standing in the desert faded.

Fist clenched in affirmation, he heard Rusty walk outside and retreat into the night behind another corner of the building.

"Say hello to my little friend!" Rusty shouted to no one in particular.

Bob shook his head in glee.

"These crazy sons of guns. Damn," he whispered to the stars.

She had sensed this earlier, she thought, as she watched him bound up the steps leading to her front door.

She rubbed her aching, unrested eyes, noting how refreshed and vibrant he appeared in his tan slacks and green-and-gold jacket.

In stark contrast—as was informed to her by the full-length closet mirror—stood exhausted, lifeless Amy.

"Dang it," she cursed at the sight, dismayed that, despite the leave of absence she'd taken from work beginning that day, she hadn't been able to recover even in part.

She'd had to resort to unplugging her phone from the wall when Ron called her at 1:00 a.m., then 3:00 a.m., then 4:00—each time angrily asking for money.

The call she'd made to home prior to the onslaught had been of no assistance either.

Her mother had informed her that Andrea had just recently been released from the hospital—the victim of yet another assault by some ill-tempered, jealous, low-life scum.

Her twin sister.

Wow.

Maybe it would've been easier to trade places, take a few of the lumps herself.

Couldn't be any worse than this sleepless fit the attacks had induced in her.

"Damn Ron anyway," she cursed as she cinched her robe about her, calling to mind the flamboyant fashion with which the wealthy man ran through many.

Just like his dad, she asserted, referring to the overachieving male who had propelled an itinerant construction company into a titan despite his hard-drinking tendencies.

Nouveaux riches, she hissed.

Unfamiliar with good fortune, trampling over everything in their quest to psychologically distance themselves from all they'd been given.

Afraid to feel *superior.*

Stupid.

She was happy that the Vance money had begun accumulating in the late nineteenth century.

No problems assimilating there.

"Ron," she shook her head as the doorbell rang.

He cared only about three things:

One: touting his chiseled physique behind the bar, looking for them.

The Man, she laughed—the one who lived his customers' dreams.

Two: fighting without being cut.

Three: sex without falling in love, consuming without becoming addicted.

All bull.

Hell, he was more helpless than even the weakest, dumbest fool on the barstool.

Charm and slyness he had revealed at eleven—bludgeoned by narcotics and the realities attendant to sleeping with married women by two.

He was attractive, though.

Someone she liked to be seen with—at most times.

Not like this, Bob.

This doting loser.

Driving that ugly car.

That stupid silver tooth.

God, they'd run him out of West Queens in a minute—canceling his car insurance as they did so, she smiled.

To hell with him.

He wants to appear like he can stay in my path *sans* consequences.

We'll see how he feels after Ron sees him here.

Nah, no need for violence—at least not yet.

The destruction will be ingested by him internally.

I'll have him composing love songs in my honor within days.

"Mi Ami, oh, my Amy."

Some country bullshit, she chuckled.

She suppressed her mirth as she opened the door, feigning surprise and happiness as she greeted him.

"Bob! How ya doin'?"

"Good. Yourself?" he asked gruffly.

"Okay, come on in."

"Sounds good. I tried to call you, but the operator said the phone was disconnected."

"Yeah, I..." she started to explain but decided against it.

We'll keep all this a surprise, she informed herself.

Spring it on him without warning.

"Man, I landed a good job in Andrews—coaching and counseling," she heard him explain.

"Guess I ain't so screwed up after all."

How, she asked herself as he rambled on, had she allowed herself to fall prey to men like him?

Even then, she'd worked too hard, been too smart, she thought.

Pity, probably.

"Have you eaten yet?" she asked, touching his arm. "I need to get out of here."

"You don't want me to drive you around in my ugly car?" he asked, looking at the floor.

"Let's walk, then," she said, dropping her robe onto the carpet.

"I'm no princess, Bob," she informed him somberly as she turned around, already fully dressed. "I'm not too good for you. If anything, you might be too nice for me. Who cares about what type of car you drive, really? You know I was only kidding the other day."

"Thanks, Amy," he said as he opened the door for her.

Confidence seemingly renewed, he resumed his dissertation on the beauty of opportunity.

"I feel blessed. No way I thought I'd get a second chance to be with my boys—my Amy," he said with a grin. "Bet you never thought you'd have me chasing you around when you took this job here, huh?"

"It's been no bother. In fact, it's made life more interesting," she said, clutching his hand.

"Wow," he whispered, apparently feeling that the awe with which he uttered the word made additional speech unnecessary.

"Your hands are shaking," she laughed as they drew near McDonald's. "Are you all right?"

"Yeah, I'm all right. Just hungry, is all."

"That's all, huh?" she grinned.

"There's just something about you…" he uttered, his voice trailing off into the restaurant entrance as he released her from his grip.

"What do you mean, *there's something about me*?"

"There… there just is. This aura, you know?"

"An aura, you say? How so?"

"Number Two combo, large vanilla shake, please," he said to the attendant.

"What can I get you?" she asked Amy.

"Just a large fry and a small vanilla shake," she said, reaching for her purse.

"I'll get both of these," she heard Bob say to the attendant.

They stood in silence until the food arrived and the bill was paid.

I wonder what he's trying to say here. Keep pressing, Amy, she implored herself.

When he turned around, food in hand, she engaged him again.

"I exude some kind of magic power, is that it?" she smiled.

"No, it's just that you intrigue me. You're my little research project. *Rich Girl 101*, you know?"

"Pretty hung up on the money thing, aren't you?' she asked matter-of-factly, suppressing the confrontational speech she felt building within.

"You see me living in a condo? I probably don't have any better housing situation than you. Where do you l ve?"

"In a hotel room in Rice," he sighed, exasperated. "I could never see you living somewhere like that, in the sticks."

"You'd be surprised."

Boy, will he, she mused.

"As a matter of fact, I'm not working right now. I'm just so burnt out—I could really use a friend like you. Good friends are just so hard to find. I've never lived outside of the city. How about if I come and stay with you for a while, *friend*?"

"Damn it," he cursed as the shake slipped from his trembling grasp.

"Gotcha," Amy whispered to herself.

He felt as he always had with her near—propelled into action.

Thus, downward he pressed, pushing until his chin met its sweet target.

His eyes automatically shut upon glorious contact.

He experienced an immediate oneness with his surroundings.

The sound of the afternoon traffic dissipated, lost within the shrieking din of ruffling silk.

"Mmmmm," he groaned, rolling his head to his left, seemingly drowning in exhilaration.

"Everything about you is so compelling," he found himself whispering as his hand moved along the back of her—

"We won't need that dress," she laughed as he abruptly pushed himself away from the closet.

"It's a bit *risqué* for 'the sticks,' don't you think?"

"Yeah, you're probably right," he uttered sheepishly, excusing himself as he strode past her on his way downstairs.

"Gosh damn that girl," he muttered. "You want me to put the television in now?" he shouted over his shoulder.

"Can you move it yourself?"

"I can try."

He smiled at the relative ease with which he was able to place the television into the rental van.

The mere touch of the form-fitting cotton Lycra knit garment had seemingly increased his strength twofold.

Maybe she wasn't a *princess* as she had informed him last night, but, he assessed, as he gazed upon the neatly pressed clothing hanging within the velvet interior of the vehicle he'd rented for her transfer—she did rule his current world.

"Dammit," he cursed as he shut the door.

In a previous era, he couldn't even look to the southeast without thinking of her, absolutely aching with curiosity.

And now this.

"Wow," he whispered as she came into view beyond his left shoulder.

Unable and unwilling to move, he stood utterly motionless as she drew near.

The sight of her in the one-piece black dress, black-and-white skirt, black leggings, and shoes shook his stoic resolve.

"Uhhh," he whispered aloud as if wounded.

"All set, huh?" he somehow managed to utter.

"That would be all. We'll see you later, then?"

"Definitely," he replied, leering.

"I wrote the address down for you here," he stated, slipping the restaurant matchbook between her polished, manicured nails.

"It'll be easy to find—the hotel on the hill on Highway 3."

"Thank you," she replied sweetly as she slipped the card into her purse.

"It may be early in the morning before I get there."

"I'll be up."

"See ya," she smiled as she opened the door of her car.

"Definitely."

He moved toward the driver's side of the van, still gazing at her.

"Hey, thanks, Amy Lou."

She smiled and shut the door behind her, securing herself within the seatbelt.

He watched her pull away, then climbed aboard his own gateway—inclining in an exaggerated fashion on the armrest to his right before driving off with his bounty.

To Rice?

What could he have been thinking?

The last taste of defeat he had ingested as a high school athlete had been placed upon his plate there—by those Red Raiders.

He could still hear their testosterone-saturated cheers, could see himself in the first base box, shocked, as Gouthier was called out.

"It's all right, dude," he comforted himself now, inclining into the comfortable seat as he turned left onto the avenue.

It was still superior to the stuff he'd gotten covered in the previous days at the old farmhouse.

That pervasive shame.

Sad, he guessed, but he always felt so liberated when he departed from there.

Was so relieved when he convened with his family on neutral ground—especially when his boys were thrown into the mix.

Yes, his good thoughts had begun only with the arrival of Ms. Amy some eight years earlier.

All preceding memories would not hearten him.

High school, the hood—all irrelevant.

Wild days without merit.

"Twenty-two disappointing years," he muttered as he departed the city limits.

Slumber.

Sleepwalking from cradle to grave.

That's what he had been doing before she woke him in the middle of the night.

Now he couldn't fall back asleep.

He envisioned it all again, as he had hundreds of times since.

Always beginning with her slow, trancelike movement toward him in that dress.

The progression of her fluid movement.

Slowly enveloping him.

The warmth of her body so near—*so unforced*.

That was the word.

But not *natural*, for nature he could take for granted.

Could escape by merely walking indoors.

She walked through—oblivious to the cynicism, depression, fear, and anger he had erected to shelter himself.

Could find him anytime, anyplace—impacting upon him at will.

Yes, he had been correct in telling her at Matt's that he was screwed by the force of her memory.

It appeared that she had been confined by it as well, he smiled, gazing upon her belongings.

Kicking her vulnerable little ass right back into his grip.

"Wow," he whispered as he stomped on the accelerator.

As the bell sounded, he staggered automatically toward the alarm clock, his desire—as always—to extinguish the hissing, mocking sound that rudely woke him daily.

The voice that informed him that, yes, he was still alive.

That he would have to wade into the midst of yet another uncompromising day.

He acted now as he would then, swearing as he slammed his fingers into the messenger, squelching its taunts in exchange for nine more precious minutes of sweet oblivion.

As he walked away, this time, the bell continued to toll—torturing him within the relentless din.

He stumbled back toward it, then realized the sound was coming from behind him.

"Damn," he chuckled as he reached for the phone.

"Hello?" he mumbled.

"Bob?"

The simple, elegant aspiration floated toward him.

"Yes?" he answered, dazed.

"I'm just outside of Leville. Do you want to meet me somewhere in Rice? I need to pick up a few things."

"Yeah, meet me at the Texaco. It may take me a little while," he said, slipping rapidly into his shower shoes.

"Okay, thanks. Bye-bye."

He was set into motion within seconds, his sandals mocking the shag carpet as he skated toward the shower.

His glimpse at his surroundings reminded him somehow of some long-ago Christmas morning—the meticulously arranged setting presented in anticipation of the Santa that conferred gifts upon him in tribute to his virtue.

The bright, feminine artifacts placed carefully about the room fully enhanced the surreal effect.

Where was he? He wondered as he swaggered into the shower.

The hot water that hit his heaving torso an instant later caused him to wince with pleasure, the aching, stiff muscles—induced by his preparation—now made pliant by the simple salve.

Despite the sensation he induced through the massage therapy, within a few short minutes, he would find himself breathlessly reaching for the van door, shirt in hand.

He grinned as he did so, looking down upon the illuminated village before beginning his exhilarating descent.

He drove the half-mile in seconds, the swirling energy created by the ride exacerbated by the sight of her sitting in repose in the sparkling white car beneath the Texaco sign.

An involuntary expiration of breath escaped his pursed lips as he flexed his right arm, circling his clenched fist vigorously above his contracted bicep.

The gesture summoned forth the vision of Dante Bidette initiating the same after hitting the game-winning home run in the inaugural game at Coors Field in 1995.

He'd imitated the movement a hundred times since—attempting as he did so to vest himself with the energy to conquer the mundane.

This was the first time, however, that he could recall having done so involuntarily.

"Uh-oh," he laughed aloud.

He parked and unfurled, sauntering toward her window.

He placed both hands atop the car and leaned forward, his eyes following from the hem of her dress up to her blue eyes.

"All set?" he asked casually.

"Yes."

"It's right up the hill here."

"Okay," she replied drowsily as he stepped away.

Atta boy, he congratulated himself, proud of the poised way he had presented himself to her.

He put the van into gear and sped off, beating his chest with his fist.

"My, my, my," he shouted aloud, pressing the accelerator into the floorboard as he began his ascent, temporarily losing sight of her headlights in his mirror.

He slowed until he regained sight of her, then negotiated his right turn.

He pulled in close to his front door, then sat, staring smugly at the full moon above, in awe at the way the heavens seemed to be fusing together his past, present, and future—leaving in their wake only promise and hope.

They might ask of him if it was worth it—to wait three decades to finally have his fractured self made *whole*.

Hell, yes!

Thirty-two years was not even a reasonable down payment for the gift that was now squeezing upon this pretty son of a bitch emerging from the car to his left.

"Right this way, Amy," he shouted into the night, his feet touching gravel simultaneously.

He rushed to unlock the door and stepped aside, holding it open for her.

"Thank you," she replied.

"Oh, you have it set up really nice," she asserted, moving toward the closet.

"No problem," he stated gruffly.

"Want me to bring some more things in?"

"Sure," she responded enthusiastically.

He'd already moved smoothly outside.

He opened the car door.

The taste of perfume trapped within assailed him, searing his balance.

Through the stimulating mist, it registered in his barely functioning mind that he was gazing upon what could only be defined now as *his legs, his blonde curls, his lips, his night, his Amy.*

Holding a freshly laundered blanket blindly to his nose, he felt himself reeling, swaying—until he found he was looking upon the picture of the two of them together within the reflection of the bureau mirror.

Her neck, he observed, as he placed the blankets on the table, was craned to the side as she straightened her clothes.

The vein—prominent, uniting her mind and heart—daring him to whet his passions.

"What's that you're wearing?" he heard someone inquire as he moved toward her.

"Obsession," she replied without looking up.

"Appropriate," he heard the voice say again as he touched her elbow.

His tumbling viscera informed his mind that he'd made contact.

He felt as he had in the dream—he had at her couch that night after they'd left Matt's.

The olfactory pleasure perhaps ever surpassing the fantasy—the numbers still in his favor.

Vale, Cralt, and Pell—all stomping on the third base bag as he pointed them to the plate—as his lips met the same spot on her neck.

"What are you doing?"

He heard the words *pop* into his consciousness as dark amoebas filled his eyes, obscuring the lightness of her disappearing flesh.

"What?"

"Don't... just don't surprise me like that again, okay?"

"Yeah," he mumbled, searching for his countenance within her highly polished shoes before she deftly strode away.

"I've made your bed up."

Listen then, bitch, his thoughts echoed inside his aching head.

"I've got you set up in the bedroom," he stated firmly.

"Thank you," her condescending voice replied, the words trailing off as she hastened along.

He retreated to the bathroom with the folded sweatpants.

He could taste the bile in his throat as he rubbed his stomach.

He stared into the mirror.

The defeated, haggard vision subdued him, induced him to quickly turn and crawl toward the couch.

He flipped on the radio and lay down, turning toward the wall.

"What the hell? *Disillusioned punk,*" he chastised himself.

"She don't give a damn about you."

He pulled himself deeper into the couch as she walked past.

He could sense her anger even in the dark as she stomped off with the black dress on the hanger.

"*His*" dress, he scoffed.

He lay listening to her bathe, calmness gradually returning—until he fell asleep.

On two occasions, he jerked awake, experiencing himself falling off a cliff.

Shortly after the second occurrence, he heard the flow of music cease—a dead, suffocating, vindictive silence left in its stead.

He exhaled slowly painfully, and stared at the ceiling.

Sweat began to bead upon his forehead.

"Forget this," he mumbled into the blackness.

Smashing a hard line at Pell, he felt dull pain radiate from a point below his scapula.

"Man, I'm worn out," he muttered to Greg. "Think I've slept ten hours the whole week," he asserted as he received the next ball from Greg and lashed it to the left of Cralt.

"Good play, Cralt," he hollered out.

"Where do you want me to throw it?" Cralt asked.

"Second," he said as Tony hastened to the spot.

Cralt's throw glanced off Tony's glove as the young man fumbled, trying to get his footing on the bag.

"Sorry, fellas," he called out.

"Damn it, I just can't focus, Greg."

He was thankful that he'd prepared vigorously in previous days—the hours of designing an appropriate schedule had been rewarded by his players' execution of what he'd written up for them.

Yes, all was well, *despite him.*

Cralt stopping everything hit near him.

Rusty's cannon arm making accurate throws from third.

Pell's great range at short.

Brad, Bounds, and Johnny looking good in the outfield.

The pitching prospects were especially heartening—Jason, Kendall, Alex, and Pell all could be considered potential staff *aces.*

Damn it, if things were going this well with me staggering about, how much better—he pondered—would they be if I had my edge?

He'd lost it—lying awake, listening to her sleep in adjoining rooms, fighting his compulsion to climb aboard.

Of late, he'd resigned himself to reviewing his baseball notes, repeatedly, at the kitchen table, deep into the night.

He wondered what it was she had been inscribing onto those note cards in her increasingly rare waking hours.

He didn't ask.

They scarcely communicated at all.

He'd quickly lost the will to reach out to her through either speech or touch.

Her rebuff on moving today had seen to that.

Still, he could not help but feel that opportunity was straying—recalling how, at UNEI, he'd called her a dozen times after they'd met, each time ending his incursion with the words, *I'd better leave you alone.*

That innocuous phrase—for a reason she chose not to expand upon—would anger her.

Perhaps she wasn't like him.

Maybe living alone was something with which she wasn't proficient.

Didn't seem to be the case now, though.

It was wrecking him—that's what it was doing.

That pretty body, evading him, *every damn night,* was all he could think about at present.

Needed a pinch hitter.

"We gonna work on bunt defense now?" Greg asked.

"Yeah," Bob replied, glancing at his list.

"Say, Greg, who was that little blonde girl with you at my house the other day? She looks really familiar."

"Andrea George. She's from Rice."

"Good looking. She yours?"

"She's on the roster. I think she'll crack the lineup," Greg winked.

"You lucky son of a bitch anyway," Bob laughed. "Wish I had a woman like that. When I was your age, that is."

He amended his statement quickly as he rolled the ball in front of the plate.

Wow, I'm trippin' on little teeny boppers' girls. I must really be in a fog, he thought to himself as Greg sprung from his crouch and made a picturesque throw to Tony covering first.

Taboo, son, he thought, recalling how Dee had told him about the tears trickling down the guy's cheek when the jury's foreman proclaimed him guilty of statutory.

"Girls!" he inadvertently blurted as Greg returned.

"Those things can kill ya, dude," he whispered.

It was not easy for her to attain an accurate assessment of the culture of his *sticks*.

The hours she kept seemed to be in direct contrast to the ones the residents nearby lived.

On those occasions when she would drive past them, she had to laugh.

"We ain't in West Queens anymore, Dorothy," she'd chuckle, as people she'd never met before would stare—then wave.

Always that damn waving.

Appearances seemed to be ascribed a lower value here, she reflected as she set her cards aside.

People walking around in muddy work shoes, dirty baseball caps—oblivious to the residue of manifest powerlessness.

That's what it was.

She felt their eyes upon her back now, in the restaurant booth.

This isolated area—like some odd social club.

Non-members were allowed within but would forever be confined to less *than* status by the offspring of the charter members.

"Doesn't matter," she mused as she sipped her coffee. "I can leave whenever I please."

For now, she'd adjust—as always—creating opportunity to achieve within an unfavorable environment.

Their shunning of her would only serve to enhance her ability to develop her book—the fictional account of a powerful woman's quest for serenity.

She could be relentless in the pursuit.

Keeping him at bay.

Exiling him continually to the kitchen table with that dumb *Baseball playbook*.

It was probably an act, she reflected as she stood.

But he seemed to be resigning himself to defeat.

Not speaking.

Not touching.

He was, it seemed, breaking himself down.

Stealing her job.

She did not want to relinquish the role—the power in her heart within.

It was time, she smiled, as she set the check on the counter adjacent to the cash register, to force him to reveal his hand.

She'd woken even before he did on this sunny Saturday.

She watched as he slept, still fully clothed, on the couch he'd fallen into some twelve hours earlier.

When he rose, he startled her with a cheery "Good morning!" as he passed by on his way to the shower.

She could hear him singing softly now, beneath the din—the offering of optimism filling the tranquil morning air, in stark contrast to the somber, silent gloom he'd cast the previous rainy evening.

He looked like *crap*, she reflected.

Worse than usual.

Seemingly vulnerable, perhaps.

But she could not bear drawing near—saw no merit in disturbing him as she'd planned.

He'd merely turn his sad face to the wall when she tried to engage his attention, she hypothesized.

Anger seemed to be his foil—his point of departure from comfort.

Depression—defeat—he could share his home with.

Provoke him when he's on an upswing, when he's rested—then drop him.

Make it *really* hurt, she thought.

She heard the water cease to flow, and seconds later, he emerged, toweling off his balding head.

"What do you have planned today?" she asked him.

"I've got to go see my assistant coach later. I should take you along—show you off a little, you know?"

"Sure, we can drive my car," she responded, quickly determining that he'd just handed her an opportunity for readily avenging her defeat.

What's it feel like?

She could picture herself shouting into his angry face now.

Ruin my relationships, my reputation with the force of your greed, will you? she whispered after she'd stepped outside.

Leaving those stupid messages—not even stopping to think that I would probably have a companion. How damn blind can a grown man be?

She shook her head as she placed the keys in the ignition.

She'd see that all that would not occur again—would create within him the same contempt he'd placed inside of her.

Hitting him from nowhere.

Repeatedly.

Until he could no longer bear the thought of her.

He climbed in tentatively, adjusting to the unfamiliar seating arrangement.

"Hey, I appreciate this," he said as he engaged the engine.

"De nada," she smiled.

"These guys—these kids I'm coaching—are pure magic," he said as they descended the hill. "Everything I've done with 'em has been a positive experience.

"It's strange... But the adults," he continued after a minute of silence, "well, it's different with them.

"I feel uneasy around them.

"You see, I used to get drunk and stupid in the bars in Andrews—passing out in ditches, wrecking cars."

She noticed how he stirred uncomfortably as he spoke, his mind twisting like the beaten path they were following now.

She could again sense his defeat.

Could envision him being set adrift by a flood of regret.

"You can move the seat back if you want," she informed him as he twisted again to his left.

"I'm okay," he whispered.

"My cousin runs the park here. Has the same B.S. degree I have—as does my cousin, Chase, in California.

"I respected those two tough sons of bitches enough to try to follow in their paths.

"I just couldn't secure opportunity for myself as they did," he sighed.

"My friend D.C. grew up there, in that house to your right.

"A damn good man—would do anything to help me out.

"I had an opportunity to help him out a few years back, but I choked," he winced.

What in the hell is this? she thought to herself as she looked into the mirror at the farmhouse.

He's acting like he's drowning in a sea of remorse.

It was time to put an end to this façade.

Time to reel him in.

"The past—it is not genuine," she informed him.

"Let it dissipate—burn off like morning fog in the glow emanating from your ever-brightening future.

"By all means, keep yourself perpetually in motion.

"Do not stop and wander about.

"It's difficult enough to reflect upon good days.

"When confronted with that which has the potential to make you anxious versus that which can depress you, always choose the former.

"At least then, you can feel the pain is a consequence of your attempts to introduce positive change into your life."

She saw his eyes quickly begin to regain the hue present within earlier that morning.

That ought to do it, she mused, suppressing a smile.

"That's good. I like that!" he blurted a moment later.

"I know it is," she asserted smugly.

Gotcha yet again, she thought.

"Let me pull in here really quick," he stated softly as they drew near the entrance to the convenience store.

"I want to introduce you to my mother."

She followed him into the midst of a swarm of lifeless patrons—all making unimportant decisions.

Pepsi or Mountain Dew.

Chips or pretzels.

Fueling up for the purpose of traveling deeper into the heart of nowhere.

The parlance—flat, monotone—seared her ears.

"Hi, sure is nice out today," these beings would say to one another.

Upon seeing him, more than one inquired, "How's the job going, Brad?"

On the third such query, he whispered to her that this was his brother's name.

"Still working at Perkins?" one had asked.

"No, I'm not, John," he replied.

"I never did," he whispered to her.

How, she pondered, could he have made such an insignificant impact in such an isolated, restricted setting?

Population: 711.

Miles from the nearest mall.

The nearest theater.

The only people traveling through would appear to be former and current residents.

Hell, they couldn't even remember his name?

Big man on campus, he was not.

"I'm going to work for the school," she heard him tell an older man.

"Oh, I guess I did hear that," the senior replied.

"Robert, what are you up to?"

Amy jerked when she heard the name pronounced.

"No good," he smiled as he looked at the gray-haired woman behind the register.

"Just goofing off today," he said, pointing over his shoulder. "My friend is hanging out with me, letting me drive her car.

"Say hi to Amy, Ma."

The look of surprise that met her gaze startled Amy, causing her to glance self-consciously to her left at the group of motorcycle riders standing restlessly at the counter.

"Pleased to meet you," she heard the woman speak softly.

Amy stared at the pyramid of beer the riders had set near the cash register.

"She's pretty shy, Ma," she heard Bob laugh.

"Oh, sorry. Hi," she said, staring into the mirrored sunglasses the biker had set back upon his face.

Amy shuddered as she turned quickly around.

"We'll see ya, Ma," Bob said, hastening to hold open the door.

"Okay, take care," his mother replied.

What was that about? she wondered.

The flustered look upon the elder woman's face.

The sunglasses shrouding the large man's eyes.

She looked down at the floorboard until the car stopped.

Looking up, she noticed that they were parked in front of a café.

"Let's stop in here for a minute," he suggested, jumping quickly out of the door.

She shook her head and raised herself slowly from her seat.

"Oh, God," she moaned softly.

She reached the door of the establishment in moments, but the time elapsed seemed much longer.

One hand on her swirling stomach, she pulled firmly.

Her strength quickly vanishing, she walked slowly inside, head bowed.

Slowly, with all the dignity at her disposal, she raised herself upright.

She scanned the room, eyes narrowed, still frowning, until she spotted him in the corner, conversing with a white-haired gentleman.

"Who's this?" the man asked as she wandered over.

"My cousin?" Bob smiled.

"Your kissing cousin?"

"I wish," Bob replied.

"Hey, Rusty you look tired, man. What'd you do— swallow a bunch of beer tabs last night?"

The redhead he'd addressed the question to didn't even bother to raise his head from the table as he mumbled his reply.

"Nah."

An adolescent whom Bob had earlier referred to as Greg laughed at the spectacle.

"Old Monica kept him awake all night, probably."

"Shut up," Rusty responded languidly.

"Hey, Pell," Bob hollered to a tall, strong male standing nearby.

"What happened last night?"

"We went to the mall to see *Die Hard IV.*"

"Any girls there?"

"Yeah, but we had to get out of there quick. Some Rutgers guys started messing with us because of our ball caps."

"What'd you say to them?"

"Vale and I told them to 'bring it,'" Pell said, gesturing toward the cowboy in the booth next to him.

"What'd they say then?"

"They took off—flipped us off when they left the parking lot.

"We figured they were going to get more guys."

"Cralt," Bob turned to address a shorter, yet equally solid male.

"What are you doing for graduation?"

"We're having a party at our house."

"Tim's springing for that? He never thought you'd graduate, huh?"

"Guess not. I'm paying for some of it, though."

"What, you're buying half a keg?"

Cralt laughed, then resumed talking with his friend, Mike.

"Hi, Marge," Bob shouted into the kitchen.

In the bar portion of the *joint*, a younger man sat drinking Budweiser with a slightly older patron.

Upon catching a glimpse of Bob, he shouted, "Sellers, don't teach them how to hit, okay?"

He laughed, lifting his beer in tribute.

"Okay," Bob replied with a wide grin.

He then took a step to his left, stopping abruptly at the pool table as he heard—

"I'll be damned. Sellers has a woman!"

Winking at her, Bob responded, "That's right, Wolfman."

"He's lying, Wolf," she said beneath her breath, peering at the man through the smoke.

"You ready, Amy?" she heard him ask as he stared.

"Certainly."

As they headed toward the door, a man in his mid-twenties called out, "Sellers, you seen your brother around?"

"Not lately, man," Bob sighed.

The question seemed to have deflated his temporary cheerfulness, Amy observed, as he somberly held the door for her.

The hint of vulnerability revealed did hearten her—even if only momentarily.

The solemn nature in which he made the trek south seemed deafening when placed against the backdrop of his frolic within the café.

Hence, the need for her to think, to act, seemed even more compelling.

Why would she be accosted by the past now, in the light of day, in this setting?

Just no connection, she breathed in.

No reason. It was just a look—one she'd gazed upon hundreds of times. Big deal. Get a grip, she derided herself as they drove onto a gravel road.

Hell, she'd seen it on his face just now—the way he'd looked upon her thighs—leaving no room for doubt.

Perhaps he was taking her somewhere.

Somewhere secluded from intrusive variables.

So what?

She felt no fear.

She would prevail, she assured herself.

She would ensure he'd not have his way with her.

She would out-think him.

Then why that overwhelming pain earlier?

There was no time to assess now, she bristled, as he pulled before a farmhouse.

It was time to prepare a counterattack.

"Why are we stopping here?"

"I just want to show you where I grew up. Before we go to my friend's."

"Is anyone home?"

"Nah," he replied as he reached for her hand.

"Hey, I'm not going to help you with this. I meant what I said at Matt's. Not on a dare.

"You just don't do anything for me, that's all.

"This trip down memory lane has your brain all twisted.

"I can sit out in the car while you go play make-believe in the bathroom—or wherever."

"WHAT?" he responded angrily.

"Who the hell do you think you are?

"Moreover, who do you think I am?

"Some dumb-ass hick who thinks West Queens ladies are willing to be with someone like me?

"I was just trying to show you some sights, get you out of town."

"Sights? A dilapidated farmhouse in the middle of nowhere?

"Gee, thanks," she said sarcastically.

"Forget you," he said as he angrily opened the door.

She saw him grab two apples from the refrigerator from her view behind the screen door.

She noticed no residue of trammeled family relations as she looked—

The absence of which surprised her, contradicted the angst he seemed to feel at most times.

Most people like him, she surmised as he turned around, would have come from homes like she'd visited while employed with DHS—

Second- or third-generation alcoholics raised in an unkempt, beaten environment.

Holes punched in walls.

Broken glass.

Kicked-in doors.

The manifestation of futility.

Ensnared.

Yet this place looked orderly.

Unscathed.

Even *loving*.

The force of good had charmed the beast.

Most likely, then, the medium of that kindly looking woman at the convenience store.

That look she wore.

Amy shuddered as he passed by her now.

That startled look.

How could that fleeting touch have become such a triggering mechanism for her?

It's over, she reminded herself quickly as she stepped outside.

Let it go.

He stomped angrily to the car and slammed the door for effect after he'd entered.

"Be careful!" she shouted.

"Dumb ass," she muttered as he put the car in reverse.

For a moment, she thought he wasn't going to stop for her—would drive right over her—then head north, abandoning her crumpled body in this desolate Netherlands.

She breathed easier when he pulled to a stop beside her.

He stared straight ahead as she entered, fighting his ire.

You've already tipped your hand, boy. It's no use.

The past, poverty, family, sex—all sensitive issues for him.

The medium through which she'd assail him.

For now, she'd bring him back.

Place him again beneath her control.

She reached out and caressed his lower leg, feeling the tension release instantly.

"You okay?" she asked sweetly.

"Yeah."

"Where are we going next?" she inquired innocently as they sped off out of the lane.

"To Bart's.

"See that house up there?" he asked, directing her attention to a tattered house, standing amidst a fie d of too-tall grass.

"Every Friday night we'd throw a party there—would just go nuts.

"We didn't care."

"Who lived there?"

"My buddy, Henry.

"He was the host.

"He's fallen into disfavor lately around here.

"But back then—you wanted to be around him.

"He was a cynamo!

"When you saw him," he continued, his voice now laden with excitement, "you knew something exciting was about to happen.

"Inhibitions he never met—when he drew near ya, they'd leave you too.

"A guy would feel comfortable as could be, s iding down these dusty roads at 80 mph, sipping on the drinks he'd prepared—

"Thirty-one ounces gin.

"One ounce tonic," he laughed.

"Why do you think people don't care much for him now?" she inquired, twisting her body so that she now faced him squarely, ner hand still resting atop his knee.

He cleared his throat as they ascended the hill, which contained the driveway leading to a large, well-kept home, then responded—

"The same spontaneity that compelled us to hang out with him... hurt him in the long run.

"When he was supposed to honor appointments—with friends, employers, wives.

"He's a lot different from Bart.

"He'd drive people crazy with this unpredictability.

"Sometimes he'd just take off—wouldn't be seen for months.

"On one of these adventures, he lost a gorgeous fiancée.

"Collected a bullet in his forearm from somebody's jealous boyfriend.

"And lost custody of his son, who's now a talented junior high baseball player.

"It's ironic..." he laughed softly.

"What is?"

"That this *roughneck* could father a gentleman—who is excellent at a gentleman's game.

"The gift he gave to the community—such a departure from the benefactor.

"Must be the kid's gorgeous mother's fault," he concluded as he braked the car to a stop.

"Come with me, little shy girl," he smiled as he stepped out.

"No tricks.

"None of that crazy stuff, I promise," he said, smiling more broadly.

"Shy?

"How reassuring that is," she said playfully as she casually followed him out of the car.

The house, she quickly assessed, was pleasant-looking.

Inviting.

Even noble in bearing.

It maintained its prominence by remaining a significant distance from the closest neighboring home.

In that it sat high atop a hill, it bore a resemblance to the hotel in Rice.

But *this*, she surmised, was a *home!*

Complete with multiple levels, patio, and hot tub.

Multiple doors provided access to its modern inter or— and to the barbecue grill on the wooden deck outside.

"Very nice," she stated as she walked onto the porch.

She could almost hear the jolly walls beckoning her to draw herself deeper.

"Bart, you home?" he shouted.

She heard a muffled reply, then footsteps across the wooden floor.

The door opened onto highly polished ash, the finish enhanced in a complementary fashion by the sun pouring in through the bay windows on the north wall.

In the midst stood a big, muscular man.

His tousled blond hair and bare feet indicated that he'd just woken.

"Sellers, c'mon in.

"What're you up to today?" he asked.

"Who's your buddy?"

"Amy, this is Bart."

She shook his hand amiably, amused at the way his tired eyes bounced from Bob to her—repeatedly.

When his gaze became trained upon her eyes for a seemingly involuntary ten seconds, he quickly turned around and asked, "Do either of you want a cup of coffee or something?"

"Got you too," she mused, enjoying the spectacle.

"Sounds good," Bob responded.

"I need to get woke up.

"May as well fix two."

"Okay, have a seat in the living room. I'll be right in," Bart stated as he placed the instant coffee into the cups.

She sat sleepily on the couch, watching Bob stroll over toward the window.

He turned to face her, then turned around, looking out upon the town, hands in front of him, thumbs interlocked.

"What are you doing?" she asked, chuckling.

"Picturing myself looking down on the lights of the town, pressing your naked, writhing body deep into that couch with my own."

She heard Bart laugh in the next room.

"I can't see that," she said defiantly, slightly startled.

Bart appeared from the kitchen.

As he set the cups on the coffee table, he snorted, "Did he say 'deep'?"

"Well, kind of deep then," Bob deadpanned as he went and sat down.

"Why's a good-looking gal like you hanging out with this crazy fool?" Bart asked her.

"I ask myself the same question," she laughed.

"You ready for the regular season?" he asked Bob.

"Oh, hell yes!" Bob exclaimed.

"We look good—especially on the mound and up the middle.

"That's a hell of a good sign."

"Yeah, I wish we had a little more power is all," Bart responded, his eyes glancing at her thighs.

"Give it time," Bob replied.

"Cralt and Pell will get their timing down.

"Speaking of Pell, can you work with him on a change-up?"

"Yeah, sure. I'll get him throwing a circle change."

She quickly became alienated by the conversation, but within it, she discovered a great deal about the men's relations with one another.

Bob revealed his deep respect for the younger man's knowledge, combining his queries and comments with statements related to former roles Bart had performed—acting out these moments as if they validated what emanated in him.

Bart deflected such praise, looking her direction as he did so, the act belying the humility he was trying to exude.

It appeared that he had conferred great value onto Bob's life, with the social opportunities his charisma had availed Bob of.

Indeed, the success Bart had come to experience as an athlete, soldier, coach, and teacher had seemingly washed over Bob now, as he spoke joyfully of past shared experiences.

The *magic*, she surmised—the power sealed off by both from the midst of this fertilizer-laden air.

She became enthralled with this shared camaraderie—the loyalty Bart somehow had to his less accomplished colleague.

It appeared that he'd nearly fall face forward to instill Bob with the strength he possessed.

It had to be a discouraging quest, she assessed—trying to empower one who didn't have a clue.

But it seemed to be his want.

Inevitable.

Natural.

For him to endeavor as such—to compromise his potential was less a crime against his person than abandoning the man who'd appeared to become dependent on his grace.

"It would be a challenge, to be certain," she mused, as he glanced her way yet again.

But she'd seen loyalty be purchased before.

The offer presented him would be the touch of Amy Vance—

More than enough to break his heart, she asserted, as she watched Bob chatter, certain in her belief that her instincts would not deceive.

Thud!

She heard the sound resonate throughout the quiet house on this humid Memorial Day weekend.

"Damn it," he cursed the demons, subsequent to his punch.

She could envision him lying still now, in repose, taking a respite from the seemingly thousand or more times he'd pushed himself down and off the faded carpet that week.

Whatever it was he valued about that game had vested him with an intensity and focus she'd seen in few people lately.

The incentive, it would seem, was this thing he'd referred to on the paper on the fridge as his *opening day lineup*—that thing he'd amended dozens of times in the past forty-eight hours.

She walked over to it now and read the almost indecipherable print.

"Forget it!"

She heard him scream, his fist now hitting the wall.

He's lost it, she mused as she walked into the room.

She met his angry gaze coolly, staring at his now horizontal frame.

"You okay?" she asked him tenderly.

"Yeah, sure," he responded.

She knelt beside him and was immediately overcome by the strong odor of sweat in the enclosed room.

She pressed on despite the smell, instructing him to raise himself up on his elbow and turn his back toward her.

She began to rub his neck with both hands.

"You're trying too hard—making yourself crazy.

"What are you trying to do here, huh?" she whispered as she pulled herself nearer.

"I've got a golden opportunity with this job.

"To redeem myself, you know?

"I have to make sure I don't lose my fire—don't wimp out."

"Man, that feels good," he said softly, the lateral movement of his neck, along with the slowed, much more pronounced inhalations and exhalations, testifying to her impact.

"I *know* it feels good—I've got the magic right in these nimble digits," she whispered as he arched his neck.

"You just have to relinquish control sometimes,' she said, yet more softly.

Break him down, she implored herself as she moved her face closer to his.

His eyes were now closed, his teeth gently biting his lower lip.

She was again startled by the ease with which she could transform his ire into tranquility with the slightest application of her touch.

Power!

She had it where he was concerned.

She could sell him the illusion of security and worthiness—could shelter him from worry with this showering of affection.

It was all in excess of his capacity to understand—something he could not assimilate, she told herself, as she pressed her fingers harder into his deltoids, her breasts now brushing his back with each movement, painting him in bliss.

She could, she assured herself, vest him with the capability to dream—to believe that she could one day become his—would one day transcend the uniqueness, the duality, the secret misconceptions...

To *hell* with him, she angrily thought, grinding into his skin.

If it weren't for him...

"Ouch."

He flinched, his body jerking forward.

"Those nails are sharp!

"Not that I don't like the thought of your nails scraping my back..."

"You really are crazy," she forced a laugh, releasing her grip.

"Yeah, you're right.

"I've got to be, though.

"Resistant.

"Unyielding.

"I've been a whipping boy before.

"Overcoming that shit feels too good.

"I'd die before going back," he stated, his voice rising as he began to stand.

"C'mon, relax," she said, gently pressing her bare hands downward atop his chest as she deftly moved to a position facing him.

He lay back on the floor, vacant eyes locked with hers, as he mumbled—

"'Big Dog' at UNEI.

"'Ful-dog' in the hood.

"'Mad Dog' in Atlanta."

"Who are those guys?" she asked, grinning at the spectacle.

"My role models.

"Guys who never felt caved by confrontation.

"Never overmatched..."

Unlike you now, she mused, as her fingers caressed his tautening stomach.

His eyes again closed to the world.

She pressed on, experimenting with the strength she possessed—

Toying with him.

"I'll be right back."

The whispered aspiration startled her, stopping her in mid-foray.

She felt him rise and leave as she sat still on the floor.

"What the hell?" she wondered aloud—

Until the sound of running water defined his intent.

"Yeah, you do reek," she intoned as she heard him crawl beneath the tap.

BRRRRINNNNNGG!

The phone sounded inches from her.

Still kneeling, she lifted the receiver.

"Hello," she said softly.

"Who's this?" the disoriented voice demanded.

"Amy. And who is this, may I ask?" she said playfully.

"Oh, Amy, how ya doing? This is Bart."

"Oh, how've you been, baby?"

"Uh, okay. *Baby*?"

"A term of endearment, you know?"

Amy laughed.

"Do you need to speak with Bob? He's in the shower washing his filthy ass."

Bart laughed heartily.

"It's about time. Have him call me, okay?"

"What's your number, honey?"

"Honey? Man, you're going to make me blush yet.

"Amongst other things..."

Amy laughed, then set the phone down, her intent to call him up just moments later—telling him they'd been inadvertently disconnected.

See if he was still hanging eagerly on the line.

"F. Fennel," she said, thumbing through the listings for Rice.

"His dad must be named Henry," she said as she dialed.

A voice appeared on the other end.

Big surprise, she mused.

"I covet you, and there's nothing you can do to stop it.

"I'll be as one with you before the summer's over.

"Bet that farmhouse on it," she teased, then hung up again.

On the other end, one Henry Fennel sat his stunned self onto the couch.

"What the hell?" he asked, as he gazed upon the picture containing his uncle, aunt, and cousins Nikki and Bart.

"Why do I have to be so damn good looking?"

High noon.

Showtime. Gut check.

Whatever expression one used in describing these moments.

It was time—time to make the decisions that determined whether one would succeed or yield.

He'd been here before, years of pain accompanying his march tonight.

The slow, dramatic grind was impeded by his superstitious, cautious step over the chalk baseline. Memories of the final game he'd coached some five years earlier filled his mind as he climbed the hill and waved his players to the summit.

That seemingly impossible lead, he sighed.

Juhl was still throwing well.

He became blinded by the recollection, seeing the faces of Mike, Old Cralt, David, Moss, and Hayes encircling him, as his eyes looked blankly upon the actual questioning looks of young Cralt, Rusty, K.B., Greg, Vale, and Pell.

He could feel himself again being dispatched by Coach Kent, to inform all that Ashton would be the relief for Juhl. That moment, it had been decided, would be an opportune time for Ashton to prepare for his next start—to work on his curveball under actual game conditions.

He had done well with it in batting practice the day prior, he and Kent had both agreed.

Hence, the sight of the fluid movements of the lanky senior in the Brooklyn pen that evening had immediately inspired them to dream of the third-round match, putting Juhl against the less fortunate of either Martens or Wells.

"A lot of guys throw good at batting practice."

The slurred style resonated in his ears now, as it had when he'd first heard it in 1995—years too late.

Woven within the fabric of a tattered garment comprised of hundreds of inanities—like *Hey sweetheart, call me when you're twenty-one; Holy cow!; Pedro Ka-stil-uh*—that bright statement leaped out from the dull camouflage that was the sodden man's words:

"A lot of guys throw good batting practice—that doesn't mean a thing, Steve..."

"Shut up, Harry," he nearly demanded aloud now.

A nine-run cushion, he grimaced, eyes now closed, watching as Juhl, having caught a fly ball in left, threw a strike to Moss at the plate.

"He's still fresh," he whispered silently.

"Wow, that's unbelievable. Nine runs! Geez!"

The exclamation was punctuated by laughter from the salesmen he'd served breakfast to the following shameful morning.

He could be devoured by the pain accompanying that day. He was so near it.

Equally as close was he to the expressions of gratitude in the dancing eyes of the stunned yet elated Brooklyn farm boys who were congratulating Kent and him for having taken part in that "good game..."

"Forget this," he mumbled, shaking his head.

"Gotta live in the now," he reminded himself as he stared at the scoreboard glaring at him beyond the center-field fence.

Score was 1–1.

It had retained those same numbers since the first.

Here, six innings later, Kendall and the G-H pitcher remained locked in this wicked pitchers' duel.

"You're aiming, K.B.," he began, eyes still trained on the board, willing it to change.

"Groove those mechanics, man. Middle infielders, play at double-play depth. Concede the run. I know it's a gamble, but they've probably got the contact play on, as they did in the first. We won't have a shot at the plate. Vale, hold them at first. Rusty, likewise at third. Outfield, grab the lines. Alex, go get Hand to warm you up now—be ready when we call. Fellas..."

"C'mon, Blue, hurry them up," he heard Stortz's exasperated plea issue forth from the first-base box.

"Forget him," Bob muttered automatically, scraping his foot angrily along the pitching rubber.

Nervous laughter surrounded him from his position within the circle.

"Whoops," he countered with a smile. "Forgot where I was."

"Let's go," the umpire barked from behind the plate.

Bob clapped Kendall on the right shoulder, then began his slow descent.

He counted each of the twenty-seven steps back to the dugout, then turned around, ordering K.B. to walk the next batter "unintentionally intentionally."

He quickly placed the four fingers he'd held on his stomach into his pocket, then turned toward Bart, who was standing in the makeshift bullpen behind the dugout.

Before a word was uttered, Bart nodded in affirmation. "He's ready."

"Go get 'em, Alex!" Bob shouted.

Alex handed the ball to Bart, then strode confidently to the mound. His brother handed him the ball, whispering encouraging words.

"Sir!" Bob yelled out, engaging the umpire's attention.

As the umpire turned toward him, Bob shouted instructions. "Bounds, reentry for Jason. Kendall to shortstop. Pell to first. Vale to right. Cody to center."

The umpire rolled his eyes. "Freaking head case," Amy heard him mutter as she watched the young players scatter in six different directions at Bob's request.

In that single snap of his fingers, she learned quite a bit more about her target.

She saw within the act a man trying to cover all the angles of a dilemma.

Despite his apparent overconcern, he seemed to be enjoying the whole production—the "one-act play," with the subplots of him vs. his boys, him vs. the orange-clad man in the box to her left, him vs. the man in the blue shirt, and, of course, him vs. himself.

He must be winning, she surmised.

She watched him swaying and preening beneath the Friday night lights in front of the "cage" they kept him in, the one he could leave only with the permission of the man behind the mask before her.

She shook her head as she looked around, the déjà vu unnerving her as she observed the strange surroundings.

Andrews, Indiana.

Farmers.

Small-town girls.

Again, it made no sense.

She shifted uncomfortably on the wooden seat, surprised to find herself here tonight.

The glow of these beams above her acted as a prod as she drove through Andrews earlier, their lofty position beckoning her near with neon promises.

That was it, she determined.

His dancing and posturing as he worked, eliciting laughter and pleas for service.

The Tap—the place she'd left him years earlier, long after he'd stopped intruding upon her at Holmgren.

That's what this was all about—this sense of familiarity.

The sight of him moving about a restricted area, eyes trained upon him, acting on instinct in the unnatural, chaotic arenas.

Behind the bar.

In the cage.

Before her.

It was all the same.

The only places he seemed to be at home.

Two venues, she concluded, where she could not easily level him.

"Got 'em right where we want 'em, Bart," Bob laughed on the field below.

"Bases loaded. One out. Tie score."

"C'mon, Alex," Bart asserted as the hand-biting slider departed Alex's fingers.

"Sttttriiikke!" the umpire responded.

"Alright!" Bob shouted, watching as the Grable-Harden player spit and stepped out of the batter's box.

When he maneuvered his way back into the same position he'd relinquished—cleats digging into the compliant earth—Bob yelled, "Think, Greg!"

The cross-seam fastball sailed in.

The furious swing of the bat lifted the ball high into the air near the Andrews dugout.

"C'mon, fellas," Bob pressured Greg and Rusty as they gave chase to the ball.

Greg threw himself headlong into the dirt, stretching, reaching.

"He caught it!" Bart shouted as Greg smashed into the fence, his shoulder springing off the unyielding wire mesh separating the field of play from the Andrews bench. Stortz, eyeing the vacant home plate, ordered his man to tag up.

"Oh no," Bob thought aloud. "Rusty, throw him out!"

Rusty reached frantically into Greg's mitt—now at Bob's feet—finding the ball. The redhead turned and fired a strike to the plate, where Alex had arrived an instant before the runner began his dive.

The tag was a quick slap tag. Alex immediately pulled the ball up and off the orange uniform below him.

"Yeah! A double play!" Bob yelled, racing out of the dugout in his excitement.

Looking up, he was startled to see the umpire holding his arms out to his sides, palms down.

"Safe!" he yelled.

Bob felt numb.

"No way, no damn way," he muttered.

"He was out! You blew it!" he screamed, tossing his scorebook into the fence. "How can you call him safe?" he shouted as he rushed the plate. "No way!"

"Coach, get back in the dugout. NOW!" the umpire instructed him.

"No way!" Bob countered, speaking to his misfortune, not the instructions.

"You're out of here!"

The quick punch-out signal surprised him.

"What?"

"Leave now, coach!"

Bob retreated, shocked at the punishment handed to him.

"Where do I go?" he muttered, looking over his shoulder as he scoffed off toward the gate along the left-field side.

"He blows the call, then gets angry with me for calling him on it? What's he expect? Should I have just stood by and silently gone along with that crap? Was it reasonable for him to keep us from the rewards we earned with that extraordinary play? We deserve better."

He cut short his monologue as he shuffled past Bart, standing at the door of the dugout.

"Take charge, son," he stated to his assistant, saluting in jest. "I'm going out to my car. Get us some runs."

Bart's lips twisted into a thin smile. "We'll see what we can do," he asserted, reaching for the lineup card on the fence before him.

"Damn," Bob whispered at the end of a lengthy sigh as he opened the gate.

He tossed his cap at his car and turned around.

From there, he watched in stunned silence as his team was quickly dispensed with in the bottom of the final inning—under Bart's direction.

Upward he trod, offering himself in his mind to whatever god awaited at the summit of this rain-drenched section of Highway 3. His shirt, torn off in disgust, lay somewhere behind him. The sight of him now, when ensnared by the headlights of westbound traffic, tempted several occupants to shout derisively.

"Get a shirt on, white boy!" he heard someone of Hispanic parentage shout at his rain-saturated self.

He turned only when he heard a horn blare, wearily trying to catch a glimpse of the license plate in the downpour, wondering what country they were from. Unable to get a good look, he plodded on.

"Three one-run losses," he muttered. "What more do I have to do?"

Earlier in the evening, he had watched his club squander a 4–0 lead at Martens, his defense failing on several occasions to close the door on their free-swinging foes.

"Forget it!" he hollered as he walked through a puddle. I can't think straight; my mind has been cluttered by al this conflict. Parents seem to be organizing a camp. They've got to be patient with me.

He'd already had a man desert the team—something he simply could not bear. Krans had begun what he feared might become a long procession, angrily turning in his uniform during pre-game batting practice and loudly informing Bob that his dad was tired of him leaving work early just so he coulc sit on the damn bench. And with that, he quit.

Unsure how to respond, Bob quietly took the crumpled uniform, folded it, and set it on the bench near the batting cage before resuming throwing. He pretended to be nonchalant about the ordeal but quickly became unnerved at the sound of Krans's angry departure, badly missing his mark on three tosses to Cralt after hearing the squeal of tires spraying gravel onto the grass beyond the cage.

The problem worsened when Jim Bounds criticized his pitching decision. Perhaps he had allowed Rusty to toil too long, surrendering seven runs before replacing him with Alex, who, despite allowing only one unearned run in three innings, was still tagged with the "losing pitcher" label.

When Jim challenged him on why Alex had been "mopping up" for the less dedicated, less talented Rusty, Bob fell silent. He looked beyond Jim to the gray horizon, listening as the man threatened to pull his sons from a program with such irrational management of resources. Out of the corner of his eye, he caught Rusty in the covered dugout, flipping his middle finger into the air—just for the benefit of Kendall and Alex to his right.

Man, this feels like absolute walking death.

"Just a game," he could hear them all say—guys like Truro and Chase, who had stared down impending, immediate death in the desert of Iraq and the streets of L.A. County.

You don't know pain.

And they would not be silenced, these benevolent critics.

He shivered in the storm, his gaze drifting below him to the nursing home where his uncle lay wounded—the same man who had introduced him to this heartbreaking love of baseball.

The man who had traded propaganda-filled pro baseball books and magazines with a Little Leaguer.

The same man who had never greeted him with a conventional "hello" but instead asked who the preteen projected to win the Major League East.

The same man now locked away, inexplicably kneeling and repeatedly making the sign of the cross, caught beneath a tidal wave of Old Mil, wondering aloud inanely if Yogi still played (played!) for the Pirates.

Another casualty.

"Aahhhhh!" Bob yelled into the night.

Three one-run losses.

What unforgiven sin was he being punished for, anyway?

Fate conspired to beat him down, sentencing him—through mind-blowing irony—to an eternity standing alongside Tantalus, stretching for grapes just out of reach, for water he could not drink.

Powerless.

Over everything, even the good stuff.

It was all greater than his fleeting determination to adjust. Bad timing, arrogant umpires, love—preordained. He merely needed to be present at the opportune or inopportune moment, and the drama would begin to unravel.

Jill had known all this long before he did.

Yes, that's why the sign—the one with that single word, "Powerless"—had hung slightly askew on her bedroom wall. That ominous word was the first thing he would see, the first stimuli he would incorporate into his young, congested mind on those autumn mornings above the park in Younkers.

Back then, that word—the perfect economy of explanation—had signified exactly where that tough Harrison girl was emotionally.

Abandoned by an insufficient lover.

Unsympathetic employers.

Prodded awake from a fitful sleep by a colic-ridden baby.

He had lain still, observing how the tough old Harrison girl was being forged—like the steel in the foundries outside that same city's limits—into something that, despite its apparent elegance, was far more fortifying and practical than it was beautiful.

He chose not, he sighed, to stay around to watch the development. He did not have the resolve to risk both life and sanity by toiling inside the impossibly hot oven that was the eroding apartment. He would not be present when, nine years later, she secured the high-paying nursing position that was now hers; would not reside in the new house; would not ride in the new car; would not watch the healthy, happy child frolic.

No, that word—"powerless"—was designed for him, not her. That's why she placed it there; he was certain now.

Disillusioned where she was cautious.

Reckless where she was vigilant.

He kicked at the mud.

What was he thinking?

Why did he yield to the suggestion of his peers, the ones who told him she was cursed—this manipulative, brash entity?

Why didn't he hold fast to his initial belief that he could secure a future with his levelheaded, loyal buddy?

Why?

Because he needed everything to be either very good or very bad, to fit quite readily into these mutually exclusive mental files. To this, he could adapt. Unfortunately, his thoughts were now liquid, flexible—much like the aforementioned steel—diluted by too much education.

The compulsion to understand inhibited these mental constants from assuming a distinct, useful shape.

Nothing here, of course, could be all good following all bad.

But close.

Either way, it sucked the life out of him.

As did potential—he grimaced, recalling how "Big Dog" loathed the word. That highly hyped football prospect who'd snorted away a promising athletic career at the age of nineteen.

Yes, expectations and ego kill, the Zen masters implied.

"Lower the scope of your goals," Robert M. Pirsig told them—that was essential to peace of mind.

"Humility," they preached in the clubhouse.

Fine, fine, he muttered.

But then, in all later experiences, humility becomes implausible.

Overwhelming.

Numbing you, even as it wraps about you.

Your attempts at recreation—impossible.

"Damn all this!" he cursed, raising his eyes to the melting sky.

"It'd be a lot easier to just endure one conclusive ass-whipping!"

She spotted him as she crested the hill.

His staggering, drenched form startled her.

Was he drunk?

It wouldn't have been inconsistent with the shocking letter he'd left on the kitchen table—an initial draft of his resignation from Andrews Community High School.

"Unable to fit the image expected," he'd written. 'I step down and away to allow a more competent, capable individual to assume control."

He felt he owed at least that much to his alma mater.

The note sat open before her, unmailed, unfinished.

No way.

Despite its apparently sincere tone, she knew he'd never discard his only opportunity. The despondent message wasn't a declaration—it was bait. Designed to elicit her support.

Each sentence, carefully placed atop her notecards, painted her into a corner.

If she refused to sympathize, she would confirm what he already feared—that she'd been using him for her own gain.

If she comforted him, she'd only reinforce his belief that she'd always be there.

Either way, she lost.

Yes, she could see it clearly: her calculated cruelty, meant to hurt and repel him, would instead be dismissed as an aberration. A fluke.

Proof, in his mind, that she still cared.

She was losing patience.

Enough of this.

Impulsively, she grabbed her keys and left, gripping the wheel tighter with each mile.

What a challenge, she sighed.

She hadn't expected him to take it this far—to put his own health at risk.

She pulled alongside him, rolling to a slow stop.

He squinted through the rain.

"Who's that?" he demanded.

"Get in, Bob. I'm taking you home."

"Why?"

"What the hell do you mean, why? It's pouring out."

"I'm alright."

"Bullshit!" she snapped. "Get in. Please."

The urgency in her voice made him comply without hesitation.

He slid into the seat beside her, shivering, startled to realize how far from home he'd wandered.

★ ★ ★ ★ ★

He awakened early the next morning, both physically and spiritually famished. Fixing himself a simple breakfast of eggs and toast, he sat down to eat and watch Amy work.

"Good morning, little white girl," he mumbled between bites.

"How are you feeling?" she asked without looking up, her hand moving vigorously, pressing ink onto notecards.

Man, she is focused, he mused. *"I'm okay, thanks."*

"Good," she replied, effortlessly retrieving another card.

"Damn, you look good this morning. Makes me almost wish you were mine. For an hour at least."

Her face revealed no trace of emotion.

He stood, placing his dishes in the sink.

"Guess I better leave you alone," he muttered to her bowed head.

Then, abruptly, she jerked forward before resuming her posture.

Still has an impact on her, that phrase. Makes no sense—eight years removed, and nothing's changed.

He really did feel like leaving her alone today. He needed to regroup. This playful bullshit wasn't going to get him back on track. Hell, if nothing else, it looked good having her around, even if he couldn't slobber all over that pretty body.

Why waste energy trying?

His boys deserved better than what he'd given them so far.

Determined, he thumbed through the old suitcase.

"Where is that Zen book?" he muttered, digging through the contents. He needed insight. Wisdom. Now.

As he parted the last layer of papers, he cursed.

He was always misplacing stuff.

It made no sense.

"Ramblings of a Mad Man," he read aloud, staring at the orange tablet at the bottom of the case.

"Appropriate," he whispered, mind drifting back to Younkers, three years ago. Vacation time. Bored and disappointed.

Junking out on Braves and Cubs games in a hotel room.

Walking around like a ghost.

Nobody remembered his name.

Nobody to talk to.

That was the only way he could keep himself from bolting—to sit in that damn student union and write. He knew that if he left disappointed, he'd never return.

Had to connect somehow.

So he wrote.

A fictional, triumphant baseball team.

Interwoven with real-life observations.

A la Pirsig.

Not a bad decision, he reflected, as he walked toward the kitchen.

It changed his karma.

The next trip back had been great—running into old friends, girls.

Regret replaced by creativity.

He should do it again, he mused, sitting down with the tablet in hand.

Pouring himself a cup of coffee, he flipped to the first page.

"Poverty, baldness, envy, fear—all gave me an edge. Made me resistant to the latent self-doubt that once haunted my every waking moment...

Whipped so bad lately, it's hard to face me anymore.

Guys like Joe Kjos, Dick Williams, even pot-bellied Howard taught me survival was contingent upon my ability to metaphorically knock people back off the plate.'

Joe.

Bob smiled, remembering the grumpy S.O.B.

Tough to bear on a hot summer day—shouting, cursing, setting orders atop the kitchen counter.

But inspiring.

Toiling day and night in food service and janitorial work.

Always searching for more of these horrible opportunities.

Never expressing pain.

Always enduring.

Scoffing at those who took *sick days*.

A fighter.

An abrasion on the collective psyche of his less weary colleagues—who'd spare nothing in his quest to prosper (monetarily).

Howard was no less mysterious.

Showing up an hour before his shift.

Positioning himself at the minimum-wage trough.

Thriving—somehow extracting enough from the scraps tossed his way to live comfortably.

And stripping Bob of excuses.

"Jackass," Bob muttered.

How did he do it?

Laying his heavy ass down every night in the corner of that crowded, alcoholic flophouse.

Abstaining from both drink and smoke—all because of a mere doctor's suggestion.

Unaffected.

Sanity intact.

Bob whistled, calculating his own odds of doing the same.

And then there was Dick Williams.

The man who revealed his method for managing the lunacy of professional baseball.

Putting himself "on edge."

Creating team unity by making his players unanimously despise him.

Sacrificing popularity.

Deliberate estrangement.

That had to be tough.

Severing himself from the affection of his charges.

Fighting with younger, stronger men who rebelled.

And yet—prevailing.

Not just beating them.

Mocking them.

Scoffing at the limits of their resolve.

All for the sake of winning baseball games.

Yes.

The trio had revea ed the truth.

The best defense? Be offensive.

Don't wait around to lose.

Go all out trying to win.

Unsparingly.

Be empowered with passion.

Defer assessments and consequences to a later time.

Bob closed the notebook, exhaling sharply.

Yeah.

He had his answer.

He turned the page.

The question before him seemed to jump off the paper, striking his consciousness.

"Amy Lou, where are you?"

He smiled, glancing toward his blonde muse in the next room.

"Would you remember me if your very existence depended on it? Like a dream from which I never want to wake. I feel your l ps locked with mine—a controlled collision borne of desperation, confusion. Yes, where are you? Probably weakening someone's resolve with that seemingly innocent smile..."

Now that's longing, he thought, his eyes drifting back to his words.

Glad that's over.

The next line caught his attention.

"Henry."

Contribution: 60 mph emergency brake slides, hesitantly turning a corner and flipping the old Mercury with me inside.

Analogy/lesson: Pitch too fine, and you walk in the winning run. Throw the heat—eyes closed, mechanics grooved, instinctive—and pick up the save.

The kid was what they all wanted to set free within themselves, but fear held them back—an aversion to social sanction.

Small-town *dumb-down*.

Static patterns repelling creativity.

Now, deeply inspired, he continued reading, recognizing the influence of Pirsig's *Lila* in the following passage on the fallacy of romanticizing his daredevil friend:

Static vs. Dynamic.

Dynamic: *UNEI taught me the value of being free, open-minded. A $27,000 lesson.*

Static: *Then staid conservatives like Dan, Dad, and the Andrews baseball committee rescued me every summer, in the process making the pursuit of further improvement possible. Helping also when I ultimately fled Younkers and my unavoidable financial demise.*

Dynamic: *Kjos. Irate when duped out of $20 worth of jewelry in the 'hood, yet placid in the wake of having $200 worth of clothing stolen from my car in the same minority community a month later. Why? No hustle attended the latter act—only loss.*

He'd read Silverman's *Criminal Violence, Criminal Justice*, the one where he stated that the only thing a badass fears is getting old.

Kjos disagreed.

"The only thing a badass fears is being conned," he had countered.

Implied within was the idea that passivity in a competitive setting was the ultimate sin.

When the locals had hinted that they were probably cops *infiltrating*, Kjos had insisted they not act in a manner inconsistent with the allegation.

"Any edge," he had told Bob. "Especially one attained without effort."

Bob turned away from the page and walked to the screen door behind him.

He looked out at the two semis descending the hill to the south.

"Sorry you're gone, Kjos," he whispered to the sparrows in a nearby tree.

"You showed me a lot."

It was ironic, he reflected, envisioning the redhead fretting over the junk necklace he'd let the black man "hold"—the man's promise to sell it at a more lucrative profit pushing Kjos into consenting.

Victory was right there.

Kjos had it figured.

"Just had to wait it out..."

Sellers had felt the same.

Ruining the fact that he hadn't been able to make that one decision—the one that could have allowed him and his to prevail.

Larger margins of defeat—like a damn carjacking in the 'hood—couldn't have possibly produced such angst.

Not to a true *competitor.*

He turned the page, feeling secure now in his decision to give his team, and himself, the day off.

A fresh perspective was coming into focus.

A review of his past self.

Dynamic: *UNEI, Jill. Didn't like 'em initially—felt weak-kneed, hopelessly smitten—then came to resent the hell out of 'em.*

Static: *Closing the door on both—an act eliciting feelings worse than any other once you've been in love. Wish I'd never met 'em. Should have never left them. The sentiment expressed, inanely, within the same expiration of breath as I travel northeast each April.*

He could, he realized as he looked toward Amy, become addicted quickly.

Like the ACOAs.

Loyal to the wrong things.

He would be vigilant.

He read further.

Dynamic: *J.C. Dude would tell you he loved you—even when he was sober! Told me I "thought too much" when he pulled the beer out of my hand that night, when I was acting in defiance of the Twelve. Didn't he realize you weren't supposed to do that? Haven't had a drink since, though.*

Dude had married a woman with two kids.

Driven to Dallas in a beat-up station wagon—despite a mechanic's warning that it might explode.

Just up and quit his bartending job at *The Tap* and took off.

Impulsive as hell.

A perfect blend of confidence, faith, and humility.

Unpretentious.

Rewarded within days with a high-paying sales position.

Did what he felt was right—ethically—without reflection.

And won big.

Static: "Consider the consequences," J.C. had uttered as he pulled the beer from my grasp. No small matter, these rejections—life-threatening even.

Having trusted in the wise counsel of his loins with Angela and Marley, Sellers had almost been undone. Certain they were throwing the heat, he'd swung too freely—way too early—all his weight over his right foot, in an inferior position to challenge their change of speed.

Angela—he knew, just knew—that she, Amy's twin, was inviting him, sans words, to join her later in Holmgren for the purpose of reenacting the Valentine's Day drama of a year prior. For the actor and actress almost directly resembled the pair present on that hallowed day. When the curtain fell—somehow, during the first act, lowered by an angry boyfriend—he knew the show would not go on.

Marley: She compromised a well-fortified friendship with a single sentence: "I'd make love to Bob anytime." No shit—that's what she informed mutual friends at her party.

I was cool, though, waited for her to recant, to qualify, to state that she was only kidding. Hey, I'd have laughed with you if you did, content just to have a pretty friend like yourself, Marley. But instead of laughing, you offered me the opportunity to stay over. Hell, I only lived a block away—had walked a mile from the clubhouse to get to your place.

Then, when you came into the room where I was sleeping, lying on the floor at my feet—damn! I had no chance, no choice, even after you challenged me for drawing near. Hey, I felt as if I'd been victimized. No way I could honor your curt dismissal, your pleas for me to leave. No way. It was too late. The friendship, the trust, the well-wishing we'd shared up to that moment had vanished. Forever.

It made no sense—none of it.

"Sex, man, anyway," he mused.

He already knew the words that followed, the thoughts provoked by the touch of the enticing duo—the ones he'd felt he'd never gain access to. The upset, a valid word in such cases—the sports metaphor that referred to one's defeat of an opponent to whom, prior to the conquest, one had been deemed inferior. Nothing felt better than to administer the upset.

Amy. She had become his upset victim back at UNEI. Angela and Marley—tantalizing near misses. No way he could forget them. He would bring the experiences into each subsequent liaison, ever at his peril. For the reverse of this phenomenon was that nothing felt worse than being defeated by one you'd deemed inferior to yourself.

Hal McRae had been taken to task in USA Today by La Russa for having bitterly criticized his Royals for losing to Tony's "second-division" A's. L.C. had scolded Sellers and his roommate for assigning relative numerical values to the girls who walked by in the 'hood. He'd been dismayed at the sudden rebuff of the overweight girl who'd groveled at his feet for the preceding hour at the club one night. The remedy, it seemed, was to treat all with equal amounts of respect—being exceedingly grateful for each victory.

La Russa—he smiled, thumbing at the A's jacket behind him on the hook on the wall. The lawyer was Sellers's favorite manager now that Sparky had retired. He was a man who knew static patterns were illusory, that Earth revolves even as we attempt to stand still. Rivers overflow, tornadoes devour hundred-year-old structures. Yes, nature—like Tony—seemed to loathe the status quo.

Daily lineup changes. Quick removal of tiring pitchers from the mound. Three-man pitching groups. Creative in the face of adversity. Kicking ass in a "small market." Revealing to all in his placid manner that, yes, it could be done.

Cool.

He'd introduced so much change into his life at his own command that he'd become immune to the external deviation that was free-agent movement.

Static: Bart Cox. Set lineups, pitching rotations. Dance with the one who brought you—large-market mentality. Cool, effective, yet somehow uninspiring. It wasn't until his fourth consecutive postseason with the Braves that he finally won it all—utilizing his bench, Devereaux, backup closers, Borbón—realizing, finally, it seemed, that players can't grow sitting on the pine, locked into fixed roles.

He paused after reviewing this passage, placing his hands behind his head and gazing at the ceiling—a mannerism borrowed from the chairmen of the old clubhouse in Yonkers. It was a movement he associated with relaxation, confidence; thus, when initiated, he would often become locked within an almost trancelike state.

He began to count the tiles on the tattered ceiling, then closed his eyes.

"Just win, baby!"

The old Raiders' motto met his consciousness as the candlestick-like winds swirled about outside. That's what he needed now—a win—of any kind.

That, he surmised, would put an end to the morale issue on his team.

Can't win cooperation. That's confusing ends and means—of this he was certain. Why cooperate within a team context if you're not to be extrinsically rewarded?

That's why Amy was here. That's why any of the women in his life had ever been there. When he'd been gaining on a college degree, they drew near. When he bought them drinks, they drew even nearer.

Projected earnings, he mused as he stopped by the sink and began washing the dishes—she'd be nowhere around without them.

He paused to look over his shoulder at "her," his "babe."

Man, she looked good.

I'm a lucky man today.

"Just win, baby."

The thought reached him again, evincing memories of long-haired "Snake" Stabler throwing to "stickum"-saturated, long-haired Biletnikoff, cheered on by the late Matuszak and Alzado, all directed by the comedic John Madden. They'd take others' castoffs, "free spirits," and beat all challengers—bending rules, snubbing convention in their quest to establish their own traditions. A "tradition" of excellence.

Moving when and where they wanted—Oakland to L.A., L.A. to Oakland—the ultimate antitrust mongrels.

Al's boys.

That damn bay, he smiled. It seemed to inspire lunacy.

Charlie O. The mustachioed crazies destroying the Big Red Machine. Reggie.

That's what got him hooked on the game—the broadening horizons imparted to him by these boys in the hippies' backyard.

Karma. It had to be.

Cincy—they still didn't allow facial hair.

Incarcerated Orlando Cepeda quoting the tenets of Buddhism.

Barry. Dusty. Saying how he liked surrounding himself with a team of "bad boys."

Friggin' "Prime Time" Deion.

Oakland A's—1972–74, 1988.

Raiders—1977, 1984.

49ers. Four times.

Champions—all within his lifetime. All beginning with his first gaze upon Dick Williams's A's in the 1972 World Series. The influence would not be offset.

Dynamic they were.

And certainly, he would become too, by establishing—then utilizing for all they were worth—old cars, jobs, interpersonal relations, and pitchers.

Thus, always ensuring he had an alternative escape route when the resource was depleted.

I.e., a relief pitcher.

Hell, he'd always been that way when he was at peak performance as a player.

Swinging viciously at life's curves. Reaching base when the third strike he'd just accrued eluded the opposing catcher.

Passion, he surmised, was rewarded.

Fears were self-fulfilling prophecies.

Head-shaking, head-hanging blueprints for destruction.

"No free rides," he'd told Rusty in his second year of coaching, seven years earlier in Galva.

Six pickoff attempts later, he was still shouting the same to this swaggering redhead pitcher.

No sense giving in—not that Rusty would have anyway.

Internal fortitude, forged by brawling with two large older brothers, was so damn ingrained. Might as well capitalize on it. Make that base runner pay.

That's why Del's static manner, effective as it was, did not mesh well with his style that year.

Bunting. Always pushing the ball into play. Using contrived outs to move runners.

It seemed almost a sacrilege to Sellers when the fence was so close.

Del was a former Andrews star, though. That's why Sellers sat idly by as his volunteer assistant gradually assumed charge—as the victories remarkably accrued.

To him, the game could be controlled, honored, conquered—as always.

Sellers, in contrast, merely closed his eyes and flailed, flooding the field with movement, noise, desperation.

It had, he concluded, to have been confusing to his players to have been subjected to these mutually exclusive methods of instruction.

He sighed—at both the thought and the next on the page.

"Static: Guilt—Culpability, Legacy of Shame."

Catalyst: Not allowing a kid to play enough, then finding out the strong affection they had for the game—watching it wane. E.g., Ped six years ago.

Remedy: Research. Don't presume to know another's capability/desire.

Looking up from the notebook, he saw her gazing at him. When she turned her head to reach for yet another note card, he started to speak—then thought better of it and returned to his review of past philosophy.

It was better this way, he decided.

He knew that Bart and Klein had turned it around for old Ped, placing him in the starting lineup the subsequent year. He'd excelled within the advanced role, and Sellers had been pardoned. Bailed out.

This would not be so with old "Crazy Man," however. His inability to properly teach the youngster how to position himself at third base on a steal attempt had resulted in the youth having his leg fractured.

Bob winced, seeing himself again, watching helplessly while Crazy Man twisted in agony on the field.

"Damn," he whispered, angry that he didn't immediately apply ice to the site.

Klein in the stands, admonishing him not to move the leg. It's too late.

He'd really messed up—had failed his boys at a crucial juncture. This he knew.

This was his legacy. A legacy of shame.

"Screw it," he'd written, attempting to soothe himself.

Baseball is a perversion of the body. Shoulders destroyed, ankles pierced by spikes, elbows torn. Infielders sent flying by runners attempting to slide through them in their attempts to 'break up' the double play. Line drives hit back up the middle off pitchers' heads. Foul tips bending catchers' thumbs. Home plate collisions.

Happens all the time. The price paid for the privilege of attaining success within the lines.

Yes, but he'd never paid, he reflected now. The only price borne was this silver cap on his tooth—the memento from a ball he'd lost in the sun in his third-grade year.

Big deal.

Under his watch, players had suffered broken thumbs, legs—even Del's nose had been broken by Mike's errant warm-up toss. Kids running out of the batter's box, subsequent to being hit by a pitch—

He himself had never been hit.

"I'm sorry, Crazy Man," he whispered as he stared out the window.

He thumbed to the next page—the last one he'd written in that notebook.

Skipping past a list of his all-star team of former charges and a thesis on the perfect relationship with a woman, he read the quote he'd been looking for:

"Lloyd McClendon, addressing the fact of having missed postseason play for the first time in four seasons: 'Don't look back. It'll make you mad.'"

Following that, he had written:

Excellent. I'd been angry with Jill for not inviting me to spend time with her here this week. I'd been trying to recreate the energy of 1986. Hell, I bet Doc Gooden does the same, he of the then–World Champion Mets. Time doesn't care, Dwight. It has amnesia. I'd been a good Little League and junior high player but couldn't do anything right on the high school fields. Why? Who knows? Who cares? Yesterday is gone.

He closed the notebook and carried it to the bedroom, somehow less anxious and more determined.

Sellers had now been made privy to the fact that he'd been in a bad way in the era in which he'd written—but was still going, driving through the pouring rain with no windshield wipers.

Sans incident.

"Forget it," he smiled and dropped the tablet into the open suitcase.

She'd looked up only after he'd departed in his black-and-white suit.

"Where was the game to be played on this night?' she wondered as she stepped before the calendar.

"At Clancy at 6:00," he'd inscribed within the day's box.

North on 11, a half-hour drive.

Maybe she'd go—take a respite from this work on her book. She had to select from among two possible alternate conclusions anyway. The break would allow her to gain perspective regarding the most practical course of action here.

Things were going well, she decided as she stepped outside.

If she could publish her novel, she could profit doubly from this sabbatical—simultaneously extinguishing him and replenishing her dwindling savings.

"Ten million dollars," she sighed. "What kind of cache was that anyway?"

On Monday she could call into work, tell them she'd be willing to return within a month. That would be long enough to implement her plans.

Bob out of her life. Book complete. Ron at bay.

"Bony," he'd called her in Matt's. "Her bony ass."

She gripped the wheel tighter, her eyes narrowing to complement her frown.

As if he had the answers.

"Stupid ass," she muttered as she pressed on the accelerator.

"Little white girl." "Princess."

All words he employed to attempt to demean her.

He would pay, even though the words did not upset her; he would be assessed a penalty for having merely uttered them in her presence.

"Boy, will you ever pay," she whispered as she spotted him while turning into the ballpark drive.

Sitting with one leg crossed over the other, hands resting atop his neck, he seemed to be quite relaxed. Driving nearer, she could see him staring into the sky.

The only movements he made were occasional pats on the backs of his players, accompanied by words of approval.

He looked less affected by the events unfolding than did the spectators in the stands to her left.

Within moments, they were all walking off the field.

She heard Bob congratulate a "Kendall" on some sort of "one-hitter."

Her eyes flashed toward Bart, who stood on the dirt portion of the field, talking to that redhead kid who'd made advances to her in the café one night.

Now, she told herself, as she stepped out of the car and advanced upon Bart.

Now was the time.

"Amy!" she heard him cry out.

"Okay then," she whispered. "Not now."

She turned her eyes toward the beaming Bob, who was heading toward her from the left.

"You made it!" he exclaimed.

"Why, yes, I did," she replied playfully. "Congratulations."

"Thanks. It feels good to get the first one. Hey, can I catch a ride to the house?"

"Sure."

"Bart," he turned to address his colleague, "you have me covered?"

Amy's eyes engaged the young coach's. He nodded in affirmation as he looked at her.

Tomorrow, cude, she whispered silently as she turned and opened the car door.

She paused before entering, ensuring that his eyes were still trained upon her.

When she detected that he hadn't moved even a little, she smiled at him and climbed into the vehicle.

Bob entered moments later.

"You're happy tonight," she stated as she studied his relaxed appearance.

"Definitely," he asserted, then amended his statement. "I'm more relieved than anything else, really. I mean, f we hadn't won, I think I would have resigned—would nave just taken off."

"You're kidding."

"No. I've been here before—seven years ago. We'd lost fourteen games in a row over a two-year period, and I'd had enough.

You should've seen me on that night after we'd won.

Seventeen to sixteen. I got so excited that I felt guilty and damn near apologized to the opposing coach.

Yes, I was going to walk over and explain the personal significance of the triumph—that stay of execution from my own hands.

I couldn't, though. I just kept partying, my pant leg still covered with dirt from the slide I'd taken."

"What slide?" Amy asked as she drove south.

"Well, you see, it was kind of embarrassing, but I got so excited at the chance of seeing us win that I lost my composure.

I was running step for step with Mike as he ran, egging him to go faster.

When it looked like the play was going to be close, I shouted at him to 'slide!' I was so hyped by that point that I slid myself—just as Mike slid across the plate with the winning run.

This game will do things like that to a man."

She mirrored his grin with her own in the darkness, laughing at the manner in which he lived vicariously through these farm kids.

Overwrought in the wake of their adolescent fluctuations and fancies.

Life was never going to be easy for him, she thought.

And, she concluded, she was about to make things worse.

★ ★ ★ ★ ★

"Booyah, buddy!" Bob exclaimed, the utterance evoking for him memories of hyper Mike shouting the same some years ago.

Bob's zeal stemmed from having watched his boys expunge a five-run deficit in the first inning against Rice.

"Your arm tired, Bart? You've waved in a hell of a lot of runs already."

Bart smiled. "Feels like a wild one today."

"Hell, yes, it does. Come on, Pell," he shouted, training his attention on his starting pitcher.

Pell, he knew, was a great athlete, excelling in four sports. Hit for power and average on the diamond. Good fielder. However, he was more a thrower than a pitcher, with his stiff-leg, fly-open style. His methodology resulted too often in his being "wild high." When the umpire was averse to giving him the "high strike," as was the case this evening, Pell was guaranteed a frustrating night.

"Bend the back! Land on the bent leg!" Bob shouted automatically before realizing the words would have no effect. Pell was simply unwilling to compromise, his large muscles for once not serving him.

Kendall, in contrast, a relatively small man, had an ERA below 2.00—his proper execution imparting proper movement to the pitch, which offset his lack of velocity.

He looked past his slight shortstop to the scoreboard.

"The score's six to five after the second. Pell's thrown fifty pitches," he whispered aloud. "Gonna need some long relief tonight. Who do we use, Bart?"

"Jason's probably the best choice. Rusty could mop up, save Cralt for Missoula. Of course, we could start Alex then, also."

"You've been thinking ahead, son," Bob replied in mock condescension. "Very good."

"Ready for anything, that's me."

They watched as Pell walked the second of consecutive batters in the third.

Bart instructed Hand and Jason to warm up. "Guess this is why they pay me the big bucks," he muttered.

Twenty-five pitches later, the Falcons returned to the dugout, trailing 8–6.

"Man, his strike zone is small!" Pell exclaimed, looking over his shoulder at the ump.

"It's those high strikes," Bob said softly. "Just aren't gonna get them tonight. How're you feeling?"

"Good," Pell replied while moving toward the on-deck circle. "Let's get the lead back, guys," he begged his teammates.

Consecutive home runs in the inning by Pell and Cralt enabled them to do just that.

They led 10–8 after the third.

The game, Bob mused as the teams exchanged roles to begin the fourth, resembled the fourth game of the 1993 World Series—the one in which Philadelphia simply could not score enough runs to subdue Toronto.

They ultimately surrendered fifteen, six of which were earned at the expense of the "Wild Thing" Mitch Williams.

He could see poor Mitch cursing as the ordeal evolved, marching deeper into the abyss, victimized by the fickle temperament of the game, the memory of his previous postseason success obliterated.

Before him, Pell hit the leadoff hitter with a pitch. Two outs later, he surrendered a towering two-run homer to center.

"High fastball," Bob muttered. "Hit it again, Jason Mix in the curves. They've seen only a handful so far tonight.'

When Jason reached the bullpen, Bob called a timeout and began the trek to the mound.

"Let's talk, Pell," he said when he arrived. "You been throwing many changes?"

"I can't get a good feel with that circle change Bart showed me. In fact, that's what Jones just hit into the damn river."

Bob was about to chastise Pell for his choice of adjectives but, upon closely examining the large man's sweaty, disappointed expression, opted not to.

"Thumb still hurting, huh?" he asked instead, referring to the incident in which the digit was stepped on by the lumbering Rice first baseman on a pickoff attempt in the first inning.

"We have relief on the way," Bob said, turning on his heel and nodding toward Jason.

"Don't pull me, Coach," Pell implored. "I'll find it."

"Okay, Horse," Bob smiled. "Just keep them within a touchdown, all right?"

He walked off immediately, having learned long before that a determined pitcher is a valuable resource.

Old Cralt had asked for the ball in both ends of a doubleheader years earlier versus Wells, expending a week's worth of pitching eligibility in one evening. It was heartening—man, was it heartening—even if it prompted him to start an experienced Mike against a tough Grable team the following evening. He was assailed for eight runs in the first.

Bob could recall scanning his bench for relief. Finding no suitable replacement, he summoned fourteen-year-old Bart into the game, even though he'd been in Arizona for two weeks and hadn't thrown a pitch in half a month. What a walk-a-thon that turned out to be. They still laughed at the wild display Bart put on that night.

Bob had never pitched; therefore, he had no clue why some of the pitchers he replaced during games had tears in their eyes. Neither could he identify with Cralt and Pell, who, offended at the mere sight of action in the bullpen, would plead with—or even threaten—Bob to leave them in, willing to pitch until they collapsed.

He waved Jason back onto the bench, settled onto his perch, and leaned lazily against the protective screen behind him.

"What'd he say?" Bart asked.

"We'll have to shoot him to get him off the hill, that's what."

"Well, all right!" Bart exclaimed.

Throughout the next three innings, it appeared that whoever battled last would emerge the victor in the contest—a pleasant thought for Bob, standing as he was in his hometown.

At the end of the fourth, the Hawks led 13–12, and then 17–14 after the fifth.

In the sixth, Pell, on his 150th offering of the night, yielded his second home run of the inning. It was all Bob could bear not to call time.

"Let him gut it out," he implored himself.

Valiantly, Pell coaxed the next two hitters to pop up his cross-seam fastballs before Jones took his next pitch to the very top of the left-field fence and strolled safely into second.

"Keep 'em in the park, Pell! Think it through, Greg!" Bob shouted to his exhausted battery.

Greg had called a good game, Bob assessed. Hopefully, now he'd provide Pell a low target.

Man, he contemplated, why was it that every time Greg didn't indicate he'd heard a message, his heart raced, his anxiety palpable as he watched, helpless?

Crack!

He hadn't even seen the pitch, awash as he was in reflection. The ball was smashed into right field, where Cody, charging hard, scooped it up in a single motion and released the offending sphere back toward Greg at home.

Vale leaped to intercept the throw. The batter, caught unaware by the intrusion, slipped in his endeavor to impede his momentum as he rounded first. Vale alertly dove to the ground, where the runner lay prone, reaching desperately for the sanctuary of the first base bag. He arrived there an instant before Vale applied the tag.

"Damn!" Bob cursed. "Almost."

His perspective, like that of the plate umpire's, was obscured by Vale's outstretched frame. In the resultant collision, the runner had been knocked free of his post. Vale held his tag throughout the shoulder-to-shoulder meeting. When the base umpire arrived, he saw the runner off the bag, beneath the ball secured in Vale's first baseman's mitt.

"What the hell?" Bob queried as he saw the umpire's punch-out sign.

Both Rice coaches rushed onto the field to protest. The umpire stood, arms folded across his chest, defending his position.

"That run had to count, didn't it, Bart?"

Jones had scored before the out call had been made. Bob could not hide his surprise when the decision to deem the runner at first out was upheld, and the umpires considered the run inadmissible.

"Wow, we stole one," Bob whispered.

The Falcons were "retired" in order in the bottom of the inning and took the field leading 17–16 in the final frame.

"Kendall, finish this one," Bob said as he approached the home plate umpire. "Johnny, take short."

Pell was clearly through now, already wrapping his elbow and shoulder in ice packs.

"Good job, Horse. Hell of an effort," Bob said to Pell as he looked over his shoulder.

"Thanks for staying with me," Pell replied.

They all watched nervously as Kendall, forced into action without the benefit of a preparatory period, gave up two hard singles, then bounced a curve into the dirt, allowing both runners to advance. The Falcons were fortunate that the batter swung at the errant two-strike pitch. One out, thus, had been secured.

As Rice's leadoff hitter approached the box, Bob called time and ordered an intentional pass be given. He then walked to the mound, motioning Alex in from center field as he did so.

"K.B., take short. Johnny, go center."

Kendall handed the ball to Alex as Bob instructed the infielders to play at double-play depth.

Alex was asked to induce a ground ball via a curve or two-seam fastball.

"Gut check time, Greg. I know you're tired, man, but I have to see you stop everything now. They've shut us down on offense. This could be our last chance to win."

Greg nodded, wiping the sweat from his forehead.

"Need a drink?" Bob asked.

"Nah, but it'll soon be Miller time."

Bob laughed, then looked toward Kendall, who appeared inconsolable as he clawed at the dirt with his spikes.

"Shake it, Kendall. I hurried you in here tonight. It's not your fault."

"Man, K.B., don't you realize you're too gifted an athlete to be fretting like this?" he asked the earth beneath the third base line. "Leave that playing-not-to-lose bul shit to me," he mumbled as he looked back upon his slight, capable shortstop.

Bob was aware, as he watched Kendall cautiously pick up the first of Vale's practice throws, that he could easily have lost the opportunity to avail himself of the young man's pitching.

This was no arrogant youngster. It took coaxing to induce him to initially hoist himself atop the elevated patch of dirt. Yes, it was exasperation and the flawless movements of the ten-year-old afield that spurred Bob to act upon his vision of placing Kendall there, against the youth's wishes.

"Gosh damn, he was good," he'd exclaimed back then to George, mere weeks after he'd sent Kendall into the fray in Wayne.

"Draw a line from the pitching rubber to the center of the plate; don't open up so much," he could hear himself shout to the child, feeling quite inspired despite the unfavorable score as he preached the gospel of St. Thomas Seaver.

For he knew just then that he had been correct in his assessment. This was no raw juvenile material with which he was experimenting; this was an elegant athlete capable of transferring his refined skills from other aspects of his game to the mound.

He was, Bob assessed as he sat down, a refined animal who'd wait patiently for the optimal time to swing into motion. This preserving of that which he'd attained was a blessing to those fortunate to have either preceded or followed him to the plate.

Alex and Greg must have averaged a stolen base per Kendall's plate appearance. Pell, an extra RBI—all as a result of their colleagues' willingness to read via the humble, time-consuming base on balls.

The self-assurance that somehow bypassed the modest Kendall affixed itself to and now ran amok within the insides of Alex. Tempered only slightly by the influence of his well-mannered older brother, the potential for gaudy external display was redirected instead into the placid quasi-swagger he employed when maneuvering within the lines.

Bob watched him deliver the last of his warm-up tosses from the set position, recalling how, on one visit to the mound in some Little League game long ago, he'd somberly informed struggling "young Alex" that he'd be forever placed under the awful weight of his community's high expectations of him.

"I'm awesome," he recalled the precocious youth responding in jest after striking out the side.

"Strrrrrikkkeee!" the umpire's voice rang out now, testifying to Alex's recurrent proficiency.

"He'll go pro!" Bob could hear the eldest of the four Bounds brothers assert with a reverent whisper as the nine-year-old departed the mound after yet another scoreless half inning.

The information was offered so freely, unforced, that Bob himself had pondered on more than one occasion which team would select his "homeboy" and in which round.

"Young Alex," he smiled as the count rolled to 0 and 2.

This, Bob decided now, would become his new byname, the same one Ken "Hawk" Harrelson and Tom "Wimpy" Paciorek had affixed to Chicago White Sox player Alex Fernandez.

The utterance of that same pair of words would not only evoke for Bob memories of the fluid way the humorous WGN duo painted the nocturnal summer air but would also serve to permanently preserve this initial excitement at what he'd seen as the glorious prospects of his athlete.

Crack!

He looked before him to experience more of the confident, perpetual flow of power as Alex's pitch—and his brother's redemption—was delivered rapidly to the right of second base.

Kendall's momentum carried him toward the bag as he snared the ball. He leaped for second, executed a perfect pivot, then fired the ball to Vale to complete the double play and the game.

Fists clenched above his head, Bob, with Pell and Bart, hastened to the mound, where a relieved Kendall had draped an arm over his young brother's shoulder.

Bob glanced at his watch. "11:30—wow! What a marathon. We get paid by the hour, right, Bart?"

On Friday evening, it was time to execute her plan—to "take out" the white trash.

Quite satisfied with the flow of the words on the notebook, the determined, unimpeded expression of conflicted emotion, she knew—just knew—her art would sell. All she needed to do was obtain an agent.

In the interval, she informed herself as she signaled to turn left, she'd be steadfast in her endeavor to punish her "stalker," representing herself in the de facto trial in these backwoods.

"Screw him up," Amy could hear the little self-designated "gangster bitch" whisper in her ear as she peered into the darkness at Bob's parents' home, wondering how many times he'd wandered aimlessly along this path, confused.

She herself knew exactly what she was doing in this rocky terrain.

"Down you go, punk," she whispered as she ascended the hill and drove up next to the front door.

Her eyes labored in the darkness, scanning the entrails for indications of life.

"Shit," she muttered. "Is he even home?"

"That you, Rusty?"

She jumped when she heard the shout carried to her by the wind.

"No."

"Who the hell is it then?"

"Come closer and see," she replied sweetly.

She saw a smile etch Bart's face as he drew nearer, his bare feet stepping carefully on the white rock.

"Amy, how's it going? Rusty drives the same type of car. I didn't want that crazy asshole to be sitting out here. Where's Sellers?"

"In town. How come you aren't?"

"Just felt like getting away. Mom, Dad, and Nikki are gone for the week, so I can really get some rest tonight."

"Don't count on it," Amy mused. "Where'd they go?"

"They're all in Oklahoma visiting Dad. He's there on a job."

Another rush of cold air descended from the hills, inducing a shudder from the shirtless Bart.

"You want to get in here?" Amy inquired with a laugh.

"Nah, thanks. You want to come inside?"

"Sure," she replied, stepping out onto the drive.

She felt her way to the threshold, enchanted both by the aura of the residence and the ease with which she'd been able to gain entrance. She swept quickly past the beer can containers and washing machines—these inanimate yet disarming door greeters seemingly winking at her as she passed by in her pursuit of justice.

Seating herself in the dining room seconds later, she investigated the basement walls beyond the stairs, spellbound by the exposed interior of the unfinished façade, internal knotted wiring revealed sans compunction.

Serenely, she smiled and lifted her head in a silent, self-assured laugh, then looked out upon the lights of the quiet town below through the polished glass. She slipped out of her shoes and rested her feet on the adjacent chair.

Bart returned from the next room, holding two beers.

"Can I get you anything else?" he asked as he opened the bottle and handed it to her.

"No, no thanks. Not right now, anyway. You're a good host. So polite. No wonder I want you so much."

"Whoa," Bart laughed nervously, startled by her comment. "You're Sellers' girl."

"No, we're friends. That's all. Old college buddies."

"You're living with him, though."

"For now. I'm moving back to Rutgers in July," Amy countered, rubbing her foot along Bart's leg.

She purred, "You're not getting off the hook, baby. Why try?"

"Look," Bart responded as he leaned back in his chair, "Lord knows I'm flattered—pretty as you are, not to mention intelligent—but, well, Sellers is my friend, and..."

"How noble," Amy interjected sharply. "Do you think he cares about any of this? When he came home tonight, he barely paused to say hello and rushed right into the shower, singing and strutting.

"He had that glow, you know? I didn't even have to ask if you'd won. Reveling in his glory he was—he's probably in Andrews right now, triumphantly making love to some big farmer's daughter."

Bart laughed heartily at the image—Sellers and some heavyweight awkwardly clamoring about in the back seat of the old Impala.

"I doubt it," he chuckled. "I've known him for a long time, and I've never heard of him being with a woman, least not around here."

"Never?"

Bart shook his head from side to side to convey the sincerity of his statement.

"You must be special. Real special. I don't want to mess that up for him. Excuse me."

He had played his trump card; of this he was certain. If she were not persuaded to leave now, well...

"However."

He heard the word crush the silence, the careful way she enunciated, then paused, leaving little doubt as to whose plan would be implemented on this eve.

Bart sat back down and stared into the blue, compelling eyes and listened.

"The fact that he deems me to be 'special,' as you've stated, does not prevent me from being with you. In fact, it gives me free rein to do exactly this. My welfare has been assigned a high value by him. He's let me stay with him at no charge—monetarily or physically. His courtesy has allowed me to finish my novel far ahead of my original schedule. Only once has he made advances on me, and even then, he quickly retreated when I made him aware that he was acting foolishly."

Again, Bart laughed, envisioning Sellers removing his hands from her ass the way a child pulls his hands off a hot stove.

No, he surmised, she, like all the rest, would never be Sellers' girl. Just another rotator cuff–tearing fantasy that the balding, eroding, middle-aged man could not contain.

It was too bad, really, he informed himself as she argued her point—a case her body had won for her the moment he'd first seen her in that same chair days earlier.

"Paralysis by analysis," he'd heard Sellers blurt out earlier in the evening to Cralt.

"You've got the job, girl," he nearly stated aloud.

Save your energy.

What could he say anyway? He'd be forgiven; he'd offered a token defense, far more than any of Sellers' few friends would have done. In a competitive, demanding world, the weak get thumped anyway—no use sparing them.

He nodded silently as she droned on, enraptured by the crimson lips.

"As his handpicked assistant, you should realize that the happiness of his friends is more important to him than his own."

He watched her rise as she spoke, closing his eyes, foreseeing the triumph he was certain would soon empower him beyond.

His expectation—a smile etched his face, still watching the little body respond to his every whim.

Her eyes searching his, he was still taken unaware by the reality of her placing herself in his lap, arms draping his neck.

His eyes opened in surprise just as she leaned closer and whispered into his ear, "Do you have a rebuttal, Mr. Fennel?"

Bart smiled, lifting her into the air with him as he stood.

"The defense rests," he crooned and began his trek toward the couch.

Sellers' eyes met the clock for the fifth time that hour.

4:44.

The numbers hit his mind as he turned again toward the wall.

"Where the hell is she?" he mumbled.

Another sleepless postgame evening had settled upon him. Win or lose, the memory of the evening's game would besiege him, the sights and sounds as vivid now as they were at the moment of play.

He didn't mind this flashback so much, though. Somehow, they had won their third in a row that evening and were now 3–3.

"5:00."

A manifestation of inferiority to some, but in his eyes, a redeeming figure. Good stuff devouring each disappointment.

He smiled now at the memory of himself driving home the previous evening—music blaring, windows rolled down; exhausted yet elated.

"Falcon magic!" he shouted repeatedly, exulting in the exhalation, the good fortune that attended his every move on the field.

"Man, this is all right!" he'd yelled to Bart when he finally left the hallowed earth behind.

It had been a good move, he reflected, to start Cralt in place of Alex. Cralt seemed to have an inborn ability to heed instruction. Tonight, as always, he had put into practice every command and suggestion cast his way by Bob and Bart. Arm angle, knee flexion, follow-through—everything requisite to the proper application of that unearthed by the duo relevant to the art of pitching was incorporated into Cralt's movements that night.

There was to be no opportunity for poor habits to prevail as Bart made five trips to the mound in five innings, the reprieve effectively smoothing the rough road upon which Cralt had set himself.

"Three runs in five innings," Bob smiled as he uttered the figures, his mind now forming the image of Cralt being warmly greeted by the players on the bench as Alex replaced him on the mound.

The score was tied at three when that moment had arrived. With one out secured, he'd instructed the infield to play at double-play depth—then remembered he hadn't reset the defense after the exchange of pitchers.

He'd wanted his best athletes in the infield now. He sent Cralt back into the game at third, retained Pell and Cralt up the middle, and allowed Vale to remain at first.

"Rusty," he heard himself assert, "need you to go to right. Cody, go to center," he commanded.

"Screw that," he heard the disgruntled redhead mutter.

"C'mon, Rusty," Bob entreated. "You've got the strongest arm. We need our best gloves up front. Gut it out, man."

Reluctantly, Rusty had turned and waded out to right field, muttering angry words as he signaled to the bench players to toss him a warm-up ball.

Bob returned to the dugout, shaking his head.

He would watch in dismay as an Alex slider was hit on a line to right.

"Damn, the ball found Rusty," he groaned.

Rusty, still fuming, charged hard, scooping the ball up and propelling it rapidly toward third.

As Cralt applied the tag, Bob leaped out near the on-deck circle, mocking his now-smiling right fielder.

"I don't wanna play right field!" he shouted.

Even the opposing coach before him in the third-base box had chuckled in response.

"Play back corners! Squeeze the lines. Outfield, look home!" he instructed his charges.

"C'mon, Alex!"

The batter, anticipating an off-speed offering, kept his hands back, uncoiling in time to drill Alex's changeup past Vale.

Again, Rusty rushed in, jerking his arm violently forward after securing the ball in hand.

The tremendous one-hop throw he unleashed to Greg at the plate had Sellers running onto the field once more.

As the emphatic "OUT!" signal rang in his ears, he approached the sheepishly grinning Rusty.

"YES! YES!" he shouted, applying a firm palm slap into Rusty's outstretched throwing hand.

"Told you I like playing outfield," Rusty told Bob.

"Yeah, sure, my ass, Rusty," Bob laughed.

He could see the sky lighten in hue as he placed his hands behind his neck and lay supine in the middle of the large bed.

5:01, the clock indicated.

"Damn," he sighed, recalling how old Merv had told him that the loneliest times in an addict's life were the hours from last call to 6:00 a.m.

"Screw it," he cursed, forcing himself to resume his recollection of the game.

It had been 3–3 going into the bottom of the seventh, and an excited Bob had set the script to those around him.

"Pell will get on. We'll pinch-run Jason, who will steal second. Cralt will then drive him in to end the game. If they don't..."

He cut off his sentence, playfully glaring at his RBI leaders, feigning anger. The two seniors, both far superior in strength to Bob, laughed at the gesture, promising to deliver.

Pell promptly singled. Jason, having already stretched out in anticipation of opportunity, sprinted onto the field to replace Pell.

"Here we go!" Bob yelled.

To his dismay, however, Jason lost his footing on the initial pitch and thus lost the ability to achieve the "jump" requisite to advancing to second.

"Damn it," Bob cursed aloud as he watched Jason retreat to first.

Cralt, badly fooled by the subsequent 0–1 offering, hit a weak ground ball toward second, forcing out Jason. An arid, choking feeling enveloped Bob's mouth and throat as he watched the slower Cralt replace the fleet-footed Jason as baserunner, now with one out.

This had not been part of the dreamy manuscript he'd drafted.

"Shit," he cursed, dreading the potential devastation that would be wrought by allowing the contest to lapse into extra innings.

His eyes met the scorebook in his hands. Jason and Bryan, he quickly discerned, were the only nonstarters who'd been allowed to participate that evening.

Wrong.

That's what it was, he surmised, as he slowly gazed upon the alienated faces of his reserves.

"I've seen that look on me a thousand times," he whispered, reciting the title of the George Strait song he'd never heard but was dead certain he would understand.

These guys deserve better, he thought.

Why should they be arbitrarily separated from the pleasure of stepping between the lines he'd placed before them? He'd been there himself, as had his sister—both victims of a coach's presumptions.

"Lee!" His words rushed at his rationalizations as Kendall stepped to the plate. "K.B., Lee's going to bat for you," he stated matter-of-factly, his calm manner belying the anxiety building within.

He met Bart's gaze evenly.

"I know, Bart," he whispered, looking away. "The kid's 0 for 2 with two strikes, but hey, the big guys had the opportunity to close the door on this one. What the hell?"

He spat as he watched Lee swing and miss badly at the first pitch.

He then gasped as he spotted the slow-footed Cralt hasten toward second.

"Son of a—"

The expletive was abruptly terminated in response to the umpire's call of "Safe!"

"Good call, Bart! Way to hustle, Cralt!" he shouted.

Good old Bart, he smiled, pleased with the result of his assistant's bold command.

The man had balls—that's why he was out there, and Bob remained in the cage.

But how, he wondered, could they possibly score Cralt?

He looked up in time to watch in horror as the next pitch sailed at Lee's head.

He'd been crowding the plate; it appeared there'd be no way for him to prevent the misfortune about to occur.

Somehow, as Bob cringed, Lee willed himself to stay upright, leaning his head far to the left, flailing in self-defense.

Bob became numb as he watched the ball sail inexplicably past third.

"What the hell?" he asked aloud, bolting to his feet as Bart waved Cralt around third.

The left fielder had secured the ball quickly in his glove hand as Cralt's foot hit the bag.

Bob reached out and secured the screen in both hands as the picturesque throw darted past Cralt's left ear and his station five full steps from home plate.

Not a chance, Bob muttered, his joy fleeting as he looked for a seat.

The catcher, however, had been late setting for the throw and was still trying to establish his base.

Cralt's expansive form descended upon him.

Preparing for the inevitable collision, he was unable to lock the ball into his mitt.

The ball bounded away, and Cralt touched the plate.

Bob propelled himself jubilantly into the air with the hand that remained on the screen.

The rest of the Falcons sprinted toward second to convene with the exultant Lee.

"Oh my!" Bob shouted as he watched Bart shake Lee's hand.

"How about that!"

He heard his own words echo in his head as he climbed out of bed now, his sluggish gait a contrast to the haste with which he'd crossed the floor a few hours earlier, bound for the café.

He'd told Amy that he'd be there, that he'd be back.

So it was with disappointment that he entered the house at two, unfulfilled despite the revelry borne of recapping the highlights of the contest for all who would listen that evening.

She needed to have been there for him tonight, to have allowed him to literally retain this winning streak for as long as possible.

God, she was beautiful; this was beautiful, he reflected as he gazed out the window, looking for her.

He cursed the fatigue that threatened to close his eyes and end what had been a potentially superior night.

"Forget you, Amy!" he cursed, pivoting on his heel and heading toward his bed, well aware that the tide was already turning.

★ ★ ★ ★ ★

She watched as he drove away, assessing the feasibility of packing up her belongings and leaving as she did so.

For it seemed, overnight, he had once again become the jerk she had suspected he was—the inconsiderate person exuding rebellion, anger, a combustible, misogynistic brew filled with rage.

That morning, she was certain, was a manifestation of exactly that. The beginning of an envious ordeal for him that would culminate in an unhappy ending.

Walking in on her as he had, sans clothing, as she bent her own naked, soaked frame over the bathtub to shut off the shower.

"Damn it!" she'd cursed, shuddering in fear and contempt at the image of him behind her as she reached for the towel.

"What's up?" he'd muttered then, one hand smoothing the whiskers on his face, the other partially shielding himself from her line of sight as he shuffled toward the sink.

He'd offered no apology, nor revealed any intention of leaving as he placed the toothpaste on the brush before him—her brush!

"What's the idea?" she'd inquired, bristling.

"You know how it is," he'd replied, bringing the toothbrush to his mouth. "Got to get my day going..."

Yes, she reflected, she knew exactly how it was—recalling how he'd stood stoically as he stared into the mirror, acting oblivious to his changing shape, the gallant, brave ruse he had temporarily worn now brought to ruin by the realities of a youth lacking intimate opportunities.

It had just been too quick—that's what was troubling her, she thought as she paced the room.

Certainly, she was happy that she had attained a measure of success in her intent to do harm to him; was happy that her 7:00 a.m. wake-up call the previous Saturday had left him rubbing unrested eyes as she paraded her frame before him, still bearing the scent of his best friend.

But this was almost frightening—the manner in which his triumphs had been reduced to the mere pyrrhic victory one attained at the expense of watching his big guys fail to deliver in the damn clutch!

My, was he bitter!

Throwing things, punching walls—the change, she attributed to his changing view of "his Amy," for his boys were beyond reproach in his eyes.

Yes, she had him by the proverbial balls, but now she had to let go—not rub it in.

She could always hit him again later.

Yes, that was it, she decided as she walked toward the closet.

No sense staying around here, placing herself in the position to be rocked by that "storm" again.

For that would mean death for him.

She would have no choice.

★ ★ ★ ★ ★

"Hey, Bart, you see that?" Bob inquired as he looked longingly at the tall, blonde occupant on the top row of bleachers to his left.

"Wow!"

He walked across to the third-base box from the dugout during a pitching charge in the first of two nonconference games in O'Ryan.

He'd taken that route, supposedly to discuss tactics, but in truth, his real goal had been to attain a better view of the slender vision—a sight as visually pleasing to him as the 0 on the home side of the scoreboard.

"You need to do something about that," he heard Bart assert.

"What?" he replied with a shrug of his shoulders.

"You've been eyeing everything with breasts this week."

"You're judging me, with those hickeys on your neck?"

Bart laughed uneasily and returned his attention to the field.

Subdued.

That's what he was.

More so than normal, Bob assessed.

Wonder what's consuming him.

Cralt popped up to short to end the inning, and Bart sauntered slowly back to the bench.

"Who are we going to have relieve Alex?" he asked as he passed Bob and took a seat.

"Damn, I don't know, son. Let's just roll with him for now."

"He's tired."

Bob nodded, focusing his eyes again on the tan legs beyond the fence.

Man, it's tough to be creative when roused.

Bet Edison wasn't on the Schneid when he invented the lightbulb.

How ironic, he reflected, having Amy as a roommate and being less fulfilled than ever before.

And the absence of rational thought when he looked at her.

Man, especially that morning with water glistening on her back.

He still wondered how he'd restrained himself.

"Go get 'em, Alex!" he shouted, drowning out the flustering image.

Six more outs.

That, he reminded himself, would guarantee them a split.

Would Amy be home when they made their triumphant return?

Maybe it was time for a serious talk—time to prepare the lecture.

"Shit," he muttered as Alex walked the second of two consecutive batters.

"Better go hook 'em," Bart advised him.

"Why? He's still got the shutout."

"Yeah, but didn't you hear him earlier, saying his shoulder hurt?"

"Nah."

Bart looked away in disgust.

Stupid son of a... he whispered.

Can't keep his woman from straying, now he's letting this opportunity escape.

"Think! Damn it," he mumbled as he watched Bob stroll to the hill.

"You all right, Alex?" Bob asked.

"My shoulder is killing me now."

"Sorry, man. Better get you out of here," he stated, waving Pell to the summit.

"Thought you wanted me for the next game," Pell mentioned, a puzzled look forming on his face.

"Nah, better have you put out this fire. One game at a time."

"Who's going to throw the next one?"

"I don't know yet. Maybe it'll rain."

I've overused Alex, misused Pell. What's wrong with me?

He chastised himself as he walked away, observing that Bart was already applying ice to Alex's shoulder.

"Jason, go take center. Damn, I almost forgot."

"I've never played there before," Jason responded, rising to his feet, searching for his glove.

"Fake it, man."

He watched Pell labor valiantly but lose the first batter he faced on a 3–2 pitch.

"Shit," Bob grumbled, feeling quite unsettled.

The next batter connected weakly with the off-speed pitch, trickling a grounder past third, which eluded Rusty, who had inadvertently been holding the runner on.

Fortunately for the Falcons, Kendall had automatically moved to double-play depth after the walk was issued and was able to stop the ball in time to flip to Rusty for the force out.

"Trade an out for a run, that's right," Bob shouted, relieved that his neglect in positioning Woody had not cost them more.

"Stay double-play depth, Cralt and K.B."

Pell walked the next batter.

His initial presentation to the following hitter sailed high in the strike zone.

As the revolting clang of metal upon the ball met his ears, Bob found himself gesturing inanely, trying to catapult Jason in front of the ball, well aware that three runs would easily score if it eluded his center fielder.

Jason secured the ball on the fly, his momentum carrying him toward left field.

"That a boy, Jason!"

Two out, one run in, he quickly assessed, sighing in relief.

No sooner had the air left his lips than he saw a leaping Rusty fail to retrieve an errant toss.

Jason had gambled, attempting to retire the runner who had tagged upon the catch.

Unfamiliar as he was with the responsibilities attendant to being a late-inning defensive replacement—i.e., preventing more important runners from reaching second base—he had allowed another crucial run to score.

"My fault, fellas," Bob said to his increasingly anxious reserves.

Pell struck out the next batter, but not before throwing two wild pitches during the at-bat.

Hence, the Falcons led only 4–3 entering the final inning.

"Come on, guys, play some defense!" Pell yelled, slamming his glove onto the bench.

"Sorry, Pell," Jason offered.

"It ain't your fault. Everything's just out of control now. It's frustrating."

Bob averted his eyes from the pair, feeling helpless to alleviate the tension.

Got to keep my head in the game, he reminded himself.

Three outs later, his boys went back on the defensive.

Suddenly tentative with the leather, Cralt and K.B. allowed runners to reach scoring position on consecutive errors.

Bob ordered an intentional walk for the next hitter, then called time, uncertain as he walked to the mound as to what to say or do.

He observed Pell pawing the pitching rubber with his foot as he drew near, resembling a bull preparing to charge.

Cralt stood nearby, hands on hips, appearing upset as well.

With the potential winning run on second and no outs the situation for the Falcons was discouraging.

"Infield, play in, throw home for the force. Be ready, Greg, keep the knee bent. Don't bother blocking the p ate. Outfield, come on in—we're playing for the win. A sacrifice fly kills us. Pell, throw the hook, get the ground out. Good mechanics now," he urged the massive pitcher.

He noticed Kendall blessing himself in the background, begging for divine powers to intervene on the team's behalf.

"I heard that, Kendall," he whispered as he departed.

"Afraid God is rooting for O'Ryan tonight, though."

Two pitches later, his fears were realized as a hanging curve was smashed into left, landing in front of the diving Alex as the uniting and prevailing runs were scored.

"Son of a bitch," Bob cursed as he watched the O'Ryan team celebrate at the plate.

He kicked hard at the garbage can before him.

The resultant thud became the theme music for his opponent's impromptu party.

Thoughts of escape filled him as his dejected crew wound their way through the dugout.

He remembered just then—Plummer at Salem, upset at an umpire's call in the second half of a miserable nonconference doubleheader, loading up the equipment and walking to the bus in the third inning, leaving in his wake a confused and angry mob of Salem fans.

"Bart, can you get them ready?" he asked as he opened the door leading out of the diamond. "I'm going to get a Coke. You want one?"

Bart silently shook his head.

"Oh, let Rusty throw this one. Cralt can go to third. Pell to short, K.B. to second. Rest of the lineup is already in the book."

He scanned the bleachers as he spoke.

She, he noticed, was nowhere in sight.

He walked onward toward the concession stand, his own words echoing in his head.

"Make your move with women as soon as you feel the need or else pay the price of lost opportunity."

He had uttered those words in the hog barn to his brother-in-law's brother years earlier, reciting to him the trench his reserved manner had dug into his psyche through the medium of Ann, Angie, Jackie, Karen, Kathy, Steph, Stacy... all gone forever.

Except for Amy.

The most powerful becoming the one exemption; inexplicably.

A reprieve he must not destroy, he reminded himself with a nod of his head, thoughts and stomach swirling with memories of that morning by the shower.

Bart was already hitting pregame infield, so Bob settled slowly onto the dugout bench. Slowly, he turned to watch Rusty and Hank in the bullpen.

"How do you feel, Red?" he asked, observing Rusty fumbling with the knuckleball grip as he reached into his glove.

"All right," Rusty replied.

"Hey, just go as long as you can, as hard as you can," Bob requested, quoting some pitcher during a recent pennant race.

"You got it," Rusty responded—a verbal commitment his physical actions would soon honor.

He pitched six long innings, taking his knocks so that the more capable arms of Alex, K.B., and Pell would be fresh for the upcoming conference games.

As the crazy youngster calmly walked off the field as the teams exchanged roles at the end of the sixth, Bob stuck out his hand.

"Way to work hard, Rusty," he said, having long ago conceded defeat. "That goes the same for all you guys. It ain't easy keepin' your composure on bullshit nights like these. Appreciate you all staying together and not fighting amongst yourselves. Makes my job a lot easier."

He muttered incoherently as he watched his preening, posturing, gloved foes take their positions before him.

Another minimum-wage ass-whipping, he reminded himself as he grabbed his crotch in defiance.

Kendall doubled to left on the first pitch.

Bob clapped his hands as he watched Bart flash the steal signal.

"Take that!" he shouted across the diamond to the opposing dugout, the weight of the double defeat now bringing his blood to a boil.

He watched as Kendall stole third uncontested, from which station he scored on Rusty's opposite-field single to right.

By the time Pell doubled off the center-field fence, Bob was excitedly pacing the dugout.

Second and third, no out, he observed.

With a base open and a seven-run lead, his foes opted to pitch to the accomplished Cralt.

The entire Falcon bench sprang to life when Cralt connected solidly with the first offering.

As the ball hastened to land in the trees beyond the center-field fence, Bob's shouts pierced the air above his troops' commotion.

"Damn! Hell yes, Cralt!"

He remained standing, hands above his head, fists clenched, as Cralt rounded the bases, and remained standing motionless as the relief pitcher entered and began his warm-up tosses.

Both heartened and shocked by the comeback, he felt scared to move, not wanting to disrupt the flow.

Tony surprised O'Ryan with a bunt single, then promptly stole second.

10–6, soon to be 10–7, Bob surmised. Still no outs.

Vale moved Tony over with a groundout to the first baseman.

Alex's haste to reach the plate connected Bob immediately with the positive memory of Alex doing the same in Little League games—sparking rallies with his unyielding, cocky air.

Surely, he could summon the same strength now.

Bob leaped involuntarily, spilling sunflower seeds on the floor at the sound of Alex's bat connecting with the ball, the rude interception sending it on a journey toward left.

"Get out!" he shouted, entreating the ball to conquer gravity and the wind blowing in over the left-field fence.

His request was ignored, however—the sight of the left fielder settling under the ball at the base of the fence compelling him to silently turn and begin packing up the equipment for the disappointing ride home.

He glumly reached out his hand to grab Tony's helmet. The young man entered the dugout after scoring on Alex's fly.

He listened rather than watched as he worked, uninspired by the additional run the Falcons scored.

When Rusty grounded out to end the game, he bitterly hoisted both the bat bag and helmet bag upon his shoulders and left the premises.

There would be no postgame address, for he was still trying to make sense of it all; he felt that he had put a proper spin on things before the seventh during his concession speech.

He'd found his analogy by the time his players began to enter the bus.

The proverbial female "tease"—destroying perspective, wasting time, leaving him frustrated and bitter.

A one-two-three inning, and he'd have been halfway home and cognizant of what he was feeling.

"Just miss" grad school requirements, job interviews, January thaws—he recited silently; these unexpected events whose net effect was to infuriate and compound.

He felt himself taken to a moonlit night five years earlier, watching Juhl after he had been removed from the hill when Martens knocked his pitches senseless.

Weary and dejected after a day at the restaurant, Bob had sat near, cursing the opposing coach for having inserted a less capable pitcher into the game.

For he had wanted nothing more than for the ten-run "mercy rule" to be invoked in that certain loss—to not have to prolong the misery by virtue of watching Andrews score a pair of meaningless runs.

He could see Juhl's shocked face in response to the words that had left Bob's lips.

"What the hell is this? Get that other guy back in. Let's go home."

But Juhl, he whispered, looking away to the west, failure is inevitable.

Why did accomplished athletes have trouble watching this bald ass surrender in bad times?

The whirling lights before him momentarily distracted him, capturing his attention as they did, wayward passersby beckoning them to the casino.

Truro, he recalled, had been employed there after returning from the Gulf War—the same Native American boyhood chum who had informed him that politeness was hardly a trait deserving of reward.

The stateliness of the prose surrounded him now in the darkness, as did all that emanated from that man, now a direct result of his valor beneath that sea of sand...

Equally profound to him now were the words of the old country song he enjoyed.

"You know the lady's a lot like Reno... she'll draw you in... play with you awhile... but there ain't no way to win... I know..." he sang aloud.

A wise message.

Hell, he still went to the casino twice a month, humming that same tune each time he arrived.

Futile, yet strangely invigorating, this gambling.

Certainly, he harbored concern, as one of the former Miss September Playboy centerfolds had of becoming a victim of "the fever," for he had seen how even the most innocent could be lured forth from their quiet homes.

Those who had never bowed to addiction of any sort were now awash in the gleam of the blinking lights, which exposed the certain foolishness of their otherwise rational souls—souls who believed salvation to be in their trembling grasp, a mere token away.

It was no easy task, he surmised, placing these temples lowering the gap of chance in the middle of fertile farmland.

For large stretches to the north remained unscathed by the games.

To the east, Harrison had fled in haste, carrying away the 85-year tradition that was their annual fall festival when that city's fathers were told they could not prevent the ghastly slot machines from entering the fair gates.

What did everyone fear, he asked now of the night?

As Bart placed the bus upon the interstate, the same light that shone in the eyes of this sleeping community had also awakened them to the possibility of amusing themselves 24/7, giving relief to the lonely insomniacs and alienated second- and third-shift workers.

He need not have asked, as he already knew the answer.

He was ingesting it now—that fricking taste of loss, the desperation it instilled within, the deflating aftertaste assailing his palate as he became separate from that which he'd accrued, cherished, valued...

"Damn it all," he cursed, recalling how Webster had defined gambling as "exposing to hazard."

Hell, looking back into the dark entrails of the bus—or when you're on the bottom—you're already living in "hazard," getting kicked about all day long.

May as well swing, then.

Leave your ribs unprotected in the effort to fight back.

Who knew?

Might just get in that lucky punch.

And for those S.O.B.s at the top, they couldn't throw it away fast enough, stocked as they were with an endless supply of chips, tokens that could be regained with ease.

Michael Jordan addicted to that game.

Please.

He'd get a year's worth of assets back with the next McDonald's commercial...

Crash!

He jumped at the sound—the unmistakable response of asphalt breaking the fall of glass.

Almost simultaneously, he saw the red lights invade the blackness of the northbound bus.

"What the hell was that?" Bart cursed as he drove the bus to a stop along the side of the road.

Through the rear window, Bob could see an annoyed yet restrained highway patrolman walking toward the bus.

Bob sat pensively in his seat as the officer stepped aboard, preceded in confrontational impact by the flashlight in his hand.

The man's demanding eyes immediately found Bob's

"Coach?"

"Yes?"

"Are you aware by any chance that your players have been tossing beer bottles out of the window—one of which almost struck my car?"

"You're kidding!"

"Not hardly. You do not want to know the punishment I was prepared to invoke if that bottle had connected and impeded me from performing my sworn duties."

"No, sir," Bob muttered, watching as the man shone the light upon the faces of Rusty and Vale.

"As it is, I'm issuing you, Coach, a mere citation for endangering moving vehicles as well as littering. Do you have any identification?"

"Yes, sir," Bob answered, his heart sinking as he reached for his wallet.

At least Bart was not being hassled, he thought.

But why did those little jackasses have to mess up on my watch?

He handed the license to the officer and listened as the man called out the number into his radio.

Why?

His mind demanded, seeking a connection between the night's frustration and the odd manifestation.

Adolescents, psychologist David Elkind said, respond to the stress of loss by self-castigation.

Drug abuse, suicide...

Hell, that couldn't be it, he reflected as the officer began to write.

There was none of that among them—that was his trip.

Ahhh, but that old boy had also posted that in lieu of acceptance, of defeat, the teenage psyche would also lash out in excessively inappropriate and defiant competitiveness (gambling, rebellion) against the "system" that subdued them.

Yes, he asserted, as the ticket was handed to him, that was the option his boys had chosen...

"Sorry, sir," he said to the representative of "the system."

The front-line defense against assholes like him, who had increasingly less to forfeit by playing by their rules.

"Always in my damn pockets," he muttered as the man walked away, a smug, satisfied air about him, diverting funds from the poor boy to the sinkhole that was the fund financing the administration of county affairs.

"Screw your redneck ass," he muttered into the night as the state car sped past them—on his way, certainly, to damage more lives in a capricious, arrogant, unthinking fashion.

Bob slammed his fist into the seat as Bart pulled away.

It was powerless, ineffectual ventilation—unfulfilling.

For he knew it was time to discipline or be disciplined.

Another no-win situation.

Thorson versus him, him versus his boys.

The real squeeze play of life.

If only.

Ojalá.

Ahh, but it was, as always, too damn late.

Caught off guard again.

"Dammit!" he shouted before he could stop the word, his fists now pummeling the back of the seat before him.

Lost leads, lost games, lost money, lost esteem, lost security...

He flailed away at all that which he'd forfeited already tonight.

"Next!" he shouted when he stopped, his breathing labored, forehead matted with sweat, feeling very much alone on the crowded bus.

Having just disclosed the details surrounding the unsettling events, Amy breathed easier.

She was thankful that her problems were no longer known to her exclusively.

She had not been prepared for the disquieting event, had not expected anything like the shambles that was now her apartment.

Door glass was strewn about where forced entry had been made, blood and glass resting atop her scattered belongings...

A criminal act that the police could neither prevent nor resolve.

She had to finally admit now that she'd been beaten, sabotaged by her own misguided will.

It was time to get back on top.

"First things first," she whispered as she turned toward fellow social worker and confidante, Kathy.

"I have to get back to Rice," she said.

"From what you've told me, maybe you'd better lay low for a while," Kathy suggested.

Kathy's was a voice of reason, her self-assurance molded by socialization within the worst end of East Harrison.

Neglected and mistreated in her parents' home, she had graduated to being beaten to the point of requiring hospitalization by two separate male suitors as an adolescent.

She had somehow thrived, to Amy's surprise, mustering enough care to receive her degree from UNEI and establish a career in this new city.

She now launched a counterattack against the same forces that had previously assaulted her, lashing back at them from her bunker at the Council Against Sexual and Domestic Abuse (CASADA).

When she lectured on the real "battle of the sexes," Amy was attentive.

"I can't believe someone trashed my place," Amy sighed.

"You know it was Ron, girl."

"Why, though?"

"He's a rock star, that's why."

Amy laughed, despite her predicament, finding humor within her friend's choice of words—the ones she christened those afflicted with addiction to crack cocaine.

It was, Amy concluded, a term consistent with the Afrocentric dialogue Kathy used in communicating with each of the residents of this conservative community.

Integrity, hostile culture or not, those E'son roots were not about to be eradicated.

"What's your projection here?"

"About Ron, you mean? You got anything to pawn or sell in the house?"

"No, not really. The television's the only expensive item I own, and that's at Bcb's."

"Then I guess that boy will be duckin' and dodgir,' all paranoid, trying to keep away from Mr. 5-0. But when that body starts begging for that 'cane,' he'll come around, bet that up—probably as soon as tomorrow."

"Doesn't he realize that I've been away for two weeks?"

"Doesn't know, doesn't give a damn. He's running on instincts."

"Shit, now what do I do?"

"You can lay up here if you want. Give yourself the chance to get your crib fixed up or move. Whatever..."

"Thanks, thanks a lot, Kathy. I wish that I'd gotten everything out of Rice. Just didn't have the strength. Would you go with me there tomorrow?"

"Yeah, we can do this. I'll make sure I'm strapped first. Got my gat over at my sister's."

"Not a bad idea. I'd hate to see anyone get hurt, though."

"As long as it's him and not us."

Amy nodded, now sitting silent, wandering through the marsh created by the outpouring of negative emotion from these two desperate male fools.

Kathy, despite her bravado, appeared deep in thought as well.

It was she who finally broke the quietness, grinning as she asked,

"Why didn't you just sleep with Bob and not his assistant?"

Amy pursed her lips, shrugging her shoulders as she turned to watch the sunset beyond the hill, unable to answer.

Bob watched stoically as the raindrops beaded upon the windshield, his even-tempered manner belying the anxious feeling brewing within.

He rued the logistical imposition he forever equated with summer rain, envious of how the other seasons, the other games, were not touched by its presence.

Coupled with Amy's inexplicable departure, it formed a combination of elements that further dampened his already eroding foundation.

He stared listlessly at the ring upon Bart's hand as the man drove, still dazed by how empty he'd felt that a.m. when he awakened alone.

Shit, he'd done it a million times in Bluff.

Pointing upward to the ceiling, asking—begging, really—that his God watch over his self-destructive ass.

Nothing to it.

Boy, not today, though.

If it hadn't been for that damn Type C bullshit hovering over his veritable deathbed, he'd probably still be lying there.

Damn Thorson, he spat, recalling how the man had responded to his remorseful apology.

"We'll resolve this later..."

Who the hell did he think he was, talking down to Bob like that?

Did he feel it was easy, taking the knock for that O'Ryan Wednesday night road trip catastrophe?

Mr. Principal, asserting once again his distrust of Bob, letting the younger man know that he did not deem him worthy of any leadership role.

Damn Elkind's theory.

Foreseeable, unavoidable phenomenon, inducing anger and anxiousness that could only be shut down by confrontation of the offending matter.

Hell, he still felt bad.

Yes, it was all pain tonight, he reminded himself as he peered through the rain while the bus ascended the hill.

He longed suddenly to be out there, walking along the gravel road by his parents' home.

Analyzing... free...

He looked behind him to the drawn faces of his players, wondering how his speech of the previous day had affected them, if at all.

He was merely venting, tripping on those virtues he deemed necessary to his own survival and his ability to see them develop as athletes.

He'd initiated that address by reminiscing about that cold December night when he'd ultimately left his old college town—that fateful event when the jagged metal of his withering car ripped apart his tires, leaving him stranded in Carson, halfway to his parents' home.

Bad karma.

Should have turned back to the east, he told them, but instead, he limped westward, onward toward his Andrews baseball team.

He didn't tell them that when AAA and AA enabled him to finally reach his childhood home, he had arrived there with tears in his eyes, utterly saddened at the lack of comfort he felt.

The following morning, he had fled into the woods to the east of that hearth, fully aware as he fought the wind that he had just made a huge mistake, that the sense of loss that greeted him that Christmas season just might never fully depart him.

He had winced at the sight of his brother evacuating the farm, bound for that war—the one that would forever bestow upon him the self-designated status of "coward," certain he'd never recover.

Days later, he confessed he was down to begging, informing his brother-in-law on that New Year's Day that the $100 he had in his wallet was all that insulated his now overeducated ass from absolute dependence upon his already overburdened parents.

That, he informed his boys, would have been an unbearable shame.

He was still ashamed a month later, the physical labor engaged in on Dan's farm in Martens offering little in the form of relief.

He was, he recalled, miserably lost without Amy.

The benchmarks that had heretofore structured his life had disappeared, leaving in their stead a shapeless timeline—a haphazard, meaningless sequence of calendar years that could only be busted up by the manifestation of his own mortality.

"All this for you guys," he repeated.

It would be all over by May Day, this rural servitude.

Released from further service, he had immediately sought out Kent, hoping to secure his assistant coaching internship.

When Kent quickly consented, the momentum seemed to be his.

But once again, he was to be let down.

"Go apply at AT&T,' his hometown girl advised when he had told her of his unemployed state. "They're hiring."

And so, he hastened—unwittingly—into the cauldron in which he'd soon be broiled.

Oh man, did he regret turning west as he departed that phone company's building, forever equating that direction with pain, seeing the sun set upon his spirits, above the restaurant's "help wanted" marquee.

Hell, he'd sensed it within moments that day.

The lifeless features of the place could not possibly have offered anything else in his eyes—nothing, that is, other than misery.

He was prescient, watching in dismay as an angry cook slammed his hand to the counter after Bob improperly presented the customer's breakfast order to the kitchen help.

The sinking feeling he felt then would not leave for a year.

The scraping apologies he made to the cruel demons that guided the chef's actions had served only to heighten his self-loathing.

But somehow, still, he remained as summer yielded to fall, long after the baseball uniform and graduation gown had been tucked away, seemingly forever...

Long after D.C.'s pleas to leave the pit and move into his house in Indianapolis fell silent.

"Stupid, play-it-safe bullshit," he'd muttered with a shake of his head when he recounted all this to them, scoffing at how the orientation had propelled him to move even closer to the jaws of the beast, armed only with a blanket and the television Vale had given him.

Yes, he'd slept on the floor of that old farmhouse, waking to the prospect of having to run about the place he'd come to despise—that compensation-depriving, fight-breeding, patron-alienating, physically depleting asylum.

He grimaced as he called forth the vision of frowning co-workers dodging buckets set on the floor to catch the rain leaking through the defective roof.

Outdated neglect, the lords of the institution sitting in repose one hundred miles to the south, filled their pockets without having to look upon the deterioration of previously healthy personalities within the building that bore their name.

"Absentee ownership," he spat, creating a void that swallowed up the screams of their charges.

The responsive, empathetic guidance he sought was, to his disappointment, replaced by an informal hierarchy— the relative positions ascribed based on how much one could endure before revealing evidence of breaking down mentally.

He himself had surrendered within mere months, moving down in rank subsequent to having his barber give him a "Boz" haircut.

His snickering colleagues were correct in attributing his altered physical state to a foray into madness, he confessed.

It was, he assessed, an action that indicated the overwhelming disgust he had for the control the lords had over his body and mind.

He could still see himself hacking at the offending marks with a disposable razor, laboring through bleary eyes to summon the will to gaze upon the ridiculous presentation he'd left in his stead.

Indeed, the two-inch span of bare skin, the distance from the top of his ear to the portion of his hair that escaped his wrath, left then in his mind no doubt as to whom—himself or the well-insulated duo—wielded more power.

And so, he had informed his young charges, they had the right to inquire as to why he continued to go there each day, serving up his displeasure.

Because run away, he would not, if such an act meant somehow missing seeing them develop on the playing field.

Once again, he thought he'd been rescued when Call-USA called, represented by the soft, kind voice of Sandy, asking him to come to work there.

He giddily turned in his two-week notice at the abyss that day and sauntered across the street to what he was certain then was the promised land.

Within the hour, he was walking back in disbelief, shocked at the $1.50-an-hour pay cut to which he'd just consented.

Thank God, he whistled in relief.

They'd agreed to take him back at the restaurant.

Shame and a more gripping poverty would soon be his lot.

He was driving his dad's hand-me-down car and wearing the Payless shoes Vale had bought him because he couldn't afford them himself.

Paying rent in $50 increments, no bank account.

All for what?

To see them beneath the glow of the Friday night lights.

When spring replaced winter that year, the soothing warmth coincided, to his pleasure, with an $80-per-month reduction in loan payments.

But the breath had scarcely left his lips on his sigh of relief when he was told his home was to be razed, bulldozed into the ground with his now fleeting hope.

"Forget this bullshit," he'd cursed then.

When Weston's purchase of the lot halted the inevitable destruction mere days before the deadline, he rejoiced, exulting that he and his were still intact.

He celebrated by having cable television installed.

A genuine smile had etched his face for the first time in his recollection, a serenity borne of the memory of the five placid months he spent supplementing the viewing of the major league game with live observances of them.

Yeah, he'd just chilled the hell out, reclining in the old house, cooled by the early evening breeze drifting through the screen door, content to stand pat.

The feeling of bliss was only fortified more that autumn by the weekly sights of them tearing up the gridiron.

When he spent an unfulfilling week in Younkers on a short vacation, he finally became certain he was in the best environment for the times.

But within days of the final football game, the cold winter air had him shivering in dismay.

He had been made aware of the fact at Dan's mother's funeral; hence, he had come to always associate the change with misfortune and irretrievable loss.

Wow, he sighed.

One block away.

That's how close his brother had moved to him.

Guilt.

The memories of the scissors incident at the farmhouse became glaringly relevant, despite the vivid, surreal blanket of gray he'd wrapped himself in.

He dug in and dug out throughout that record cold season, scraping away at both unyielding ice and tales of endless self-destruction by his sibling at the corner bar.

"Champs," he scoffed.

They'd beaten him, though, those irreverent aliens, sending his thoughts scurrying toward UNEI Grad School, new cars—anything that would pave the way for a one-way trip away from all this.

And yes, he'd told his boys, in a halting fashion, that suicide—for the first time in years—had come to be seen by him as a possible option.

By February, he had failed three grad school exams, endured three wasted job interviews—two worthless ones with CASADA and one at Call-USA for a supervisor position.

Each time, he felt the door slam on his desire to leave.

He went back to his couch with the final rejection, had been lying there for three days, combining yet another false sick day and a weekend to form his isolation from his disgusting surroundings.

Thank God for Rusty and Cralt, he sighed, looking upon the duo who had finally interrupted his twisted slumber by knocking on his door that fateful Sunday evening.

For it was then that he had ultimately decided—all the social, financial, and sexual deprivations, all the cab rides to the laundromat, all that inane bullshit—was worth enduring because he was around them.

And now that he was in uniform in front of them again, he'd be **damned—damned to hell—**if he would throw away this opportunity merely because he couldn't constrain the manifestation of their collective insanity.

Neither would he dishonor their memory by allowing such a meaningless incident as the bottle-throwing fiasco to be an excuse to pretentiously penalize them.

Hell with feeding the appetite of a few randomly placed, bloodthirsty morons.

Forget 'em.

He had been so buried in reflection that he became startled when the bus now pulled to a stop.

They were in Bennett already.

Looking out, then up, he observed that the rain had ceased falling, and the sun was shining.

It was showtime!

They'd watched from the motel room adjacent to Bob's, waiting patiently for him to depart.

Finally, three hours later, there he was before them.

A preoccupied, distraught countenance was captured within Amy's sight as he pulled the door rapidly shut behind him.

Wonder what's wrong.

"Whoomp, there he is!" Kathy exclaimed, the words pronounced so suddenly and forcefully that Amy's shoulders jerked involuntarily forward.

"Wow, I guess love is blind," Kathy laughed.

"Screw you," Amy scoffed as Kathy poked playfully at her arm.

She simply did not share her friend's perspective, was not amused at the dynamics of her relations with Bob or all but precious few men, inhibited in getting here by a barrage of stimuli.

Visions of incest, domestic assault, and obscene phone calls filled her now, each flex of her trembling fist bringing her nearer to that defining moment in her life.

"Think he's leaving for the night?" Kathy asked, appearing now to be quite challenged by the silence and tears emanating from her friend.

"Yeah, he's gone for a while," Amy whispered as she watched him turn right out of the drive in the direction of the city.

"Then it's on!" Kathy shouted as she moved out the door.

Amy managed a smile as she watched Kathy swagger.

It was, she reflected, funny that they had used such undercover methods to get to the house, the elaborate designs sketched out by Kathy and herself early that a.m., in stark contrast to the assertive manner they had envisioned themselves employing as they confronted their world.

She envied Kathy the manner in which she could apply humor to pain as if it were a proper salve.

Herself, she could not, could only survive through magnifying that which Kathy made light of, her intent to better know her enemy in an effort to more effectively contain, then destroy them.

Yes, research would always be her weapon of choice.

She turned the key in the lock, trembling with sudden rage as she entered his place.

Damn, she hated him.

The way he had forced her to prepare, to defend.

Why couldn't Terry see that he'd never relent, would never stop intruding, despite her consistent, forceful rejection?

It wasn't her fault...

"Damn, this place is depressing," Kathy announced as she examined the contents enveloped within the bare gray walls.

"Mundane. No pictures, plants... It just ain't happenin'. The radio's set on KG109, stale pop music. A couple cassettes—both George Strait. No diversity at all," she said, moving toward his closet.

"Man, what's he have, ten white shirts? Afraid he'll offend someone by living in the nineties and wearing colors? Payless black shoes wearing, no-pattern boxer shorts owning, boring, thirty-something man. Probably no Playboy magazines up in this mug, just that silly-ass baseball playbook there on the bed. No wonder he's about to bust," she concluded, again terminating the speech with a laugh.

A moment later, as they began to load the television into the van, Kathy offered a final prophecy:

"You don't need to worry about this boy, in my opinion. He's just frustrated, bottled up, I'm guessing. Doesn't know how to deal with a pretty woman like you; feels like it's a fluke that you're near. Deep down, he doesn't think he's man enough to keep you. Subconsciously, he's chasing you away with his messed-up behavior. Preemptive strike, but not a violent one. You've been in enough hostile war zones on your home visits. You know what I'm saying?

Fortunately, this place doesn't have that karma. Trust me; if this SOB wanted to beat ya or jump on ya, he'd have already done it, would've rationalized it afterward."

The assertive, uncompromising manner in which Kathy presented the words served to soothe Amy so much that she began to feel no regret in placing pen to paper in an explanatory note.

"What the hell," she whispered as she penned atop the discarded envelope on his table:

Bob,

I felt like I needed a change. I didn't have the heart to tell you Thursday. Came by with a friend to pick up the rest of my belongings. Thanks for everything. Stay in touch. I'll mail you the key.

Amy

She smiled as she set the pen down.

She had overreacted, she assured herself, let caution and one bad moment, one bad man, cloud her vision AGAIN.

Read non-verbal cues as certain precursors to action.

Who did she think she was? Psychic Suzy?

Certainly, words could belie intent, deceiving even the messenger.

But he was not this complex.

Not worthy of such highly involved maintenance.

My goodness, she said, throwing the envelope into a corner of the table as her eyes caught a glimpse of freshly written text he had written on loose-leaf paper.

For an instant, she resisted the urge to read, but as she observed Kathy nonchalantly changing the station on his radio, the compulsion took hold.

"4:49," he had written in that book.

This page number implied that all that transpired was preordained—divinely inspired.

In the army, this same sequence of numbers designated an error processing code, one which indicated an erroneous duplicate record had been generated for aviation parts on the 'hood.

The 7-11 clock before him still read 4:49.

Certainly, it was an omen, but which to be revealed—the comfort of the natural or wasted motion?

Oh well, he sighed, he was here in West Queens, may as well place the coins in the slot.

279-3...

She began to feel the rage again as she scanned her old phone number.

She had been correct; her distrust in him had not been unfounded.

The stimulus of Amy would, to him, generate all manner of inappropriate, illogical responses.

"Dead on," she trembled, thumbing the butt of the pistol now tucked inside her stretch pants.

This son of a bitch had offered no resistance when compelled to intrude upon her, was indeed stalking her, combing her old neighborhood, trying to extract a reaction.

"How does it feel?" she could hear her soul scream as she began to crumple his notes.

"Ruining me and mine," she muttered as she set her sights on the baseball playbook.

Stupid book anyhow, I'll rip it apart.

"Hey, Kathy," she addressed her friend during her advance.

She had intended to relate all of this to her now, to present this latest bit of evidence as a reason to justify her concern, her rage.

But she cut herself short as she watched Kathy search the contents of Bob's top dresser drawer.

For she realized she would not have a receptive audience for such discourse, would not sway one who had forever inhabited a world where one's priority was what was "going on."

In perpetual motion—that's how they moved there, making quick yet informed decisions, which they stood behind regardless.

Then it was time to direct attention to the next dilemma bearing down on them.

Absolutely no time was allotted to feel sorry about erroneous decision-making, for people would prey upon them as they lamented, reveling in the advantage to which the misfortune of the weak member availed them.

"Sympathy" was not a word to be found in such a hard-bitten society.

Faith without condition, she sighed, calmly turning about to secure the laptop in her arms.

That's how life should be lived.

Efficient, clean.

She could never develop such an orientation at this stage of her development.

Indeed, the cynic's burden was to be her permanent cross to bear.

Vigilantly watching over all that entered and departed her, screening so as to capture the good, shaking loose of the bad, no matter how disruptive it was to her.

She watched Kathy languidly, without hesitation, walk out of the door and enter the van.

Amy intuitively followed.

She paused as her feet met the threshold, pausing momentarily to ensure that she had left nothing of consequence behind.

She pulled the door shut and walked to the passenger side of the van.

As he stared through the darkness, he assured himself once again that it was indeed her—the exquisite belle he had seen lately only in his deepest dreams; the one he had left behind to pursue this new career.

Kelli McShelton.

An obvious Irish surname, contradicting what he was certain was a Latin American ancestry.

So damn pretty.

She would bring long-dormant memories of Ms. Hernandez throwing herself at him each time he gazed upon her in the restaurant.

He could see himself even now, scrubbing his adolescent self over the sink in the old farmhouse, anticipating a meeting with her at Andrews High.

"Forget that!" he muttered aloud, shifting his weight from one foot to the other as he sipped the last of the orange juice in his nightclub glass.

Who needed to remember that shit anyway—all those futile attempts to engage her by love letters written in Spanish, which he had sent to Mexico City.

Might as well have been addressing them to Mars.

"She's gone," he heard the voice whisper inside of him again, inducing memories of that painful morning.

It was the first thought formed by his groggy intellect as he rolled over in the double bed.

"Better learn how to face it," Hall and Oates issued the ultimatum repeatedly until he finally found the will to rise and confront what remained of the eroding day.

Solitude.

Solitary confinement.

That's where she had placed him, locking him within a rubber room lacking pretty clothes and perfumes.

All she had left him, he realized then, once again, was her TV, her window to the world.

He knew he sure as hell wasn't in the picture.

"Shit," he sighed, now leaning into the wall, recalling how his fingers pressed into the remote in the sunlit room, searching for stimuli.

MTV, QVC, Discovery Channel— all flashed before him.

Irrelevant bullshit.

"Bunch of overhyped…"

He had cut short his criticism when his eyes met the view of Fox's TV reporter holding a microphone in front of Colorado Rockies player Dante Bichette.

He did the old Arsenio Hall dog pound thrust, mocking his prior inspiration he had formerly equated with the act, as he cursed the "Dante's Inferno" he was broiling within.

He turned languidly about now in the club, the thump of the Bart Brown song in his ears, bringing back memories of 1988 as he watched a replay of the Series on the television behind the corner bar of the building.

For it was in that year that Bart reigned supreme, the same year he had, in response to seeing Amy wrapped within the shoulders of another in Sir John's...

He winced now, stirred by the unpleasant exhibition.

"Get the hell outta here!"

That's what he had told her when she finally unclenched and drew near him.

What a dumbass he was.

Too naïve to realize then that merely days later, he'd be purchasing jewelry for her, driving to Queens on summer weekends in a wreck of an automobile.

Searching in the mist borne of his evaporating sanity again for her affection.

She would become his instincts, his impulses, his schema.

It was disturbing in impact when, in stark contrast, he would, with freedom, run up and by old girlfriends, empowered, intoxicated by his indifference as he snubbed them, laughing at their presence.

The "champ," prevailing over his former naïveté.

"What did he ever see in them?" the cliché would reach his lips.

"I feel nothing," he'd utter, looking upon what they had bestowed in a dry, passionless fashion.

Debits and credits recorded in a mental ledger that followed the transactions made within the confines of the quasi-corporation that was the relationship.

"Like this one here," he whispered, turning to enjoy the sight of his Kelli, fifty feet before him.

Hell, he had been that close for three years and never spoke to her, content to merely gaze at those same soft lips speaking into the pay telephone on the restaurant wall.

Wishing, but not caring.

Happy to merely be locked within the same asylum as her, enjoying the free beauty pageant, the one in which she had never failed to win his imaginary crown.

He watched a picture of St. Louis Cardinals player Bernard Gilkey, sprawling into the dirt to avoid Bret Saberhagen's pitch near his head.

Accident? Purposeful?

Which of the combatants held the upper hand, he wondered, now suddenly transfixed by the contest on the TV.

Gilkey's face revealed nothing as he brushed himself off slowly, hands gripping the bat in the same confident fashion, feet still precariously near home plate.

She had informed him once, long ago, that once you've fallen off a horse, it

is imperative that you try to get back on.

Easy for her to say.

"That a way, Gilk," he whispered as the leadoff man lashed a line drive over Saberhagen's head.

"Rasta," the 43-year-old Jamaican shortstop, stepped in—his presence in the starting lineup a testament to his charisma and charm.

"Skip" knew what he was doing, keeping him around.

"Forty-three years old, damn," Bob whistled as he watched the man square to bunt.

"I'd quit trying at twenty-six," he mused.

The bunt was cued perfectly to the left side of the infield, leaving no option for his opponents other than to honor his intent to sacrifice himself.

Gilkey now stood atop third with one out.

"Pitch inside, Sabe, no changeups," he said, reciting the orders of the playbook as Lang walked to the plate.

He peered back into the darkness in time to see half of Kelli's shapely ass depart the club.

"Shoot, she's gone," he sung again, closing his eyes as he watched the words depart the lips of the laughing soul sister in Granny's Disco on some teen life two decades hence.

He didn't feel, however, that laughing was going to get it done for him tonight.

He looked back to the screen.

He watched the replay of the ball rolling to the wall, then Gilkey's trek across home ahead of Dante's errant throw.

The screen availed Bob next of live action of Ray Lankford standing atop second, then saw the camera search for emotion within the eyes of Saberhagen.

The composed millionaire availed no outlet for the voyeuristic pursuit.

He merely stood calmly, calmly looking ahead for the sign from Jay Hawk.

Unsatisfied, the camera next panned the placid face of Opes.

Coolly flashing signs, the SOB looked like he was modeling the purple and black uniform right out of GQ.

He was cool.

Bob had stopped bending the bill of his cap to form a reverse "U" above his eyes.

As a tribute to the man, he now wore his new cap with a stiff brim, as Baylor was now, hoping in the imitation to somehow vest himself with the same composure.

She was cool like that.

Or was she just "distant"—alienated from the passion he exuded with regard to her?

He heard her say once that she had been a model, displaying her elegant wares in front of cars.

An adolescent mannequin.

She said she had quit after it became difficult to distinguish whether it was the sleek auto or the sleek model who was being offered to the lens.

Damn, but she was perceptive.

Deep.

Nothing like his hometown girls, who used to bite on his lame lines in this same club a dozen years ago.

God!

He shook his head as he set the glass down on an empty table and strode forward.

He couldn't believe how much grindin' went on here, in his three months subsequent to and relative to the prior three years he had spent down south.

Not tonight, though.

He would not pursue, not set himself up for disappointment.

He was merely trying to connect with the memories accompanied by the younger sisters of those with whom he had danced then.

For he knew, as he watched the Rockies turn a 6-4-3 DP, that the little rich girl had once again "taken out" the white trash, erasing any advantage he had once had.

In conjunction with the losing streak, her departure had turned his stream of consciousness into an absolute whirlpool.

"0-3, no Amy."

The phrase, often repeated in the past twenty-four hours, had threatened to pull him down and under.

"Damn it," he cursed as he wound his way through his more comfortable peers.

If mere effort had been enough, he would not have been treading such difficult terrain.

Yes, he had busted his ass in the Bennett game, stung as he had been by the perversion of resources at O'Ryan.

He had been heartened by the sight of little Kendall striking down the big **Germans—**allowing only one unearned run through four innings.

When Bob had ordered Greg to bunt with Tony on third and two outs in the fifth, he had caught the defense back on their heels, and Tony crossed the plate with the tying run.

A solo shot in the sixth gave the Lions the lead again, but still, he had felt confident as the Falcons sent the middle of the order to the plate against the tiring Lion hurler in the final frame.

He could feel himself tremble once again in anticipation as he had looked first at Kendall standing atop second, then at the specter of Babe Ruth, within the body of Pell, striding to the plate with one out.

As well as Kendall had been pitching, and the big lift Johnny's sparkling catch and throw had given them to end the sixth, two runs then may have been enough to ensure victory.

He could still see the bulbs on the scoreboard as he watched Pete lash the 2-2 fastball to left, certain that the path of the hit signified only heartache for the home team.

When he saw the ball drop in front of the left fielder, he raised both hands victoriously in the air in respect to his fortune and, more importantly, as a signal for Kendall to stop at third.

One out, men on second and third.

He had already been setting up the glorious situation in his mind when he saw Kendall race for the plate.

He realized then that he had issued his directive too late.

He was now at the mercy of the left fielder's arm.

He relived his dismay now as he lay his elbows on the bar, again seeing the picturesque, mechanically sound throw make its way to the catcher's mitt, seconds before the umpire unleashed his fury in the shadows of the setting sun—both elements uncompromising in their endeavor to block out visions of a Falcon Conference Championship.

"Dammit," he mouthed the word as the smiling bartender automatically poured him another glass of juice.

"She's gone," he sung lightly as he pulled the dollar out of his wallet.

"Look in the mirror, I ain't gettin' any younger," he sang as he spoke to his image behind the bottles—the one he had seen too many times—the despicable, surrendering vagrant that he loathed.

He turned slowly and strode into the midst of humanity.

He did not look around as he homed in on the window, which revealed the eastbound stream of traffic.

"Could spend eternity here in the city... let the carbon and monoxide choke my thoughts away, yeah, yeah..." he sang aloud, watching both foe and friend slip in and out of his peripheral vision.

"Pay the devil to replace her."

Well, not quite, he assured the heavens.

He made a rapid sign of the cross, wincing at the sudden recollection of his uncle doing the same in the nursing home years ago.

"Cold-hearted little..."

Why had she been introduced into his life?

What did she say the boys in the 'hood called this?

A back alley—beat down.

Intrusive, debilitating, nothing to gain.

Like the out-of-town hardheads trying to bust into the women's prison to get with soft bodies who were imprisoned within their own persistent despair or vindictive anger.

Futile.

He watched a solitary man waiting patiently in a car across the street as his mind tumbled toward the vision of Gwim's dad waiting in his vehicle for his wife at the mall.

Old boy could sit there for hours like that, just waiting for his woman.

"Hmmph, I'd do the same," he muttered.

Like I have a choice.

And certainly, he assured himself, she would come back to him, if only to retrieve her television and laptop.

Or maybe, she had willed these to him as a symbol of her "love," leaving the typewriter as a medium for him to compose letters expressing his desire to be forever as one with her.

Disgustedly, he sat his empty glass down and walked away from the window.

Then he walked upstairs, his desire being to find a relatively quiet spot to organize game info.

For he had a hell of a mission ahead.

Sixteen days until the postseason.

Two weeks to transform his miserable, disappointed ass into a tiger.

Reeling in once more from the veritable PTSD that was the Valentine's Day massacre, that most pyrrhic of victories.

It had begun to seem more and more unlikely that he could get it done.

★ ★ ★ ★ ★

He gave everyone a wide berth as he climbed the stairs, cautious in his endeavor to avoid bodily or eye contact.

He shook his head clear as he reached the top floor, in response to the incongruent sight of two scantily clad couples frolicking in a hot tub nearby.

What the hell, he asked his eyes, which had automatically become focused on the bare skin of the most attractive of the two women.

Another lame barroom gimmick, he scoffed, like us drunks need any more reason to drop in.

But he told himself, he liked this one—would have loved to have had it be his game, a prelude to an egocentric power trip he could play on some hotel room waterbed.

"What's my name?" he should be shouting above the woman his eyes had just fallen on.

"What an upset that would be," he informed himself as his focus shifted to the backside of the other woman.

"I'm at zero balance, 'cuz," he told himself, mimicking the phony inventory ole Fuldog on the 'hood often presented to his colleagues.

"Go kill yourself, Sellers, if it's that bad," he heard the man chide him. "You say everybody's screwing ya? When's my turn?"

Biting him, that's what "the dog" was doing—for Sellers' own benefit.

The verbal punches he tossed were as effective as the physical ones once thrown by his Louisville homeboy, Muhammad Ali.

"The Godfather," Dog had aptly christened their Vietnam vet supervisor, Sgt. Smith, the same man who had told Sellers to never become a whipping boy.

"Too late, Sarge, you ain't never met her."

He could hear Fuldog interject.

"She's gone, dumbass."

"Damn this Amy Lou stuff," he cursed to himself as he sat down upon the abandoned chair below him.

He peered down onto the dance floor.

He was startled to see his cousin waving up at him.

He felt sad as he waved back, disheartened by the lack of sympathy and empathy he had toward the man he had grown up with.

"Clock in," that's what he was doing, he laughed sarcastically—an isolation junkie going into the "nod," shutting down.

As he felt his eyes close, he shook himself to a start, for this, he reminded himself, was not a place in which he wanted to lay.

He rose, rubbing his hurting stomach, holding his hand in place until he reached the Fajita Bar.

He purchased two of the steaming sandwiches, then walked again to the east wall of the building, looking down now on the traffic.

He watched a large man below walk into and out of his sight, surrounded by two attractive women.

"Hey big daddy, can you spare one?" he whispered with a smile.

"Just one," he muttered, looking back upon the traffic.

One game at a time, he had told Pell in O'Ryan, one day at a time, they had told him at the clubhouse earlier.

"One man at a time," he had told Iris, imparting his virginal morality beneath the Texas sky to the beautiful, confident Black woman.

One more, then he'd leave, one more time, one more chance—was all he asked.

All bullshit, he surmised.

He could never be satisfied with one of anything.

He wanted to be rewarded each time he worked hard to attain the paradise the Protestants assured his Catholic ass was his if he sacrificed enough of himself in the noble pursuit of their social harmony.

Hell, he could have been drunk last night at Bennett for all his effort was worth.

He turned his eyes to the video screen, finding himself wishing that old Kjos would somehow appear out of the walls, as he had on that "one" last trip to Harrison.

That son of a gun would shake things up, could beat on his disillusion.

"Yeah, right," he muttered as the screen went blank.

Kjos wouldn't waste time on reflection like Sellers had.

He'd not allow his mind to become such a stagnant pool.

And who would want to wade into the midst of the misery that was "his" pain?

He'd have to resolve this alone.

"Everyone trying to tell me what was right for me, yeah, yeah..." he began.

"My man had better love me even when I have sex with his friends, call the cops on him, ruin him..."

His words and thoughts were blasted from his consciousness by the force of the defiant, leather-clad woman on the screen.

"What the hell?" he muttered, beneath the shouts of approval from the unseen females in the darkness.

"What's up with this?" he said aloud, hastening toward the stairs.

"Forget you, bitch," he snarled as he descended.

I owe you nothing. Kiss your ass for what? Eight seconds of compensation for having to listen to your constant criticism of my inability to pay proper tribute to your demanding, demeaning ass?

Forget that...

He leaped from the second step to the floor and moved briskly toward the door, dodging patrons as his head whirled from the force of the jeering music.

"No, no, no," his mind shouted as he pushed his way clear of the club and met the night air.

He moved angrily forward, blindly, until his knees began to ache from the anaerobic exertion.

He was startled to see the topless bar just before him.

When did this place change themes? he asked himself as a cowboy walked out the door.

A serene countenance visited Sellers for an instant as the man held the door open, inviting him to peruse the contents.

"Appreciate it," Sellers acknowledged with a tip of his Giants cap.

"Why not?" he queried, hastening toward the bathroom.

The atmosphere of the place was startling in its soothing force, a stark contrast to the more conventional club he had departed.

He sighed as he unzipped, soothed by the R&B ballad that serenaded him as he pissed.

"I've had enough," he whispered.

Would rather stay on the schneid forever than feel as he just had two minutes ago—by sluts putting me on hold, recycling those competing with jerks for scrawny twig women.

"Forget that," he spat as he zipped up.

"They're God's children," he heard the soft voice remind him as he stepped outside.

He recognized the quote, knew it was Gordy's—that ex-con reminding him again why restitution must be paid to those he bore ill will toward.

"Damn, he was right, too," Sellers thought with a shake of his head.

"Don't tell pretty girls they're pretty; they already know this," Sellers smiled despite himself, amused at the sounds of Gordy holding court in his head.

"Media and bars sell the fantasy through the medium of these pretty motherf—s."

Sellers laughed.

"We're all men, say the full phrase."

He walked toward the glass door and peered outside.

His thoughts were broken by the incongruent sight of the Mulatto woman and apparently blonde companion cruising down the street in the new van.

"She's gone," he heard again, the mocking sounds escape the ebony lips, felt again the trembling of his adolescent resolve.

"Man, I'm barely keeping my grip," he muttered as he turned.

"Are you at least nineteen?" he heard the bartender ask the young man who had just walked in the door.

"I wish," Sellers laughed automatically, as if on cue, mimicking the response he had gotten from patrons he had asked that same question at "The Tap" years earlier.

"No, I don't," he told himself again as he walked near the stage.

Twenty-three, sure, that had been the time he had rubbed upon his Amy.

Eighteen? Hell no.

Ms. Hernandez? Not even.

But how in the hell did she get so good so fast, with her nineteen-year-old self kicking his mind all over?

Northeast Indiana, calling the shots, defining, scolding him?

He assumed a seat at a corner table, resting his head in his hand as he peered at the redhead gyrating on stage.

Ran him, in his prime, with the numbers in his favor, that skinny little girl, rendering him indifferent to the others.

Rich little bi...

He couldn't finish the sentence, realizing for the thousandth time that it was wasted sentiment.

Unfair.

False.

"You ungrateful asshole," he condemned himself as he watched the underwired bra hit the floor.

"Get it together," he implored himself, as he stood, rubbing his hand nervously upon his chest.

As his eyes met the dancer's, he stood still for a moment, transfixed at the power in the penetrating eyes.

He whirled away when the stripper slowly turned her features toward the man holding the five-dollar bill in his mouth.

Within seconds, he had positioned himself again before the urinal.

This time, he paused to look into the mirror, startled by the incongruent visage of himself standing to her side as they looked upon the UNEI dining center from her dorm room.

He saw the blond curls furl and straighten from his touch, felt his lips touch her tear-stained cheeks, saw his hand slide the razor atop his own eighteen-year-old jugular at Knox.

"Screw you!" he shouted aloud at the glaring portrait before him.

His temples throbbing, he slammed his fist gently into the sink.

Don't do it, his soul whispered, too late to stop his brain from ordering his hand to act out the cliché.

A reflection "too terrible to look upon," he heard them recite from the book as he connected.

He stared in disbelief, looking for signs of himself within the web formed by the convergence of fury and reality in the moment that followed, rubbing his bloodstained fingers in disbelief, overwhelmed by the sudden force of his self-loathing.

He began to run instinctively, looking for a way out.

He ran, sprinting hard, until three blocks later, he bent over, chest heaving, and grabbed his knees.

"Damn it, I love you, Amy," he whispered as the tears met his cheeks.

He carried himself into the shadows and dabbed at the blood with the crumpled cocktail napkin he had in his pocket.

He stood still for five dazed minutes, emerging in time to see the bank clock's number reveal that it was now 12:30 a.m.

In a minute, he stood once again before the strip bar door, the panic assailing him, hidden beneath the composed fashion in which he sauntered through the door.

No one gave him a second look as he walked in, his right hand hidden in his pocket.

"Whew," he whispered as he sat down at the same corner table.

"That was close."

It floored him when he saw her—little "Dreamweaver," as he had designated her.

On stage, she moved fluidly, comfortably, appearing quite well at ease, despite the hard stare she had affixed upon her face.

The applause at the end of the first song was loud and genuine, in marked contrast to the contrived, faint claps with which her co-workers were greeted prior to disrobing.

He was among the zealous, caring little when she teasingly played at the strings of her top.

He had already seen enough, had already connected.

"Talk about your upset," he mumbled beneath his breath.

He excitedly gulped down the remainder of the juice in his glass, eyes locked on her throughout the journey.

"Forget it," he whispered.

He stood and approached the stage, overwhelmed by the fullness of her beauty.

She was positioned before him on all fours, speaking softly to the cowboy below her in the front row.

The pose was inviting—the firm backside and hamstrings in conjunction with the straight blonde—all combining to remove his breath.

He stopped a scant few feet away, wiping his palms on his pant legs.

He challenged himself to action, to ultimately broach the question:

"How are you, Andrea?"

He watched as her pliant body suddenly tautened.

She calmly turned around after a moment's hesitation and fixed a firm gaze upon him.

He was assailed by the ensuing silence and had begun to avert his eye when she finally responded.

"I'm fine. Who'd you come here with?"

She peered cautiously into the darkness, scanning the room.

"I'm by myself. I ain't got no social power."

"Nah, you're popular," she said, rising to her feet as the next song began.

"Thanks. Wish I could be in better with pretty women, though."

"Like who?" she asked coyly.

"You," he said, despite himself, watching her remove her top.

She merely smiled, then turned away, grinding her pelvis again before the cowboy.

He watched intently, infatuated by the adolescent precocity, intrigued by the way she was running the show—her G-string becoming rapidly filled with five-dollar bills from "suits" and blue-collar workers alike.

He pulled out his wallet and peered inside.

He immediately pulled out the ten and blurted out her name.

"And... dream," he amended himself instinctively in response to the angry look she gave as she snapped the G-string shut on another $3 gratuity.

He watched her as she advanced, the way everything stayed in place, even as she bent down to hear his question.

"Hey, you're gorgeous. Please..."

"Do you want a dance?" she asked.

The question was disconcerting to him in its innocent evasiveness.

"Yeah, you bet," he replied, as she extended her hand and placed a high-heeled shoe on the ledge next to his drink.

"Dear God," he mused, as she draped first one, then the other thigh atop his hips.

His hand remained gently in place upon her left wrist as she gyrated, the intoxicating, repetitive movement sealing him off until he felt quite alone in the crowded arena.

His prior awkwardness vanished as he concentrated, reminding himself not to allow his hands to slip.

He wanted to do nothing as she again forced her loins further into him.

He smiled when she looked at him.

"Damn, girl," he whispered, caught with the alluring scent of her perfume.

"You like?" she asked melodically, scratching his tousled hair in wonderment.

He caught a glimpse of his reflection in the stage mirror as she rose, watched her pirouette from one side to the other from that vantage—the movements denying, then enticing—all serving to enhance the surreal effect her glamorous nearness had upon him.

When she again placed herself on top of him, her vigorous, rhythmic writhing became something he could not define. If he had been more composed, more lucid, he might have realized he'd tapped into that mystical Zen quality Pirsig had spoken of. As enraptured as he was, he'd become reduced to merely enjoying the snow. Certainly, he had not felt this way with any dancer in the past decade. More often than not, he'd sat here, lifeless and disheartened.

Perhaps he'd been alienated by the experience because the pretty gal had treated him as *scaffolding*, a step to enhance her prospects for winning the favor of the well-heeled suits who frequented the corner tables. Often now, he mused, he wouldn't even offer cash to the loveliest, preferring instead to push his back firmly against the wall of these hallowed shrines, nodding in time to the accompanying pulsations, frequently surprising himself with his unconscious, spontaneous dancing reactions to the music and choreography. When the dance was carried to him, it was quite rare that he'd offer up anything like the $15 he was now slipping her.

The rehearsed kiss suddenly met his cheek, accompanied by the mandatory *thank you*, as the music fell silent and she retreated to the stage.

He sat silently.

Cautiously and awkwardly, he sat up and rose to his feet.

He smiled an embarrassed smile as he approached the bar, pushing first one hand, then the other, against his right cheek in an effort to relax his taut neck. He gazed into the glass as the bartender approached, momentarily caught unaware by the placid look upon his own face.

He purchased a margarita and an orange juice, then returned to the stage.

She nodded silently when he handed the drink to her.

He watched as she stirred the contents with an elegant movement of her right hand. It was, he feared, an all-too-galvanizing scene, this graceful mixing of dissimilar ingredients. Finding himself wavering, he closed his eyes, feeling his consciousness slip past the horrifying image that was his heartbreaking potential, and landed inexplicably upon the vision of Ice Cube uttering in *Higher Learning:*

"We're behind enemy lines, dog."

"Don't fall asleep," the laughing directive that interrupted his thoughts made him sigh audibly in relief.

"Hey, how ya doin', buddy?" he asked as Andrea approached.

"Just great," she said, wobbling from the effects of the hours spent on high heels and, he theorized, the margarita she'd just drained.

She placed a hand on his shoulder to steady herself, then sat down in the adjoining chair.

"You alright?" he asked with a laugh, staring hard at the silky thighs revealed below the slip she was now wearing.

"Yeah," she sighed, squinting onto the stage at her prancing co-worker.

"Go, girl!" she shouted, swaying too hard in time to the music.

"Man, you move well," Bob leered.

"You like that?" she asked. *"I've got a lot more moves."*

"I don't doubt it. You could kill a man with that shit."

"You ever been with anyone as hot as me?" she asked, leaning in close.

He felt his face flush as the soft teenage laugh met his ears.

"I'm old enough to be your dad," he whispered.

"Screw my dad; he's the ass hole who put this scar on me," she said, thumbing the jagged mark on her cheek.

"My own dad," she sobbed softly, *"trying to violate me."*

"I'm sorry," Bob whispered, watching her hand tremble. He rubbed his hand upon her neck.

"Just order me another mess-me-up," she said, her body becoming rigid beneath his touch.

He waved the waitress over as he removed his hand. The sight of her suddenly filled him with pity.

What a rotten break she'd been handed, he thought. *Ruined. By a friggin' cannibal.*

"You have power over me, Andrea," he began without compunction. *"I'd like to advance, to just hang out with you, get to know you more."*

"You don't understand," she mumbled.

"Can I at least give it a try?" he interjected, placing the bill in the waitress's hands as she set down their drinks.

"You ever been in the back room?" she asked suddenly as she stood.

"No," he replied as he followed.

His hands found the small of her back as he rose.

The soothing strains of the *Luther Vandross* song surrounded him in the dim light, and he was set in motion again.

God's little clue, he called it, challenging himself now to stay calm.

Think of something else.

"Alright, cuz," the black voice uttered from the corner as she opened the door.

"She's just a kid, homes," he told himself. Use your head.

He knew he would not be the last, was certain that her adolescent form would be wrapped within arms even older than his, probably as soon as tomorrow.

It would be foolish to resist yielding to the lure of such fortunate genetic endowment, he assured himself.

He was already unbuttoning his shirt by the time she opened the door onto the stairs. He was taken aback by the sight of the duo illuminated within the bright lights.

A *Tom Cruise* likeness and his scantily clad redheaded companion nodded in his direction as he entered.

"Is this heaven?" he asked. *"Mrs. Cruise."*

"No, it's Iowa. But that there is the field of dreams," the man intoned with a nod toward Andrea.

"Good one," Bob laughed, feeling giddy at the affirmation of his plans the man's words had created. *"A good man's fault"* they would call it, he assured himself, as he pressed his lips to Andrea's cheek.

He slipped his fingers beneath the G-string as he did so, then quickly removed them in shock at the rigid non-response. His mind hurtled toward the vision of him with Marley on that disquieting evening. He braced himself for the worst. He was almost taken aback when he felt her yield and lean into him. No sanctions were forthcoming.

He followed her through yet another door, floating over the threshold accompanied by the DJ's announcement of "Last call." He captured her profile within the lamplight as she slipped gently down upon a queen-sized bed.

"Damn," he sighed as Andrea released herself from her slip in one hand, G-string in the other.

"Do you have to go home now?" she asked.

"Hell, no!" he said.

Removing his belt, he felt his knees buckle. The *changeup* she threw him with her offering was in such stark contrast to the *high and tight fastball* Amy's departure had delivered that his head would not stop spinning. He knew, beneath the din, that he was powerless now to regain any sense of balance.

"Jiminy Christmas!" he sighed reverently as he removed the last of his clothing.

The innocuous words caused her to smile. He returned her look with an embarrassed grin.

As his knees gingerly met the bed, he knew he'd certainly climbed these stairs to a lofty level he'd never have expected to attain—ascended to a station from which he must at some point gently descend.

"Forget it," he said aloud, as his hand touched the pillow. *No way I can afford to walk away now.*

A long drive from Wayne to Rice lay ahead—an opportunity, Amy surmised, to devote her full attention to the task at hand. She'd tell him she'd come merely to return his key in person, but the ulterior, intangible motive was the one to be served.

It had struck her competitive core to vacillate, to flee, with respect to Bob. She had, in a sense, failed to put this away, to properly attain the closure she coveted. She needed, somehow, some way, to feel as if she'd left on top. It was almost with a sense of urgency that she sought to do so now that her transfer request had been submitted to Indiana DHS, and her completed manuscript had been forwarded by her former UNEI instructor to his literary agent friend. She was certain to be off to bigger things, more vibrant places. She cared little if she ever returned to this tumultuous terrain. It was just that she did not want to leave feeling this way, to enable him to pay such a small price for his transgression.

"Envy, lust," she mused, reciting a list of that which she'd futilely attempted to inject into him. Touching him and Bart was not enough, did not induce the mania she wished to see in him, did not have him begging for her love.

It surprised her in reality, she admitted, recalling the irrational acts of real men, who, having discovered her in the presence of other admirers, had shed blood—and on one occasion, tears—in a wide variety of settings. Indeed, she'd seen men destroy themselves, spurred only by the realization that her loyalty was not to be easily won. It was as if the baneful blows they struck, as she watched powerlessly from afar, were administered as a symbolic means of vanquishing this distressing fact. The gift, she smiled, these beautiful eyes, face, hair—the whole package—had quite an effect on even the strongest man. How many times had she observed the air expire from men's lungs when she pulled near, heard them call out in involuntary disbelief as she lay unaffected?

She'd caught two more in this Kramer County, she assessed—the two strong yet divergent characters of Ron and Bart. Bart, charismatic, upright, composed, successful. He'd been reduced in a hurry, his stoicism a distant memory, washed away by the torrent of pleas he'd left on her answering machine.

And Ron, that alluring creature—even within the grasp of crippling addiction—had slid blindly nearer, finding her at Kathy's apartment the previous eve, his red, relieved eyes desperately thanking her for the $20 she slipped into his bloody hand. It was obvious to Amy that it was her mere appearance that arrested the insane, furious car-window-breaking spree he'd embarked on in the complex's parking lot.

So how in the hell, she asked herself, could weak, shy, indecisive Bob remain so in control of her psyche, be able to take her on and off the pedestal he'd erected? Why had she been so ineffectual in warding off the persistent chill of regret which surrounded her when she thought of him?

She inhaled deeply as she descended the hill, frowning as she spotted the town of Rice's water tower in the distance. She exhaled grudgingly, longing to bask in the tranquil New England countryside of which she'd always dreamed—that same site in which she'd set herself in the concluding chapter of her novel.

"Damn it," she swore softly, reassuringly touching the pistol that lay hidden between the seats. "It's going to take a miracle to get this done."

"What are you doing?" he heard her ask playfully as he pulled into the parking lot. "You know she's gone."

"Pay the devil to replace her," he sang in a distant reply, surprising himself with the melodic fashion in which the words echoed off the apartment building glass. He watched intently beneath the blue sky at the incongruent blend of Sunday churchgoers and irreverent beer drinkers, feeling a pang of both longing and regret as his passenger rubbed her hands atop his thigh.

"Would you like to dance? You move so well," he heard her whisper.

He waved into the dugout as he drew her nearer. "Check me out, fellas!" he shouted into the darkness. "Don't tell anyone," he pleaded.

He smiled and turned the key, despite the labored sounds emitted from the engine.

"You're the icing on the cake, Amy... er, Andrea," he spoke to the ephemeral figure.

"I ain't no bellhop, dude," he heard the man shout.

"Uh oh," he whispered to the large, glaring, bandana-wearing man before him.

"You need some transmission fluid, cool," the man whispered back in surprise.

"Hell, you better get a ride outta here!" his companion warned him as the intimidating dude approached the car.

"White boys be kickin' it," Bob called out to the b-boys. He watched in shock as one delivered a forceful knockout punch to the bystander who'd dared pass before him in his journey.

"Yo, you holdin'?" he shouted to Bob, kicking the fallen man out of his way as he walked.

"No, sir," Bob replied, intent on not dissing anyone.

He watched nervously as the bandana-wearing man began to speak into a cellular phone. *These jerks were going to kill him, were calling for reinforcement, blocking his escape,* he anxiously informed himself. Again, he turned the key, heard the knock of the engine.

"You wanna date?" the polished youth to his left inquired.

"5-0," the man behind the sheet shouted derisively before slipping out of sight.

"Gotta knife for me, girl? This dude's tripping," he heard the stage whisper of the prostitute's friend.

"That boy's okay," he heard the bandanaed one address him, pointing to the bartender from Max's, that bug-eyed, disheveled, yet still handsome man, staggering before the car.

"You ain't though," the man concluded with a shake of his head.

"Forget this," Bob muttered.

Pulling away, he heard derisive laughter surrounding him, saw an angry hand hurl a full quart of Budweiser at his back window. The sound of shattering glass serenaded him as he left the lot.

"Alright, cuz," he spoke to himself as he gazed at the blank faces before him on the sidewalk, pressing the accelerator to the floor, his eyes trained on the windowless brick building ahead.

He woke with a shake, eyes staring vacantly at the curtain stirring in the gentle afternoon breeze.

"Wow," he mumbled, surprised that he had fallen into such a deep slumber at mid-day. He had scheduled an evening off, but still, he rose hurriedly.

"What a weird dream," he laughed as he stepped toward the pop machine. "I must be working too hard," he smiled, reflecting on the marathon victories he'd secured on consecutive nights preceding this day. *Both upsets too,* he reminded himself as he pressed the coins into the slot. He'd overcome logistical obstacles, big innings, late-inning scares... *Damn!* He just wanted to reflect now, to savor each fortuitous bounce, to pay homage to each frame.

He carried the diet soda back to the chair he'd placed upon the deck outside the front door. Easing himself down, he turned his attention to the Lata game.

He'd stood, prior to that Monday night game, behind the wire mesh, anxiously watching a Little League game. It was 5:15, and the Lata players were already warming up beyond the outfield fence. With an inning and a half to play, Bob knew there would be no time to drag the old fence panel over the rough infield. *Rake and run,* that's all he could do, wincing at what he was certain to be split lips and bad-hop-induced black eyes.

The angry comments of his foes reached his ears again.

"Look at this cow pasture. What a joke."

He'd scarcely suppressed the will to not respond as he listened. He'd decided it was best to disappear beneath the bleachers, to organize the equipment he'd needed to delineate the field. He was not quick enough in his retreat to escape the sight of the Lata coach.

"This field hasn't even been dragged, and it's time for us to take infield," the man hollered out to Bob as he approached.

"I know," Bob replied, stopping in his tracks. "This game's lasting longer than I thought."

"Can't you drag it real quick?"

"No, the truck's way up at the school."

"Guys, let's get this thing going," the umpire called out as he glanced at his watch.

"Okay," Bob replied, stumbling inside to secure the equipment.

"Damn it," he heard the Lata coach mutter and walk away.

"Forget you,' Bob whispered, "forget you and your well-kept, city-maintained field. I'm no farmer."

"Ain't no good host either," he mumbled as he stepped outside. *It's a friggin' distraction, making sure all is in order for your enemy guests. The only advantage is last at-bat, and you've got to wait forever for that,* he mused as he pushed the chalk dispenser toward the plate as the last out of the Little League game was recorded.

He'd lifted the wheels of the cart from the dirt when he'd reached first base. He'd laughed, despite his frustration, as he began drawing the running lane, amused by the sight of the Lata players pacing excitedly within the visiting dugout. He called to mind blissful childhood days at that moment, remembering how, when appointed leadoff man for Little League road games, he'd stand, helmet on head, bat in hand, positively tingling with anticipation for the cue "Play ball!"

Really, he reflected, as he took a drink from the can and scanned the traffic, *it was that way in all facets of his life. Fleeing the familiar, being catered to by strangers, especially those he'd never see again.* No need to tell the truth then, he'd smiled, recalling how he'd so often alter his past, his future prospects, and his income to the girls he'd meet on his Michigan vacations. *Hell, they were probably lying to him also.*

He saw himself next walking behind home plate after sketching in the third base line. He'd sighed, disheartened by the wavy lines before him.

"I flunked both geometry and art," he informed the stone-faced umpire.

Yes, he was happier away from home, was far more at ease in the company of females at their homes, able to, as in baseball, focus his attention on the game, to let them recite the "ground rules."

He heard the six o'clock whistle blow now, just as he had the night of the Lata game when he hastily wound the twine about the spool and threw it at the base of the dugout. Angrily, he'd gathered his players about him as his foes ran onto the field for their delayed pre-game infield warm-up.

"Fellas," he addressed them, "this field's not game-ready," he said, looking over his shoulder. "I don't want to hear any excuses, though. We practice every day on that damn rock pile behind the school. This field's a helluva lot better than that one."

He'd hit his pregame ground balls harder than normal, much harder, mocking the way his opponents had tested the battered earth. Cralt had one ricochet off his chest and one off his wrist. Each time, he calmly retrieved the offending sphere and fired the ball over to Vale.

"That a baby!" Bob had yelled, particularly inspired by the sight.

The Falcons would have an auspicious collective beginning, however. Rusty, the starting pitcher, could impart little movement to his fastball and was scored upon five times in the first two innings as a result. He escaped unscathed in the third only because of the brilliant 5-3-5 double play Vale and Cralt alertly hooked up on.

Bob had leaped to his feet at the sight of the surprised baserunner being tagged out and moved rapidly out of the dugout toward both men. He was caught unaware by Cralt's irritated look as the man sauntered past Bob's outstretched hand on his way toward the bat rack.

"Cralt, what's up?" Bob asked.

"They keep complaining about the field. They are really pissing me off."

"Forget it, man," Bob advised. "Give them something to really worry about. You're leading off."

A determined Cralt promptly drilled the initial pitch to the base of the left-field fence for a stand-up double. Bob applauded Cralt, who, like his older brother, was capable of parlaying his ire into exemplary play.

He smiled now as he stood and stretched, recalling how the whole team had rallied around old Cralt after he was denied a home run for allegedly missing third base on the trot following the first home run of his life. He could still hear the *pop* of the catcher's mitt the next inning as Cralt angrily finished his complete-game 6–5 victory.

Pell's single scored young Cralt, and the merriment began on this more recent victory. Those Falcons who could not hit wanted out on errant tosses and took their base on balls, from which vantage they would be sent across the plate by the knocks of their more capable colleagues. Under Bart's direction, all ran the bases with abandon, the foolhardiness of the more plodding eliciting shouts of dismay from Bob—shrieks that drew laughter from the hometown fans when players like Vale wistfully crossed the plate, smiling as they looked into the dugout.

Rusty, then staked to a comfortable lead, was able to labor well into the late innings. He would ascend the mound for the final inning with a five-run advantage. The first batter singled to left. He scored on the subsequent pitch when Rusty, having dropped his throbbing right arm, failed to get on top of his curveball. The *3–9 o'clock* pitch hovered over the plate until it was smashed handily over the left-field fence. The following batter singled up the middle, then promptly stole second.

Bob had made the move out of the dugout at that time, initiating the journey that was to end with his relieving Rusty of his pitching duties. He stopped abruptly, however, at the sight of the redhead whirling and throwing to Pell at second in time to pick off the Lata runner.

It was not until after the next hitter received a free pass to first that Bob replaced Rusty with Kendall. With the Falcon advantage now at three runs, it was a save situation for K.B. Bob's move was seemingly to be rewarded as Kendall coaxed a weak pop-out to Pell from the first batter he faced. The Falcons' collective composure was eradicated a minute later when Kendall lost the next hitter on an errant *3–2* pitch.

The potential tying run, represented by the powerful first baseman, was now in the batter's box. He stood to the first-base side of the plate, flexing his arms, glaring at the right-field fence. It was a barrier he'd cleared twice already that evening. Each of the five runs he'd driven across the plate had come from Rusty's fastballs.

Bob gestured for Greg to order a curveball. The hook arced down and in. The beast waited, coiling, poised to strike—triggered by the sight of Kendall's left elbow driving his body forward on the delivery. The man unfurled and connected solidly, his body motions singular in purpose and lethal intent.

The ball quickly fled from the plate, its low trajectory followed by Alex in right, who then stood motionless, helpless, as the ball left the playing field into foul territory! Hands on hips, cursing his fate, the demon watched two Andrews kids retrieve the ball.

The collective sigh of relief heard in the Falcons' dugout was quickly silenced, however, when Bob asked freshman Kevin Millen to enter the game as pitcher.

"Go get 'em, Lefty," he'd remembered yelling out, exhorting the inexperienced southpaw.

Kendall's face suggested surprise when Kevin met him at the summit. It had to have been a shock, Bob admitted, for the senior to be replaced at such a precarious standpoint by a kid who'd never before pitched in a varsity game.

"You sure about this?" Bart asked after they watched Kevin's second consecutive warm-up pitch bounce into the dirt before the plate.

"Yes, sir. Have to have a lefty-versus-lefty matchup. Keep the curveball away from his. *Vis-à-vis.*"

"He hasn't thrown in a game this year, though."

"I know, man," Bob had whispered. "This cowboy told me about training his puppy by putting them in a cage with a wolf..."

"Play ball!" the umpire ordered, drowning out Bob's tale.

Greg looked to the dugout. Another deuce was ordered, a strike called.

"Yeah!" Bob yelled.

The next two pitches were intentionally thrown low and away—the intent to induce a defensive swing and miss. No such luck would visit the Falcons.

"This ain't going to come easy," Bob muttered.

Kevin then returned to the mound after descending to retrieve the ball from Greg. He glared into the mitt, appearing very much enthralled with being the Falcons' man of the moment. His body swung confidently into motion; the timing of his movements was exact, flawless. His abbreviated stride moved slightly to the third-base side, and the down, back, and up motion of his throwing arm—with his elbow above the plane of his shoulder—as he made his fateful descent imparted perfect motion to the ball in a direction away from the club in the big man's hands.

"Dang!" Bob yelled in admiration, a split second before the giant's feeble attempt to intercept its path fell desperately short.

"Yes!" Bob yelled as the ball was secured safely in Greg's mitt.

"Yeah!" Kevin exclaimed, pumping his fist, his elbow at a 90degree angle on his left side moving back and forth, pulling the plug on Lata's hopes.

"Good call, son!" Bart yelled, grinning at his beaming colleague as both men ran onto the field.

The next evening, they climbed the hills to Grable, arriving a mere ten minutes before the scheduled 6:00 start time, sans practice balls. Instructing his players to warm up with rocks equivalent in mass to baseballs. Bob had no time to reflect on the daunting task ahead inside the fence. Indeed, as Hamsten approached him, the gold G emerging triumphantly from the regal purple background of his cap, there was no time for Bob to recall his 1–8 lifetime Little League mark against the man. Even the lone victory was tainted—a joyless triumph in which he'd watched from the bleachers after an on-field argument with Del regarding baserunning philosophy. He'd been nearly inconsolable then, even as he watched his squad excitedly celebrate after old Cralt struck down the last of the Grable hitters he'd subdued that day.

No, the past simply did not register within his mind as Hamsten asked the rhetorical, "You ready, Coach?"

"Yes. What time is it?"

"5:55. We've already taken infield. Y'all go ahead and do the same, then we'll get started."

"Yes, sir," Bob responded, feeling fortunate that his team would not have to go on defense first, would not be buried before they had their bearings.

The Falcons were retired in order, and Hamsten began his glorious march to the coaching box, carried by the cheers of approval from the hometown fans. It was just then that the deflating déjà vu enveloped Bob. Even with Kendall atop the hill, Grable managed to score twice in the first. They held that two-run advantage through the third.

"What's new?" Bob asked sarcastically as Bart walked to the coach's box to begin the fourth.

In retrospect, he thought he should have been proud of his charges, secure in the knowledge that even in the face of certain defeat, his team was fighting. Hell, he'd not allowed them to retain their dignity with his tardiness and shoddy preparation. They, as always, deserved better. And there they were again, making him look good.

He began pacing on the porch, brimming with pride at the recall of their defensive effort, for that had always been his forte—his only concern. His diving catches in the outfield as a player had caused his peers to overlook his minuscule batting average in junior high; he had attained satisfaction in only losing 4–0 in wrestling; had been grateful after 2–1 and 3–2 defeats as a coach. But why, he asked himself? It was as if his whole life's purpose was to keep the really bad stuff at bay. Who the hell even thought about winning? No "slips" back to the bottle, no late bill payments, no job terminations, no illness, no homelessness, no babies—he recited the list. It all made him look "nice," responsible, but it wasn't fulfilling.

He smiled smugly at the sight of himself in bed with Andrea. He'd owed himself that break from convention, he assured himself.

His boys, he mused as he sat back down, they were different—molded by differing life experiences, differing expectations. He was definitely not attending to a team of his clones. They were cocky somehow, diving headlong into the competitive setting, invading and intruding upon enemy enclaves.

Indeed, he scarcely recognized this new breed of Falcons—that inning, that black-and-gold cohort who ran with abandon until a dozen runs had crossed the plate. He watched in stone-sober awe as they raged on under the direction of Bart, who was conducting a veritable symphony from the third-base box, playing Taps for their vanquished foes. Damn, the boy was good!

When the two sides exchanged roles, the Falcons led by ten. The Andrews voices sang out to one another, enveloping Bob within the mirth. He'd slapped Bart's hand in approval, oblivious to his surroundings, as he shouted, "Man, we're making this look easy!"

He regained his composure when Hamsten's steady gaze fell upon him. He stopped mid-strut, snapping to attention as Hamsten's question landed.

"Coach, what do you have for a score?"

"What the..." Bob started, looking over his counterpart's shoulder at the blank, unlit scoreboard.

"It's broke. My boy says you're up five."

"No way," Bart asserted.

"Let's see," Bob began, suddenly deflated as he counted the shaded diamonds in the scorebook. "We're showing we're up... nine," he said, averting his eyes in an unspoken apology.

Hamsten remained still, his expression unmarked.

"I can take my book over and compare if you want."

"No," Hamsten countered. "We'll use yours."

Bob seated himself on the bench, shaken. Was this merely gamesmanship? Certainly, Hamsten wouldn't have tried to defraud him. But the S.O.B. was tough, fiery. It would not have been in the Falcons' best interest for him to feel he'd been ridiculed.

Fortunately, the Birds had not been privy to the conversation between Hamsten and himself, and they were still playing liberated, aggressive baseball. They challenged the Grable offensive. Two runners who had reached second base were exhumed by sparkling, unrehearsed pickoff plays. Bob recalled watching in wonder as Cralt and Pell alternately feigned covering the bag, while the other broke in behind the runner to take Kendall's throw.

The difference was still seven as the Falcons took the field in the bottom of the seventh and final inning. There was palpable tension on the dirt, however; a more subdued air surrounded the previously dancing Andrews crew.

They seemed to be yielding to the pressure attendant to retaining their advantage.

Bob looked upon Hamsten in the third-base box before the first pitch. The man still stood upright, calmly urging his boys to do the seemingly unimaginable. He appeared almost serene as four runs crossed the plate at the cost of only one out. A runner stood close to second base, glancing pensively at first Cralt, then Pell, when Bob called "Time" and walked to the mound. It was, he decided, time to be creative.

"You all right, K.B.?" he asked the tiring Kendall, his hands now resting on his own knees.

"If not, I have an idea," Bob continued, winking at Greg. "We'll bring Greg in to throw, put you behind the plate. Who knows, it just might work."

"I ain't doing it," Greg spat.

"You're gonna let us down?" Bob responded, winking again at Greg from behind Kendall's back. "Kendall's got nothing left; he's too tired. So what if you fail? We'll only have lost by one."

"I'm okay," Kendall interjected, snapping upright. He pounded the ball into his mitt. "Let's go, Greg," he said, waving his hand.

"You're sure about this?" Bob asked, wide-eyed.

"Yeah, yeah, of course," Kendall said hurriedly.

Bob suppressed a laugh as he followed Greg off the mound. He smiled at each of the consecutive strikes it took Kendall to finish off the Grable attack. He calmly stepped over to Hamsten and shook the frowning man's hand.

"Good game, Coach," he said firmly, then returned to the dugout.

"Fellas," he said aloud, "you just beat a damn good team."

"Yeah!" Woody shouted.

"Good job, guys!" Kendall asserted.

"Don't show off until we get out of here, though. We've got plenty of time to enjoy this on the way home."

Bob smiled and stood up, content to watch the sun wind its way toward the horizon, now from his vantage on the porch. He turned and went inside, intent on showering. As he retreated to the bedroom, he removed his shirt. He stopped as he bent to remove his shoes, certain that he'd heard a faint knock on his door.

"Opportunity?" he shouted toward the sound in a laughing voice.

"What else could it be?" he whispered.

Amy steadied herself, waiting for the door to open. She would need to adapt spontaneously to an overabundance of emotions. She promised herself now that she would be unwavering in the face of his potential accusations, would shield herself with her assertion that she had overestimated him, misread his capacity to care for her... whatever bullshit it took to soften him. "Stoic, unflappable," she could hear herself use in misreading what was, in truth, his cowardly inability to convey his true thoughts toward her in this house.

She could not have been more surprised, having readied herself as such, when the door flung quickly open, revealing the cheery individual before her. The beast stood to the side, offering her safe passage within his domain.

"Amy Lou!" His voice reverberated against the wall, echoing his excitement. "How are you? Have a seat," he said, pointing toward the couch.

"Thank you. How's everything?"

"Good," he said, as he threw a blue towel across his bare torso. "Excuse me a second," he said, retreating toward the bedroom. He ventured out a moment later, now fully clothed. "I got your note," he began, "didn't expect to see you."

"I decided to return your key in person," Amy broke in. "I was afraid it might get lost in the mail." As she spoke, she studied his body language, examined him in hopes of discovering some hint of vulnerability. Not today, she informed herself cheerlessly as she watched him swagger toward the kitchen.

"That's pretty nice of you; then again, what else should I expect from a pretty woman like you?"

Here we go, she thought as he turned around. Preparing his intrusion. "Shy guy"? Whoever tagged him with that moniker at UNEI had never seen him in situations like these. She stood as he droned on, her intent to reduce the symbolic advantage he held by standing overhead. Looking into his eyes, she proceeded to place him in a more passive position by supplanting him as speaker.

"I need to talk to you. That's why I'm really here," she said assertively, impeding his facile attempt at seduction.

"Okay, okay, have you eaten yet?"

"No."

"Let's go to Andrews, to the Ritz. It's time to celebrate."

"There's nothing to celebrate."

"Yeah, there is. I'm on a fricking roll."

"Why, what happened?"

"We won two games in a row, I got laid, and the blue-eyed, prodigal daughter has returned."

"These are special events?" she responded, feeling a bit overwhelmed by his soaring spirit.

"In my world, they are, baby!" he exclaimed, shaking his head in affirmation.

As he drove, he'd been lecturing about winning—the joy of making sound decisions. You just had to create the right "atmosphere," he counseled her.

She resisted the urge to lash out, to ridicule his laughable dissertation. What the hell does he know about success, she mused as she looked out the window of her own car. For him, a triumph was an aberration, a short-lived experience. No matter how exultant his manner was, she informed herself, he'd soon find his spirits waning—would become again the same lifeless being who had scuffled along, head bowed past the "Scotts" and "Mikes" who had entered her dorm room some eight years earlier.

It was merely the timing that bothered her, she mused, nodding her head to the rhythm of his giddy, galloping words. She could not bear having this be her legacy here, could not tolerate her inability to detect even the slightest evidence of negative emotion on his pungent carcass. How could this be? Certainly, there had to be some debilitating ideas mingling about with all these positive ones in his head. His pessimistic orientation surely could not be reversed by the mere visitation upon him of a few well-played little guys' ball games and this girl. And who would want to assume the role this unthinking female had? To entangle themselves with this awkward-looking fool? She cringed at the sight, wishing she could lash out against the dumb slut who'd sabotaged her plans by altering the flow of his miserable existence.

Could it be that he was lying? Considering what Bart and others had hinted, she assumed that he had somehow drifted into the fantasy world he'd nurtured and developed during his lonely late evening hours. His idealized self was probably now possessing his soul, obliterating his unendurable reality. *He's probably never...*

Did he just now employ the term *romance* in his endeavor to define that alleged trust? It was not a word that fit well with the adolescent prose with which he'd described the jaunt. Certainly, he was familiar with the symbols, could maneuver the attendant "props," but he did not have a clue as to how to create the energy, the vibrations that were the essence of such compelling drama.

She did. That's why she knew the multisyllabic words he utilized were a cover—a desperate attempt to mask his inexperience. There would never be enough time to redeem himself either, she surmised, as she envisioned the disheartened man being pulled reluctantly into middle age, scratching his brow in celibate, self-contemptuous wonderment.

It was sad, she thought. Too bad he hadn't worked more fervently, been more cognizant of the fact that there was this substantial penalty to be assessed for failing to win the favor of her refined class. The gaudy, heart-shaped necklace he'd sent her, with the crude "A" engraved into the fallacious gold exterior, would never sway those who inhabited her elegant world. He needed to have literally gotten "real" if he wanted to have a chance, she concluded, suddenly heartened by the belief that he'd soon be at her mercy.

He was still lying when they arrived at the restaurant. She would pick at this story, confound him until he confessed that there'd been no such foolish victim, no romantic tryst. Then she'd tell him about her and Eart— that would upend him, would leave him in a heap.

"Tough break, boy," she whispered as he stepped out and walkedaround to her side of the car. He opened the door and took her hand, then helped her up the high curb. He then held the door as they stepped inside. He waved at the hostess as Amy passed the threshold.

"Marley, can you get us a good table?" he inquired flamboyantly.

"Of course. Right this way, sir," the gray-haired woman replied, mimicking his contrived actions. "Can I get you anything to drink?"

"Yeah, I'll have a Diet Coke. How about you, Amy?"

"7/7, please," Amy uttered to the back of the round woman.

"Have you ever been here before?" Bob asked.

"No, it's nice though," Amy forced herself to say, longing to be basking in the opulence of West Queens.

"You've heard of it though?"

"Yes."

"Hey, I've been do ng all of the talking," he said as they sat down. "What's on your mind?"

"I'm leaving town. I just want to ensure that I'm leaving on good terms. I feel like there may be some unresolved matters between us.'

"Like what?" Bob inquired as he sipped on his drink.

"I just couldn't get a read on you in the days before I moved out of Rice. You were so silent."

"Frustration, Amy," he sighed. "Standing knee-deep in water I couldn't drink, an arm's length from grapes I can't eat," he mumbled as he stared at the ceiling.

"What the hell," Amy laughed, amused at his application of the fable.

"I've just always wanted to make love to you, and I couldn't. So close..." His voice trailed off as the smirking waitress cleared her throat from her station above the table.

"All on one check, Bob?" she asked, appearing to be trying not to laugh.

"Yeah, sure. Two specials with fries, please."

The "Stacy" departed, and Amy broached the question she knew he'd never ever be able to answer. "Why me, though?"

He chuckled, then looked into her eyes. "I have no clue. Guess you're stuck with me for life. *Valentine's Day Massacre,* I call it—that weekend I met ya. The catalyst in my static life, the only spark I had for years. And then you show up here? Wow! Who the hell else gets to be rejected by their dream woman twice? Who else is stupid enough to try to draw water from an empty well? Who allows themselves to get screwed over like that?"

She watched his face turn ruddy, saw his hands shake. She was winning, effortlessly.

"I'll bet you come back a third time," he asserted. "This is a friggin' nightmare."

"Why?" Amy asked, raising her empty glass at Stacy. "Just fill your life up with other women like you did the other night."

"Did you see a lot of girls banging down my door in Rice? And besides, that girl was just a kid." He stopped short when he said the word, acting as if he had inadvertently said what he'd wished not to be known. Kid? She snook free of the thought. He was always referring to anyone younger than himself as such. The girl was probably thirty.

"You think there was no action in that room?" she smiled.

"No way," he whispered, shaking his head in disbelief.

"Do you really believe I sat there engaging in some stupid sympathy celibacy ritual with you? You had to know better."

His face paled in response. "Who was it? Who did you betray me with?" he asked, clearing his throat before nervously sipping his drink.

"Bart, obviously. The guy at the bank," she lied about the last name, but having heard that he was an adolescent bully who'd made his teen years hell, she couldn't resist.

"Oh, man..." he grimaced. He sighed, then resumed a silent tact.

Amy sat in preparation, assessing the damage wrought, waiting for him to lash out. *Wonder which words he will use. What would he throw? Come on, get it off your little chest,* she mused, staring at his pensive countenance.

The impasse was overcome by his nervous chuckle. In seconds, to her dismay, it had become a mirthful roar. The patrons at the nearest table smiled, amused by the spectacle of Bob—chest convulsing, rolling on one side of his chair.

"Bart's taken this assistant role a bit too seriously," he grinned. "I know I told him to stick the rubber on the mound, but..." He stopped, snickering as the food was set before him. "Look," he said as he cut his steak. "Bart's a good man. If you're going to be stupid with anyone, I'm glad it was him. And that guy at the bank—a married man.

Lord knows he ain't going to heaven. He better hope God forgives him. I thought what I did Saturday was immoral..."

Amy ordered a third drink. She could not believe he was not shaken by the revelation. The laughter appeared genuine. This was not going to be an easy night.

"You? Immoral?" she scoffed. The liquor was beginning to give an edge to her tongue. "Who was this chick, anyway? I bet you're lying."

"Screw you," he muttered. "Go to the strip bar and find out for yourself."

"You were with a stripper?" she laughed wickedly. "Oooh, what an accomplishment. How much did you have to pay?"

"Nothing. She paid me," he grinned.

"You're crazy," Amy laughed, disarmed by his humor.

"I know I am. No, she was a nice girl."

"Was? Aren't you going back to her? Back to the well?"

"Good one," Bob grinned. "No, that wouldn't be smart."

"Why not?"

"She's too young. Not gonna happen."

"How young?"

"I hope eighteen," he laughed nervously.

"Young enough to be your daughter."

"She looked older."

"Why did you pursue her? Were you drunk?"

"No," he replied, pausing to eat the last of his steak. "You want to know the truth? She looked like you did then— little blonde-haired, blue-eyed heartbreaker. Name's Andrea, just like your middle name. I had no choice; got no common sense when it comes to you..."

Amy sat silent, assessing her next move. She'd run to the city tonight, talk to the employees of each of the dancing clubs, meet with this possibly underage girl. The statutory—a mandatory five in this state, a dictate initiated by her father's West Queen friend, the honorable Dr. Vehlen. Open and shut. The public defender, the poor boy would have to hire, would be laughed out of court.

See ya, wouldn't want to be ya, her soul whispered to the man across the table.

"You ready to leave?" she asked, waving for the check.

"Sure. Are you staying in town tonight?"

"No, I have some errands to run."

"Tonight?"

"Yes. Do you think you can catch a ride home from here?"

"Yeah, sure," he said as they both stood, getting ready to leave.

He left the money on the table, pointed to Stacy, then followed her into the night.

Amy stepped into the car and placed her hands out for the key. He handed them to her, then stood longingly as she engaged the engine and turned on the easy listening radio station. *Perfect,* she surmised, gazing into his lovesick eyes.

"Thanks a lot, Amy," he said.

"No, thank you," she replied with a grin, then backed the car out of the parking space.

Bart sat next to Pell, adjusting the straps on the catcher's shin guards, intrigued by the man who'd supplanted him in the role of administering pre-game infield. It had been all too often, he reminded himself, that he'd seen the being with the Fungo bat get so inside himself that he'd adversely impact the Falcon morale. Yeah, their search for direction on this rudderless vessel would turn out to be a futile quest—at most times, the depression of the man looking first down, then away from them, leading them to anything but excellence.

Not tonight, though. The son of a bitch seemed to be in a "zone," resolute in his decisions, in tune with necessity. It was unsettling to see him swagger onto the field, flipping the bat around pretentiously, snaring the ball with bare hands. All were acts that elicited the scorn of his blue-clad foes, but as risky as such behavior could be in psychological warfare, it was, Bart admitted, a refreshing change.

The fervor with which Bob hit the balls to either side of his infielders, the way he'd exhorted them to attain brilliance in their moves, vested Bart with a feeling he'd thought had been reserved for the gridiron. Sellers had taken this game to a new level, transcending the traditional grinding manner in which Bart had always seen the game administered.

What could be the source of such enthusiasm? What got him to that "quality" state he often referred to? He seemed to be in total accord with his surroundings, empowered in every way. Bart had felt it of late inside of Seller's Amy. In being with her, he'd enjoyed the spoils of this winning streak, had become grateful for the opportunity to be here, on this field, now. He'd nearly resigned himself to not experiencing her again. The deficiencies of those he'd called upon to duplicate such pleasure had inspired only his irritability.

But now he had rallied with her nocturnal assistance last night, and seemingly so had Sellers. What was his recovery dependent upon? Certainly not that same blond belle. She had offered, without prompting, an admission to the contrary. But there was something external to his passion for the game that had placed him in such an emotional state.

"I'm the D.H. tonight? How come?"

Bart turned toward Pell, whose question had served to evaporate the thick pool of contemplation into which Bart had waded.

"He said something about it being Alex's birthday. He wants to give him the chance to pitch. You'll start tomorrow."

"That's okay, but why ain't I playing short?"

"He said it'd be good karma for Alex to have his buddy, Cody, playing there."

"So, I'll hit for Alex. Alex can keep his focus on pitching, will say strike three to himself continually, imagining himself hearing his favorite music each time he throws one."

"Damn, you know this stuff?"

"Nah, I heard Sellers telling it to Alex a little while ago," Pell said, as he winked at his sister directly behind them.

Bart laughed. "Hey, he's been hot lately. Look at the way he threw Kevin in against Lata. Blind, crazy luck. Why argue with him now?"

Pell nodded in affirmation and grabbed a bat from the rack. Squeezing it firmly between his large hands, he seemed quite ready to do some damage.

"Showtime, fellas!" Sellers yelled to them as he sauntered to the bench.

"We're in our Home box too," Pell responded.

"Take it to the Cinemax," Bart added.

It was a game worthy of placing on pay-television, as both teams battled for five innings without either breaking free of one another. Bart glanced at Sellers. No hint of inner turmoil graced the head coach's face. The man seemed confident as he stood talking to his sister prior to the top of the sixth.

"One to one, we have them on the ropes, boys," the man stated as he returned to his seat between Bart and Pell. "Alex is cruising. How many pitches has he thrown, Pell?"

"Seventy," Pell replied after scanning the pitching chart. "Mostly fastballs. His arm has to be fresh."

"When do you bat this inning, Horse?"

"Fourth."

"What's he been throwing you? What pattern?"

"Hooking me right away. Mixing fastballs and changes when he gets behind."

"You've made good contact both times up."

"Yeah, been just a little out in front, flying out to left."

"Jim will start squeezing his strike zone if this one stays deadlocked. Let him get in a bind with that deuce. Wait on the heat when it's 2-0 and 3-1."

"You got it."

They'd scarcely concluded their talk when the Falcons returned from the field, following a 6-4-3 (Kendall-Cralt-Vale) double play.

Bart reflected upon Bob's forecast as he walked to the coach's box, the sight of perspiration soaking Jim's shirt as he brushed off the plate on this humid evening almost certainly ensuring that this game would not take extra innings to decide. Jim would not allow it; Bart knew this. The check was probably already in his pocket.

Kendall led off with a single. Bart flashed the sign to the fleet-footed runner—right hand rubbing leg, then the letters, then the bill of the cap—a command for Kencall to attempt a steal. Kendall acknowledged receipt by touching his belt buckle as he assumed his lead from first. Come on, Bart pleaded silently.

"Ball in, Jim!" Bob's inane cry startled, then angered, Bart. Why in the hell did he break up the timing? The pitcher wasn't even looking in Kendall's direction. "Damn it," he muttered as he glared into the Falcon dugout.

He watched as Bob removed his cap and wiped his brow—a gesture that indicated he was exercising his veto power. Audibling. He then signaled for Bart to flash the bunt sign to Greg. Grudgingly, Bart acquiesced, upset that the Falcons were opting to trade an out for a base when they had Kendall's speed available.

In an instant, he came to understand Sellers' decision. The pitcher, having deceived Kendall by appearing indifferent to him, threw a pitch far wide of the plate. The catcher leaped to a standing position as he secured the ball, poised to deliver a strike to second, unencumbered by the presence of Greg, now far to his left.

The pitchout! Somehow Sellers had been tipped off. The request for a bunt ensured the Falcons that Kendall would be attentive to the action at the plate, would stand pat until he saw the downward motion of the ball off the bat.

Kendall dived in far in advance of the catcher's throw to first. He was now free to advance on the next pitch. "That a way, Sellers!" Bart yelled.

They left the request for the sacrifice in place, and after Greg's flawless execution, Kendall stood at second with only one out. With first base open, the Martens' coach elected to walk the menacing Cralt and pitch to Pell.

The slow curve, Sellers had often told his pitchers, was an excellent pitch for inducing a ground ball double play. Pell, upon seeing the motion and spin of that type of offering and mindful of Sellers' prognostications from earlier that inning, left the bat on his shoulder. The pitch looped wide of the strike zone. The next delivery ended up in the same location. Now, with Cralt and K. B. surrounding him, the pitcher pawed nervously at the rubber, a limited number of options available to him.

His selection of location and velocity on the subsequent pitch would not go unpunished. Pell tore into the 2-0 belt-high fastball. The resonance borne of metal on leather left no doubt as to what the score would be when the ball was to finally land. As it crashed into the verdant pasture south of the center field fence, Bart shook first Kendall's, then Cralt's, hand. When Pell's hand met his as he crossed third base, Bart stole a quick look at Sellers. He laughed as he caught sight of the man standing on top of the bench, arms held above his head, à la Joe Montana at the culmination of a successful offensive drive.

As he entered the dugout following the inning, secured within the glow of the scoreboard lights, which now revealed "Falcons 4, Guests 1," Bart inquired of the beaming duo before him, "Who do we get to beat tomorrow?"

"These guys again!" Pell replied giddily.

"Bring 'em on!" Sellers shouted, swaying and weaving on the bench, pumping his fists.

"Damn straight!" Bart yelled, perpetuating the revelry.

Amy stretched her hands above her head and yawned as she sat awaiting the arrival of her confidant and his friend from the literary agency on the summer morning in Queens. She had left Bart's home much later than she had planned; hence, she'd completed the long drive to Queens at 12:30 a.m. Angela had been waiting on her, and they had talked until well past two. The previous evening's research had concluded at 2:15 in the parking lot of a dangerous, decrepit establishment. Thus, when the alarm sounded at 6:30, Amy had crawled out of bed feeling anything but refreshed. But, cognizant as she was of her 8:00 a.m. commitment to meet with this duo and mindful of the consequences attending their potential reproof of her and hers, she'd hastened to reach the site before them.

She glanced at the clock—8:05 a.m., it indicated. *Where are they?* she wondered, annoyed by their lack of punctuality. *I've received less than one full night's sleep combined over the last forty-eight hours. What's their excuse?*

Little freaky Andrea, she mused, recalling the conversation she had initiated in the oasis that was her car amidst the leering, sodden losers in the gravel. *If Andrea had a brain, I could have been home by twelve on Wednesday. It was a wonder she was able to focus long enough to consent to my request.*

The door opened just then. Amy glanced again at the clock, which now revealed that the time was 8:10 a.m.

"Amy, how are you?" the good Dr. Vehlen inquired, beaming as he reached for her hand. "Sorry we're late. Damn ice storm slowed us."

She laughed at the improbable summer alibi as she placed her hand in his. She liked the bearded, well-groomed, middle-aged man—had trusted him from the beginning, would entrust him with details attending both her personal and professional endeavors. He'd always been supportive as well as accessible, never asking for compensation except for the one time at Sir John's....

"I'd like you to meet my friend, Dr. Brooks," he asserted as his colleague extended his hand.

"Pleased to meet you," Amy said as she felt the man grasp and caress her hand.

What the hell.... She wondered as the memory of Dr. Vehlen's slurred words in Sir John's came into vivid hue. He'd merely asked for what they all aspired, and she'd easily eluded him, readily accepting his contrite apology the following morning. He'd made good on his promise to not allow its occurrence to reappear, and all was well.

It was his amorous associate behind the desk who inspired her greatest concern. This *gatekeeper* of creative ideas had the means to render useless the product borne of two hundred hours of solitary nurturing. That which she had endured in yielding a commodity worthy of consumption by those alien to her soul, she would not allow. She had predetermined to be easily dismissed. She furrowed her brow, scrutinizing this broker of imaginary expulsions, searching for deficiencies she could exploit.

She need not have prepared herself as such. Dr. Brooks had formed a positive opinion of her work within the first fifteen pages of his review:

"Amy, I'm very pleased with your story," he began shortly after settling into his seat. "I concur with Dr. Vehlen as to the vast extent of your grasp of the requirements of creating and sustaining interest in the reader of fiction...."

Amy's mind drifted as he praised her, her focus shifting to the other tasks at hand. Certainly, the law professor/criminal lawyer would accept the case, would prosecute the scourge. Yes, he, the ally of all who dared to excel, would definitely do all that he was capable of to implement her goals. He couldn't resist her.

"Your abi ity to develop credible, consistent characterizations of the actors portrayed within your novel is impressive," she heard Dr. Brooks laud her. "Your application of symbolism and allegory is exquisite."

"Thank you." Amy replied. She then turned toward Dr. Vehlen, the first name that had entered her mind when the last word of the novel had been printed in Rice.

As if on cue, he launched into his laudatory address:

"You have demonstrated an understanding of the essence of developing a theme—in this instance, the disillusionment of a promising young social service professional. She cannot secure fulfillment in attaining the rewards lavished upon her as a result of acquiring a lofty position within her chosen field."

"Each time she begins to gain an inner calm, this prosperous, enticing woman is driven back, literally, to the very neighborhoods to which she most ministers. Evolving from a novice social worker dispensing food stamps to a powerful county administrator lobbying the state Senate for provisions, she is never quite able to break free from the most sord d elements of the area—i.e., those most opposed to her efforts.

"Further, rather than advancing a predictable, bell curve type of flow with respect to her excursions, you've baited the reader by lengthening the ascent of your Marley Rowe, in successive chapters, from the depths to which she had fallen. As such, the subsequent collapses become even more terrific in scope. Even the concluding chapter reveals...."

"Excuse me, Dr. Vehlen," Dr. Brooks interjected, now incapable of restraint with respect to his enthusiasm for the offering. "The use of allegory here, on page 197. She enters the bar frequented by those who have a consistent, collective disdain for those helped most by her outlays." He flipped through the loose-leaf manuscript as he continued. "She's then hurt physically by virtue of having stumbled down the steps leading there; that is the consummate metaphor for your Marley. Professional distance leveled by emotion, a desire to comprehend. In her endeavor to experience the pain she feels she has caused them, she emerges in worse condition than they—holding her fractured wrist while they walk about inside, oblivious, laughing at each other's jokes. Brilliant!"

Dr. Vehlen chose to expound upon the same theme. "Yes, how is it stated by Marley? The patrons of that establishment were insulated from the impact of those they despised through the medium of talk radio? The cathartic thrill they received as they listened to the ventilation effectively mitigated the deleterious impact these 'parasites,' as they are referred to here, would have otherwise had upon these reluctant hosts. However, these same liberating, bombastic eruptions heard across the airwaves had also set into motion the flames of their hypocrisy, in Marley's eyes. Am I correct, Amy?"

Amy nodded silently in agreement as she leaned closer to the hidden message.

This benighted band of working welfare beneficiaries, who extracted tolerable wages from those who were conferred their paltry efforts, were living the 'real' dream, from Marley's perspective. Their rantings were then, in essence, a censure of that portion of their own individual selves which fell far short of their idealized representation of the noble laborer. The first stage of widespread revolt—that's how you framed this schism of deserving versus undeserving indigent. That's an allusion to the theory posited by Fanon in *The Wretched of the Earth,* if I recall correctly.

In having Marley comment that this less tolerant group has a financial stake in ensuring that the perpetuation of the presence of the 'undeserving' underclass is not impeded, and hence kept at a safe distance from the former group's permanent wages, you further advance the believability of this enigmatic Marley. Chastising herself later in pained reflection, literally 'knocking into her head' the message that this mass of working people need not be consoled, are in no need of rescue... *If only she could act in accordance with her convictions!*

A momentary silence ensued as Dr. Vehlen ceased talking and peered at her from behind his shaded glasses. *Damn, he's good,* she mused, envisioning him working the courtroom on behalf of the State of Indiana and herself, virtually locking her into half a decade's reprieve.

Her thoughts competed in her head only with the whir of the air conditioner. Dr. Vehlen seemed to be examining her for evidence of her gratification. Her placid features had apparently produced no such result, and so he continued. "What we are saying here, Amy, is that we will represent your work pending your approval."

"Yes, of course," she replied, signing the contract set before her.

"Don't worry, Amy," Dr. Brooks asserted as he again suggestively grasped her hand. "We'll successfully place this manuscript. You'll realize a substantial profit. I guarantee this.'

The words barely reached her. Pleased as she was by their adulation, she had found their interpretation of the quasi-autobiographical offering to be quite disconcerting. *Was she really incapable of feeling fulfilled, despite her achievements?* Inner pain borne of an obsessively guilt-driven recurrent tour of the darkest aspects of her life. She had not worked with this in mind; the book had, in essence, 'written itself' when she had been set free from the demands of her job.

"If you need anything else from me, just call," Dr. Vehlen advised as he watched Amy walk toward the door.

"Yes, there is something," she said, turning slowly around. She could not believe she had almost forgotten. She shook her shoulders as the receptionist opened the door and was caught unaware by the sudden chill of the morning air.

"What might that be?" she heard him inquire. Her mind flashed to the vision of the balding, defeated man, looking out sadly at her through prison bars, hands trembling.

'Shut the door, baby, okay?' she heard the receptionist's request. She looked out pensively upon the stream of morning traffic. Her eyes became focused on the police cruiser parked in front of the Denny's restaurant.

"Oh, forget about it," Amy sighed as she closed the door behind her and walked quickly to her car.

By the time the Falcons walked onto the field to begin the bottom of the first, Bob sensed that they would win, regardless. He watched Pell peer in to receive Greg's sign as he glanced next at the scoreboard, which read 6-0, Falcons. He asked, "Do you think Pell will have control problems? He hasn't thrown in a week, has he?"

"Strrrriikkke!" the umpire responded. The batter, overwhelmed by the force of the delivery, stepped away from the plate.

"No," Bart smiled in a delayed reply to Bob's query.

Bob laughed. "Guess sitting through that long inning had no effect on him."

The first three Martens hitters had no chance, and the Falcons were soon up to bat again. They scored three in the second, and when Pell struck out his fourth, fifth, and sixth men in succession, Bob began to replace his starting players with his reserves. "Rusty, let Lee bat for you, and Hand will catch you. Stay loose." The redhead quickly consented, hastening to place his bat back into the rack.

"Cralt, Van will bat for you and play third base. Take a break."

Body slackening, Bob turned to watch his substitutes in action. He next addressed the seniors on the bench, the players who'd made the opportunity possible. "Can't beat this with a stick, fellas," he stated.

"That a way, Pell!" he shouted, heartened by the sight of yet another Martens player retreating to the dugout, bat in hand.

The difference was six when he reinserted his starting lineup into the game to begin the bottom of the seventh. The move was essentially a tribute to these upperclassmen. He reminded them before they entered the field, "Gentlemen, we have a golden opportunity to do a couple of things we've never done before, like winning four games in a week. Also, we'll be above .500 for the first time this season. Let's do it!"

The thunderous response surprised him. As they fervently rushed the field, Bart asked beneath the din, "Did I miss something?"

"Only if you don't turn around and watch this 1-2-3 inning, son," Bob smiled.

Sweet redemption, he surmised as he gazed upon the same football field where Klein had directed his junior high team to a 13-12 upset victory. Pretty much symbolic of all he'd later experienced here. Unexpected riches.

The four times Dan had employed him on his farm a mile south of here, each a necessary step in his attaining his coveted UNEI degree. Wasn't easy work. He earned his money but not the opportunity, he decided. Like the $100 he won at the Martens fair one summer, he received much that was not due him. Indeed, he reasoned, as he hoisted the helmet bag over his shoulder, it was the woman who now approached who made it happen.

In conjunction with Dan, they'd somehow prevented him from descending into what he perceived to be the valley of broken dreams. Their tattered farm home sheltered him from the gusts of self-destructive thoughts that would have certainly knocked him flat.

"Yeah, well, their faith in the apparent virtue of that 'fantasy camp' of UNEI on the state's eastern border had finally met with reward. No longer were they advancing on the hapless waiter—it was the accredited professional she'd soon address.

He walked toward the bus and met up with her at the bus door. "Good job, Coach!" his sister said jocularly.

"Thank you. What're you up to?"

"Not much. Just wanted to see how my alma mater would fare against my new hometown."

"Hope you were pulling for us."

"But of course."

As they conversed, the game had ended, and Bart and the players had filed quickly past.

"We're going to play again Monday," he began. "It's been a good week; I can't wait."

"Damn it!" he heard Bart curse, then step out of the bus.

"What's wrong, Bart?"

"The thing doesn't even want to turn over. I have no clue as to what's wrong," Bart muttered, his voice muffled by the giant yellow hood he'd lifted above his head.

"Wow, I'd better go call Thorson to see if he can get another bus up to us."

"Do you need a ride to a phone?" his sister asked.

"Yeah, that would be great. I'll be right back, Bart," he shouted as he turned around.

"Alright," was the only word he heard from the man, who by now was deeply concealed by the yellow shell covering the entrails of the disappointing creature.

When Sellers had departed, Bart backed out and threw his hands up in a gesture of exasperation. He realized that of the two of them, Sellers was the more deficient of the duo respecting mechanical aptitude. "Probably something simple," he muttered on his way to the side of the bus. "He's the head coach, yet he doesn't think to check on anything." His disgruntled soliloquy went unheeded by the players surrounding him, who now periodically posted their own theories as to why the bus was inoperable.

As the minutes elapsed, the conversation became more strained, as adolescents unable to wander about on a summer Friday night attacked the impending darkness. Rusty's inexplicable, particularly penetrating question would advance the dis-ease. "Hey, Coach, wasn't that Amy's car in your drive the other night?"

What the hell, Bart asked himself as his neck jerked about. He felt the rumblings of the players, sensed their anticipation. Bart glared at Rusty, but his impact was lost in the twilight.

He stood still, in no hurry to please his impromptu audience. He reflected upon the methods Rusty often employed to gain advantage over those in positions of authority with respect to him. Insubordinate little *asshole*, he brooded. *Trying to wreck team morale by ruining the credibility of its "true" leader. I oughta kick his ass.*

Apparently challenged by Bart's reticence to reply, Rusty pressed on. "Sure as hell looked like hers when I spotted it about 11:30 last night, too."

That was a lie, but Bart chose not to protest too forcefully. Would not walk into the minefield. He'd instead attempt to turn the tables.

"Rusty," he began, "to me you're not an adult. Not yet. Therefore, you've got no business asking me about adult situations. What's this have to do with what we're trying to accomplish as a team? Or aren't you a team player?"

Rusty merely smiled. It was a smug smile—one Bart wished to smash into oblivion, one he wished to vanquish, as the man who'd run over his dog one night last summer. *It'll soon be payback time,* he promised Rusty with his eyes.

"No excuse," he heard the indistinguishable voice reprimand him from among the crowd of players behind the bus.

"Friggin' mutiny time, is it, fellas?" he inquired firmly.

He watched Sellers and his sister pull up next to the bus. The silence enveloped him. *His "Amy Lou,"* he mused. This wasn't going to be easy for Sellers to accept. Another meaningless defeat, but an ill-timed one anyway. It would be nice if he didn't have to be dealt this blow—not ten days before the postseason began.

"Alright!" he blurted out as Sellers approached. *This will end the topic of conversation for the remainder of this season. Don't let on that you know. Let him keep what dignity he has left,* he said softly, suddenly moved by the hesitant gait of the man before him. *Let him be,* he whispered, his voice smothered by the summer breeze. *Let him be.*

Amy reclined in her chair and wrapped herself within the calming sounds of yet another utopian love ballad. As she leaned here in *The Tollbooth* on this Saturday evening, her thoughts were brought closer to her family's woe. Angela, now sitting before her, was assailed by her ex-fiancé's invectives on the phone; her brother, Alan, sitting to her left, had a civil suit pending against him for his violent reaction to one who'd dared to fondle Angela in this same club months earlier. Her mother, back home, was filled with angst as she tried to make the requisite $1,500 house payments from her now reduced station with IBT.

"Friggin' ATC," she cursed gently. *Why in the hell did they have to lay off so many upper management officers?* The severance and unemployment compensation sure disappeared quickly.

And she had no antidote, nothing with which she could inoculate them to inhibit the destruction. What had Bob called her? *The prodigal daughter?* Well, no fatted calf was to be slaughtered in tribute to her return this night, she glumly forecasted.

"Can I get another 7/7?" she asked the waitress.

"I don't wanna cry," she heard Mariah Carey start to sing.

"Me either," she whispered, sensing that the liquor would soon begin to take her past the pain. At least Angela and Alan's discomfort was beginning to stabilize, while her own was dynamic, progressive. She'd told them about her futile relations with Ron and her regret at having moved in with Bob. Angela had remembered this bartender at *The Tap,* recalled how he'd tried to seduce her in Holmgren and how she escaped. All of which was monitored silently by Al, whose clenched fists and furrowed brow made apparent what he'd do should he happen upon this Bob.

"You alright, Amy?" she heard Angela whisper as the tear fell upon her cheek.

"I'm okay," she replied, as she wiped at her eye with the napkin the waitress placed her new drink on. It was disconcerting for her to have them supplant her as their caretaker, to reverse roles. She'd be of no use to them when she moved back next month, she told herself.

As the idealistic chatter of another love song swarmed the room, Amy shut her eyes, willing her mind to pause to impede the continual analysis, the endless deductive reasoning. The effort was not to be rewarded anyhow. *They were all screwed. The hell with it.*

"I'm going to dance," she heard Alan declare. "If you need me, come and get me."

Amy hoped he would not have his hand forced as such. She did not want the cost of her security to be Alan's freedom, or worse. He had too widespread a reputation as a man with lightning-powerful fists. No one would dare engage him by any but lethal means.

"Go have fun, Alan. We'll be fine," she said calmly, her hands shaking beneath the table. Her eyes were still closed to the world, fighting to see other than the vision of one of them laid to final, untimely rest.

"Would you like to dance?" she heard the query ring down from above. For an instant, she sat motionless, afraid as to whom her blue eyes would gaze upon when she lifted her lids.

"Oh, what the hell," she whispered to herself as she revealed her blue orbs to the man.

She stared for what seemed to have been a full minute, dazzled by the thick arms and squared shoulders of the exquisitely handsome man who towered majestically above her.

"Claro, señor," she finally offered. Her anticipation of the convergence had made her giddy, enticing her to employ the other language she'd mastered long ago.

He smiled in response to the words. He smiled again moments later when she pressed herself firmly against him on the dance floor. She proceeded to lavish him with praise. The eloquent testimonial, spoken in Spanish, she punctuated by pressing her slender fingers into his back.

"Demasiado guapo, con ojos lindos," she described him aloud. It was quite implausible, but despite his having just graced her life, she felt very comfortable with the winsome character. She unearthed the origins of the sensation as she placed her hands around his massive neck.

On a poster at Bob's house was a hulking presence adorned in a yellow and gold baseball suit, upon which was inscribed the italicized letter "A." He, like the man holding her now, had neat, straight black hair and an appealing smile.

She caressed her dance partner's broad chest with her left hand and called to mind how Bob had offered that the man in the poster was born (along with his twin brother) on the same day as himself. Having fled from Cuba, the family settled in Miami, the setting in which the accomplished man was to hone the skills that would enable him to become wealthy beyond his dreams. Bob had added that this awe-inspiring creation had married a winner of a renowned beauty contest, had even been wooed by Madonna.

But he'd almost advised her, all did not go well for him. After being arrested on concealed weapons charges, the beauty queen had opted to resign from their partnership, an act that devastated him. Despite all his splendor, the man had admitted that, in the aftermath, he'd wanted to terminate his elegant existence.

She offered no resistance as Mr. Guapo pulled her in closer, rubbing her waist against his powerful thigh as a new song began. That man, who shared his birthday to Bob's delight, had rallied, becoming strong enough to accept both physical and emotional misfortune in a calm fashion after acquiring a position with Bob's beloved Red Sox corporation. While in their employ, he'd apparently done much to raise the collective hope of those who, in his native Cuba, were detained in spartan political prison camps. This impressive nabob had selflessly visited them, bestowing upon them his encouraging words and exhibitions of his athletic prowess, heartening the beaten adults.

There was definitely something about the restored man, something other than the way he struck a baseball, that made Bob proud to share his birthdate. The benevolent former "bad boy," like that guy "Big Dog" he'd introduced her to at UNEI, was, in essence, Bob's alter ego. She recalled how she'd laughed when Cody, after being informed of the shared point of origin, had told Bob, "You don't look like him, though."

"I'll say!" Amy mused as she kissed her dance partner's partially exposed chest and caressed his back. This man, like his mythical likeness, was much more impressive. The olfactory pleasure initiated by the *Aspen* cologne he wore on his simultaneously broad and trim frame made him seem impossibly suave.

From her seat, Angela watched him caress the shoulders of her mirror image—this identical twin. The intelligent, ambitious woman, she reflected as she shook her head, was being reduced, consumed by passion. Again, as she rose to take a closer look at the drama, she felt a tap on her shoulder. She turned to face the man who pleaded for her attention.

"Would you like to dance?" the slightly built man inquired, looking through glazed eyes.

Angela smiled evenly and carefully took his hand. "Why not?" she replied gently.

She led him to a position adjacent to Amy and her new beau. The duplicates of the same pretty patterns exchanged smiles, then mirrored one another in the shadow they cast on the floor as they mingled with their respective beneficiaries. From that point, the similarities ceased to be. As Angela's partner lowered his hand from the small of her back, she backed away from his hold.

"You don't want to get my brother angry," she warned him. "He's over there watching. I just consented to a nice, polite dance," she reminded him.

"If you want anything more, you're going to have to find another partner."

"Cool," the man slurred and walked away.

As she walked to the rail, freed from yet another menacing imposition, her mentor pulled even deeper into the grip of the powerful stranger, caution and foresight a casualty of desire. Angela watched the scene as light filled the room. The Tollbooth was to close soon, she mused, as Amy remained in his arms, whispering into his neck. Their journey would continue unimpeded for now. Angela walked onto the parquet, issuing the oft-spoken formality, "Amy, do you need a ride home?"

"No, thank you," Angela mouthed the words as Amy spoke them, back turned to her, still entangled within the mixture of limbs.

"I'll take you wherever you want," he offered.

"Thank you," Amy responded, dismissing Angela with a silent wave of her hand.

Amy followed him off the dance floor. She winked at Angela, who had returned to the table to Amy's right. "Wow, you're pretty," he stated after turning to look upon her. "Your boyfriend must be crazy, letting you out alone."

Amy laughed. "Maybe I should set him up with your girlfriend."

"Hey, boy!" The man turned to train his attention on the tall, Black youth who'd called to him. He playfully slapped at her partner's outstretched hand. "You playin' tomorrow?" the young man inquired.

"Damn right! I'm battin' clean-up too."

"Do you play baseball?" Amy asked.

"Softball."

"This you, Marty?" the youth asked, quickly examining Amy from head to toe.

"You know it," Marty replied matter-of-factly.

"Do you know who you look like?" the man continued.

"Who?" Amy replied.

"Michelle Pfeiffer."

"Well, I do have a 'dangerous mind.'"

"Uh oh, Marty," the youth replied playfully.

"My type of woman," Marty said, smiling at her.

"You know who Marty looks like?" Amy asked.

"Who? Tell me. Catwoman?"

Amy laughed. "Jose Canseco."

"I do believe that's a compliment, right?"

"Definitely."

"Too bad he can't hit like him."

Marty again smiled—a smile Amy found intoxicating. She jumped up suddenly on the chair before her and planted a kiss upon his lips.

"Damn," the man exclaimed.

"You ready?" Marty asked sweetly when she let loose of him.

"Mmmhmm," Amy whispered sensually.

They followed the man out of the club. Marty held the door open for her.

"See ya, you lucky knucklehead," Marty laughed loudly in response.

"Alright then, Urkel."

The man jumped in the car, then flipped him off with a smile.

"That guy is crazy."

"That he is," Marty responded as he unlocked his car. "Hey, do you mind if I stop off at my place really quick?"

"I have all weekend free. Let's go."

"Me too. Aren't you afraid I'll try to kidnap you?"

"I was kind of hoping you would," Amy grinned as she climbed in.

He engaged the engine and then drove her slowly to the east. The glow of Hilton and Holiday Inn neon yielded to the pall of dimly lit drive-in liquor stores and pawn shops as they traveled. Again, she barraged him with Spanish, her hand caressing his thigh repeatedly as she promised him he'd not regret delivering her to his house.

"Esta noche, yo paso contigo," Amy asserted sensually as he pulled the car into the lot facing his apartment complex.

She grabbed his hand as he opened the car door for her. She caressed his bare stomach, slipping her slender hand between the buttons to do so. As she released him to allow him to unlock the door, she began unbuttoning her blouse. She'd begun honoring the solemn covenant within moments of entering his living room, offering up with enthusiasm her essence in accordance with the promissory note she'd forged with the parlance in the car. It was not until deep into the morning that the igneous synergy created had been extinguished. Amy watched in the tranquility that followed, the contraction and expansion of his broad back as he lay before her in blissful slumber. She wrapped her arms about his waist and smiled.

"This is so perfect. It's about time," she asserted softly, moments before lapsing into a pleasant respite of her own.

Bob started through the diamond formed by the convergence of wire mesh, through the action on the diamond before him on which his Falcons were grappling with the Wells Cardinals, and on through his fleeting hopes for a tolerable life. The misfortune of a moment ago had crippled him, leaving him in a catatonic condition. His sagging, bent frame could not right itself now, was unable to lift the invisible oppressive, downward dynamic that had already begun to compress his resolve. "Forget this," he mumbled repeatedly, certain in his belief that any action on his part would only unleash a torrent of more devastating phenomena onto him and his.

So, on he gazed, reflecting upon the incomprehensible act. Pell was only trying to carry the game to Kendall in the only way he knew how—with conviction and abandon. It wasn't his fault...

Would they rather he had left Jason in the game? Hell, he'd pulled him even though he had a no-hitter going—his first start of the season. Geez. Yeah, but six walks and several wild pitches, the residue of his unorthodox sidearm delivery. It just wasn't good. Hadn't they breathed easier when Pell supplanted him, especially the three hitters who'd been plunked in the thighs? Couldn't they deduce from the calm countenance of the slight, bespectacled pitcher—who on each occasion did not return their glares—that there was no malice in his soul? Hadn't he even excused Wells for throwing at Jason when he'd batted in the second? And hadn't he resisted the urge to act upon the wishes of the hometown fans who were calling for vengeance? "All part of this crazy, whacked-out game," he'd told his angry charges.

"They don't know you, Jason," he'd told the young man. "My fault," he'd said as he removed him for a pinch-runner after the fourth very wild pitch sailed over his ear flap. What more could those Wells jerks want?

And so, when he summoned Pell to the hill in the third, he'd done so with a forgiving spirit. "Just keep us in it, Horse," was all he'd said as the big man began to warm up from the set position. No more. No less. He'd thrown that complete game just nights earlier at Martens. What more could they have expected? Of course, he would struggle, would leave his pitches up. Hey, he'd sacrificed for them, watched two runners cross home plate as Kendall hastened to get loose. There just wasn't enough time. Didn't they realize this? Couldn't they relate? He didn't have a chance. Yeah, Greg called for a "high and tight." There was a man on third. They were going by the book. Pell tried to spot it but was powerless, with his tired arm and all. Sure, it was too high. Okay, much too high, and yes, it was placed above the temple of the same Wells hurler who'd thrown at Jason, but any fool could see it was mere coincidence.

And why did the dummy stay in motionless disbelief? The lights were on; he had to have seen it clearly. He'd even thanked God when the fool moved at the last moment, had laughed—not in derision but in relief—as the ball ricocheted off the bat that the player had left in the air when he dropped to a knee. Pell was cool as he retrieved the ball, wasn't he? Didn't he just throw it nonchalantly to Vale, then walk off the field?

Then why this? Why, you dirty bastards? Was your boy ashamed by the Andrews fans' laughter, angered at looking foolish? He could read something in the eyes of the demon when Pell stepped to the plate. Leadoff man Pell was, and the kid was still roused, couldn't think straight, could not quell the burning passion that would complement the force produced by his strong right arm when he saw his nemesis.

Couldn't he have brushed him off first? Obviously, Pell was not prepared for this; he would not have been standing eagerly over the plate if he were. He knew he was not in the wrong, plain and simple; he had exonerated himself for the location of what was certainly his final pitch. Ever. Bob had known it was broken immediately. He was no doctor, certainly, had never had a broken bone, but still, he could tell. What an inappropriate sentence—a shattered mandible for an indignity.

"Pell, are you okay?" he'd asked, wishing he hadn't. He'd wiped away the viscous red fluid adjacent to the swelling as he knelt aghast, seeing anguish in the sunken hollow eyes of his fallen soldier. "Damn, I'm so sorry," he'd uttered repeatedly, his endeavor to muffle the groans that seared his ears.

Bart had hastened to the scene as well, calmly and firmly placing an ice pack onto the fracture. "Let's get him to the hospital, now!" he'd shouted, elbowing Bob from the injury site as he did so.

"We... we'll take him, Bart," Pell's sister assessed as she entered the dugout. Bob saw the tears welling in her eyes as Greg and Bart walked Pell near her. It was a spectacle that shamed him. This shared pain, borne of community and familial loyalty, was one he was certain he'd overcome.

And so still he remained, stunned, devastated, peering out past the Wells pitcher, the man who seemed remarkably unmoved. The typical nineties delinquent— violent, selfish, utterly devoid of trust.

He felt the searing sting in his eyes, the only active response his body had produced in the wake of this damning act, the one that pummeled his self-confidence, ran over his belief in his capability to ever manage... anything.

He hated these tears, had felt them flow too freely when the junior high bullies shoved him when he couldn't *deal* in Knox; an auspicious beginning, it was, locking him in the fetters of self-doubt and irrevocable self-loathing. *Damn! Damn! Damn!* The silent cries of his soul, which fought expression, were restrained only by the desperate bite he took from his lower lip...

"Who are we putting on third?" he heard Bart ask.

"It doesn't matter, man," he replied wanly, a response utterly devoid of hope. His mind drifted slowly, painfully, to the scene of Crazy Man's leg snapping on a shambles of a ballfield in Silent Springs...

"Cody, go to third!" Bart snapped. It appeared to Bart that Sellers had not even been aware that he was now glaring contemptuously at him. He had seen this all before, had been unsettled, filled with pity when he'd watched the man cower.

Adversity. It was the one-time catalyst of life. It was the knocks he'd taken as he ran through enemy lines, the ones that tore his knees apart and induced the migraines, which had made him the strong man that he was today. He would never be the type who would search for the sideline in life. There was no *out of bounds* in his world.

He could have avoided the second Gulf War, could have allowed his Commander to medically discharge him without a fight, but it was not his way. No way. He limped his way with dignity into the bowels of the A-P-C, his throat scorched, basked by the omnipresent thirst that drilled him in the relentless 120-degree heat. It was a son of a bitch, that daily ritual of surveying the sand for those who wished him dead. And good men, men far better than the one he now stood above, had died—honorably and valiantly—in that forsaken wasteland. *Pity this limp sham of masculinity?* No damn way.

He found himself wanting to strike the withering shell but summoned the discipline to remain motionless as he lashed out verbally instead. "Damn it! Would you lift your head up and begin assuming responsibility? Are you not being paid to take charge? This... this is not leadership. Your job is to shake this off and focus on what it takes for us to win. That's all that matters. The only thing we give a damn about."

The force of his words, the fervor with which he censored his colleague, engendered the further lowering of the older man's eyes. He seemed to be scrutinizing the makeup of the disintegrating concrete floor. Undaunted, his breathing pattern restored, Bart proceeded to advance against protected aspects of the man's life.

"You weren't the son of a bitch who broke Pell's jaw, but in failing to confront the actions of that jerk on the mound, you've tacitly defined it as a justifiable act. Why in the hell are you always retreating? Acting like losing and being servile is acceptable behavior. To hell with that. It's time to fight back. You wouldn't do it with that dickhead cook at the restaurant, because you were afraid to lose out on that *high profile job*. Who cares if someone's bigger, stronger? You still fight; you have no choice. Ever. That blond little princess is probably with *someone else* right now, all because you wouldn't put her in check. I've been that someone else with her. And now this. Letting these punks run us off our own field. No way. Man, this is what living is about. If you want to bury yourself here, go ahead. Just make sure you don't get in the way of us guys who are going for the win."

Bob dodged the barrage of apparitions now descending upon him. He parried and struck at the taunting spirits that stood in his way until he found Rusty at the dugout door. "Rusty, show these assholes the price you pay for drawing first blood." The redhead flashed him a sinister grin.

"Damn right!" he asserted, as he led the Falcons' march to the field in the top of the fifth.

"You picked the wrong man, Coach," Bart asserted loudly. "I don't think he's got the balls."

"We'll see," Rusty responded defiantly as he turned.

The lights of the scoreboard could be seen by Sellers over Rusty's shoulder. 6-6 it revealed. "Hell with the score, Rusty. Put the leadoff man on," Bob ordered.

Rusty would not disappoint. His first pitch lacked subtlety, unimpeded in its journey to the small of his opponent's back.

"Uhhhh," the man winced. He glared at Rusty, who was now walking forward to retrieve the ball. His fists were clenched, his glove held beneath his left elbow. There would be no effort made to pacify the large man.

Bob laughed at the scene. "Screw you," he sneered softly as he glared at the man. He waited for words to be exchanged, was still waiting when the man rushed the mound, bat in hand.

He stumbled into Bart's path in his haste to intervene. Players on both benches followed. The players had already encompassed the mound when Sellers extracted the bat from the Cardinal's hand. In an instant, he was knocked to his knees by a blindside tackle—a service delivered by the Wells catcher. The force of the blow stung, searing his ribs, but it was a pain he would not acknowledge, would not dignify, not tonight.

"You've got nothin'," he spat, peering into the eyes of the menacing receiver.

Still on his knees, he watched punches missing their mark, their aim throttled by the concentric combustion within the vortex of the melee. He turned to his right to see Greg, adorned in his catching gear and mask, circling the mound.

"You want some?" he asked the Cardinals before him.

He heard Cralt tell the Wells pitcher from his position behind the intervening home plate umpire, "We'll tear up Clancy, Indiana, to find ya. Even if we have to break a few jaws to do so!"

Tony and Vale remained on the fringe of the fracas, half-heartedly shoving and pushing their foes. Alex and Kendall, consistent with their athletic ability, deftly evaded the wild swinging punches of their enemies. George Bounds had rushed to intercede but opted to remain within the open dugout upon viewing. Hand, from behind, stood before the dugout door, swinging a 32 oz. bat.

"Come closer, punks," he challenged the Wells players. "Take a chance."

To the right of him stood Kevin, left fist clenched, searching for his moment to enter the fray.

"Who the hell do you think you are, starting all this bullshit?"

Bob heard the question through the surreal chaotic din and was aware that the request had come from the Wells coach.

Bob became blind to the rest of the address; it was *that* word, the adjective Jill had used to describe him a decade earlier, that had knocked him senseless. That tough old Harrison girl had shredded him with the phrase, exploiting his then-low self-regard.

Stupid bitch, he muttered. No one had referred to him in that way since. *Pathetic*? No way he'd let this go uncontested.

"Screw you, jerk!" he shouted, well aware that his anger had escaped beyond his grasp, certain that "Step Two" of the twelve could not be understood and applied as his mouth flew open again. "You assholes crowd the plate, then you blame me? You ordered this, you short-sighted, fat, mother...."

"Bob!" he heard the masculine shout intercede on his behalf. "Chill out! Cralt, shake it," the voice shouted to the man now struggling to break free of the umpire's grasp. "Hand, damn it, put that bat away!"

"Good ole Bart, taking charge," Bob whispered.

"Yeah, you guys better resolve this," the Wells assistant shouted menacingly.

No way, this shit won't end, Bob anxiously deduced. *They just keep pushing.*

"You don't tell me what to do," he shrieked. "Get out of here!"

Why did I say that? he moaned. *Now they'll really come after me.*

He watched in dismay as Rusty dived headfirst onto the assistant's knee, spitting tobacco juice onto the man as he did so.

"Aahhhhh!" he heard Jason yell out, as he too jumped onto the teacher.

Bart, by now, had subdued the Wells batter who'd charged the mound, had the youth's arms pinned to his back. His biceps contracted from the strain as he pulled this main character from the stage.

"Let it go, son. It ain't worth it," Bob heard Bart whisper to his quarry, just as he then inadvertently pulled the youth onto Bob's fingers.

"Son of a bitch!" Bob shouted as the metal pierced his skin. *Why in the hell had he still been kneeling?* He asked himself this as he watched the blood flow.

"You're gone from this game," the base umpire informed him. "You and that red-headed son of a bitch."

"Good God," Bob whispered. "That's my second ejection this season. Rusty, let's go!" he shouted to his partner, who now stood, arms folded, catching his breath near the first base bag.

Bob scarcely noticed the sting in his digits as he walked toward the dugout. When he arrived, he bent down and lifted the water cooler over his head. He grinned as he threw it onto the infield, near the now subsiding maelstrom, laughing as ice flew near the combatants' feet. He'd seen Toronto Blue Jays baseball manager Cito Gaston do this on

ESPN; he'd always wanted to do the same. "How'd you like that?" he asked playfully of Rusty, who now was strutting off the infield on his way toward the bench.

"Very nice," Rusty smiled. "Where the hell do we go? I'm not used to being thrown out."

Bob laughed. "Let's go sit on my car. Appreciate you coming through for the team on this, man."

"Anytime," Rusty answered as they traveled. "It's a lot of fun."

They watched the remainder of the contest in giddy anticipation, waiting for the next explosion. They watched Bart channel the emotion into spirited play, saw the Falcons benefit from the adrenaline that added several miles per hour to Cralt's fastball. When Kendall raced to short center field to snare the descending baseball, the Wells player slammed his helmet angrily down upon home plate. The 7-6 victory was Andrews'.

"Hell yeah!" Bob shouted, leaping atop the hood of his car. His bloody hand raised in exaltation, he watched as Rusty rushed the backstop and began ridiculing the Wells players.

"You guys must suck!" he shouted. "You lost a game and a fight!"

Four or five uniformed foes approached the screen separating Rusty from the field. "The fight ain't over yet!" one shouted.

"Yes, yes, it is!" the base umpire interjected as he slipped briskly between the screen and the Wells players.

"Get off our field, losers!" Rusty yelled out, then walked away.

As the Wells players were herded toward the bus, Bob busied himself with the task of securing the equipment within the storage shed. He tried to act aloof in the face of the taunts of his foes.

"You guys are a bunch of punks, especially your head coach, the cowardly pussy."

Bob cringed at those words. *Those connected,* he admitted. "I'm going to snap," he mumbled. Hands trembling, he dropped the ball bag to the floor. As one of the balls rolled free, his thoughts darted to the vision of Greg Maddux, glaring through the opposing hitters, busting heat in on them, scoffing.

That man would hold nothing back in trying to come out on top. An ideal team player who'd forgive even rookie teammates for yielding unearned runs, the man channeled all his energy into vanquishing the opposition. *Damn, he looked mean when he bore down,* Bob mused. *Frowning all the time, you knew he was serious, deadly serious, about trying to succeed.*

And did he ever succeed—despite his choppy mechanics and pigeon-toed gait, bouncing changeups, cut fastballs, backdoor curves—all baffling hitters so much that it hardly seemed fair. It was as if they weren't there.

He became Sellers' hero. The 30-something poor boy imitated the mannerisms of the multi-millionaire until they became habit. No, Maddux wasn't Deion Sanders or Ryan Klesko, but he was no less intriguing than these outrageous former mates. *Score three, and we'll win,* his colleagues seemed to believe, as they brashly strutted about on that veritable holiday that arrived every fifth day. *Maddux Day.* The day that delivered Sellers' mind to an area impenetrable by external stimuli as he watched above the TBS logo, the one who absolutely ruled this aspect of the...

"I'll kick his ass if I see him in the city!" he heard the voice shout again. There was no doubt now in Sellers' mind as to whose ass the man was referring to. "No more," he whispered.

Securing the ball in hand, he whirled, then leaped out of the building. He set himself, then fired the ball into the side of the passing Wells bus. It struck the panel above the front left tire. The bus screeched to a rapid stop. Sellers stood steadfast as the front window opened. Amidst the barrage of players' angry shouts, he heard the driver in an ominous tone yell, "You dumb shit! You ain't seen the last of us! We'll have Thorson, the Sheriff, the Indiana Athletic Association, and the Andrews School Board on your ass by daybreak. You'll pay!" The voice trailed off suddenly. The driver placed the bus into gear and sped off.

"Screw you; you got nothin'!" Sellers uttered as the bus rounded the bend and left the park, smiling now despite the cold sensation ascending his spine

"Rutgers 40," the green road sign informed the blonde trio. Amy looked left, past Angela and Al, out upon the calm territory. *It's easy,* she surmised, *within these hills where the number of cattle exceeded the human chattel, to lose oneself, to flow, intuitively, like the river, unhurried.*

"Shit!" she said. This, she mused, was certainly not East Queens, that centerpiece of uncertainty, wanton motion. *All,* she felt, *there were driven into action by their despair and denial. Hurrying about, looking for an 'edge.'* She sighed. *It was no wonder that these senses were so dulled.* If there were only a way to satisfy their hardened souls, to restore their faith in society.

It was as if they were living on borrowed time—two days of life charge for each day spent within the cheerless fortress, she decided. *All too rare were the enjoyable times they'd experience. What incredible pressure they feel! Relentless pain and shame, hurt which enveloped perpetual generations, tears shed in grief of decaying dreams.*

It all made them look like walking corpses, these apathy-dazed beings who'd leave at their shuffling, aching feet, implausible mature offspring who were left, by default, to preside over the rearing of their younger siblings. *It wasn't fair.* Imposed upon from the onset, the carefree right of childhood summers was supplanted by the obligation to protect them and theirs from the *drive-by.*

And they couldn't run. Fight or flight? Not relevant. Even the smallest would refrain from crying, accepting their lot as they tumbled to the unyielding concrete. After a few such falls, they'd rise while lashing out blindly, their icy stares penetrating a benighted shroud of hate. *Hardly productive.*

She'd been informed at UNEI that the initial stage in revolution against oppression was in striking out against one's equally disadvantaged peers. She cringed at the vision of an ultimate reaction—the young inner-city residents devouring their wealthy neighbors—but she was certain they'd still be turning upon one another on the eastside. *It was just too entrenched, this anger.*

Anarchy. *What a solution*, she reflected sarcastically as she watched a pair of horses run in the pasture to the right. Turning their back to the larger system, the one in which they had no input in designing. Certainly, she had to admit it looked strange when they locked into its archaic guidelines and were rewarded only by patronage and mockery. *But was this the alternative?* Anti-everything, drawing the vulnerable of the middle class into their world of leather biker jackets, punk hairstyles, gang signs. There was no admiration in the emulation, no unity, no trust, she was sure. Just another member added to an aggravated aggregate of lost persons who'd forfeited their dignity.

No escape there. No real flight, for they'd be pulled back. They all would. The original sin that was being sired into captivity in the 'hood left all their fate pending. *Couldn't break out of or into their closed ranks. And it was too hard for them to pretend not to give a damn.*

In the interval, she concluded, one could either act aloof, oblivious, or dive in loudly, concealing true emotion until one was able to empower or utilize.

But yesterday, she'd just gotten used, devoured by the excluded. Manipulated by one encouraged by the divestiture and institutional neglect that permeated their districts. One who trashed convention and fair play to appease a more cloistered master.

Damn it, she groaned in silence. *Damn Marty.* She had worked hard for him in the wake of their second encounter, instructing county administrators to expedite disbursement of aid to his "cousin" Ruth. She was nearly a saint, to hear him tell it, this poor soul who sought only what was best for her infant son. Abandoned by the father, Marty informed her in the twilight, the woman was reduced to wandering the streets with the frightened, emaciated child, begging in Spanish for sustenance.

Poor little thing, Amy hissed, sitting upright in her seat as they drove by the truck stop. *How could she have been so naïve, so fired up by the vision he sold her?* Why did she promise to deliver assistance to this deserving soul? Why?

She was going to walk right up to him with the documents, show him and, by extension, *her*, the manner in which she broke down the intricate terminology on the documents, exhibit how she'd supplied, in their language, additional related information. She recalled feeling quite satisfied as she crossed over the railroad tracks dividing the city, her fatigue, induced by her Wednesday overnight labor on their behalf, offset by the anticipation of the rapture she was certain she'd soon experience.

And why didn't she question him more regarding that dress—that damn, strapless red one—that hovered deep in the corner of his closet? She'd spotted it through the slender opening as she entered his bedroom that first time; should have seen that tacky rag as an omen, something that should have alerted her, saved her from this overextension.

Oh well, she sighed. *It was too late.* She couldn't bear losing, but it was fervor, not stupidity, that sabotaged her, she assessed. *Justified.* If her passionate pursuit of doing right led her to find her in that dress, in his arms, locked within a deep kiss, so be it. And she did hate the sight—him touching her face as they bussed. *Damn. Why couldn't the asshole have done that with me?*

The sex was good, she smiled, *but oh, the price she paid,* she sighed. She'd given him her mother's phone number, her new work number. *Shit, she could already hear the phone ringing.* "Amy, this is Marty." And then, angry as she was, she wrecked her car, slamming it into the parked car in the post office lot. She had to do the insurance company dance with the angry female employee, then watch her car be pulled into the shop for two weeks. She remembered how she shuddered when she dropped the forms into the mailbox, along with an angry letter in Spanish to his home. *Could she have been exposed to the 'virus' now?* Placed in this precarious position as a result of his intimate forays with the shaky, probably narcotic, confused slut? 'Cousin,' my ass, she simmered, lamenting now their belief that there'd be no closure attending this transfer. *May as well have stayed here in Western Indiana.*

She grimaced as they crested the hill overlooking the lights of the town. This departure was to be bittersweet now, she reminded herself—just a substitution of one sticky adhesive mess for another. Always getting pulled down by idiots.

She wanted now to have someone, anyone, feel her pain—to put a hurt on them. If she were going to be derailed, she would ensure she had company. *Would destroy someone else's desires. Trash them.* It would provide her the illusion of beginning anew. Yes, that was the answer for the moment. It was just time to find a locale, a victim. *Any of them would suffice.*

She saw the lights of the ballpark shining brightly as they descended.

Perfect. She didn't care who was frolicking there. She would induce their misery. *Gosh, damn men anyway.*

"I know I told you we'd be loading up my things tonight," she said sleepily as she turned and looked at them. 'We have the whole weekend. I'll put us up in a hotel tonight, okay?"

Her siblings silently nodded, appearing quite relieved to be spared the nocturnal labor. As they pulled near the park, she craned her neck, peering into the midst of humanity.

"Bingo!" she said aloud, realizing she'd spotted her prey. "Pull in here, Alan," she ordered excitedly.

Bob sat on the bench prior to the game in Bancroft, editing his lineup card. He glanced up at the Falcons who were warming up before him, then resumed his work. *How's this going to be received?* he wondered as he inserted Lee's name in the place of Kendall's, Hand's above Greg's, Kevin's for Vale. Brad would make his initial start behind the plate.

"Hell with it," he muttered. "It's our last regular season game. We'll go all out Monday," he said as he rose.

It'll be good to reward the reserves for their patience, he assured himself. *Besides, every move I've made lately has been successful.*

"Here ya go, blue," he said to the approaching umpire.

His decision to depart from employing the lineup that had secured him five consecutive victories was largely influenced by his experiences in the Wells game. He had suffered through a sleepless post-game eve, vacillating between defending and condemning his actions. He'd finally given in to the advice in *the book* and put pen to paper. He informed the Wells staff in the letter that no ulterior motive prompted his act of contrition; he'd merely sought peace of mind. *They need not pardon me for my trespasses, as the mere act of contacting them would be enough to provide the coveted serenity.*

On Tuesday, he issued an apology to his players before practice. He was especially sorry, he said, for what he'd done to the underclassmen.

"You guys are going to need football equipment every June when you play Wells," he grinned. "But seriously, in violent encounters, fellas, there are no victors. Who the hell wants to look over their shoulder for those desiring paybacks?"

I know it's seen as a virtue in this era of gang-banging to fight on behalf of your 'set,' but in the long run, it's best to let an impartial body dispense justice. In this case, it was the umpires to whom I should have appealed. As soon as Pell went down, I should have run onto the field and said we were calling the game.

"I wasn't thinking when I had Rusty throw at an innocent man. This ain't pro ball. There's no money on the line. We should have just forfeited. Screw it," he said softly.

He'd left them with a story before beginning practice. It was a line he'd heard in the movie *Colors* years ago.

"Two bulls, one young, one old, were standing on a hill looking over a group of heifers. 'Hey, pop!' the youngest shouted. 'Let's run down and hump one of them ole girls.' 'No, son,' the elder bull replied, 'Let's walk down and hump 'em all.'"

He recalled with fondness, now, the laughter with which they greeted that tale. He'd been especially satisfied that he'd distanced himself emotionally from the game and its overemphasis on winning. He'd been infected by watching the pros play, had gotten too juiced by the W's. He was glad he'd conferred with *the Bishop*, his old elementary teacher, earlier that day. The wise sage had told him the experience of winning had a short shelf life for the players when compared to the more durable satisfaction of being merely allowed to play.

He watched Bart smash a ground ball to Cody. Cody wasn't supposed to start, but when happening upon him and his pretty mother at the store, Sellers had inexplicably blurted out that Cody was to play the entire game. *It wasn't right*, he said, head bowed, looking upon her tanned thighs, *that I'd relegated the boy to strictly a reserve role.*

He saw Pell silently trek to the coach's box at first. Jaw wired shut, he now wore a permanent grimace. *Damn Wells*, he cursed. He watched Bart return to the dugout. He could still hear the man's challenge in his ears. *Not tonight,*

Bart, he whispered. *None of that unpleasant Wells game mood swings. I won't get roused tonight.*

And so, he watched listlessly as his youngest charges were tamed by the Bancroft hurler's fastball. He remained unmoved by the sight of them retreating, bewildered, to the dugout after each strikeout.

"Just a game, fellas," were the only words he'd used when they returned to sit beside him. "Just a game."

Alex threw nearly as well, but it was to be in vain. For when Greg, playing out of position at first base, pulled off base prematurely on a throw from Alex, with two outs, the run that scored from third was all Bancroft needed to prevail.

In the bottom of the sixth, his dull, sedate march to defeat was sidetracked by the diversion that was the large Ryder van which pulled into the grass near the Falcons' dugout. Bob had given but a passing glance, then peered back wanly onto the field. It was Vale's whistle of approval and Rusty's shouting, "Nice ass!" that induced him to take a second, longer look at the scantily clad occupants emerging from the yellow cab.

"Is that... well, I'll be damned!" he exclaimed. "Let's turn two, Bart!"

"Who's the other broad?" Bart asked.

"Angela. Wow, that girl looks good," he shouted, hoping she'd hear.

As he scrutinized the body language of the more slender twin, he remembered how easily they'd become buddies, how he valued her insight as she decoded the speeches Amy had made to him. It would have been so fair, he decided, as he stared at her—so natural, so justified— the likeness atoning for the sins of her impetuous half, bringing a sweet resolution to the angst.

"Shit!" he cursed, now watching a man speak into a portable phone, the same mechanism that hindered Angela from enacting proper jurisprudence that day in Holmgren. "449," he muttered, recalling how the cleansing act of absolution about to unfold was foiled at the eleventh hour by an unseen madman's angry call. This shrieking bearer of malevolence could have been heard throughout the room; was easily heard by Bob as Angela slipped his grasp and stood.

"Damn fate," he lamented, recalling the sight of her zipping up her jeans as she stared vacantly out the window. Hand stepped into his sight in the batter's box before him, but the fact did not register in his mind. He was still cursing the lunatic who'd cost him his chance at glory, the one who'd defeated him in his endeavor to suckle at the breast of Amy's proxy. And the anonymous son of a bitch would never know how close Sellers had come to conquering his girl, would never see how his lucky, infantile ventilation had trampled upon the intimate moment, distracting Angela from what he was certain was their mutual goal of defeating Amy.

For after that, he was forced to sit, limp, as she deluged him with questions pertaining to her relationship with *you, you sick, selfish, undeserving prick.*

"Who's the dude?" he heard the voice ask as he bottled the phantom.

"I'm not sure," he replied, unsettled by the anger conveyed in the glare of the large man whose eyes now met Bob's.

"Think it's her brother."

"Mean-looking son of a bitch, ain't he?" Greg asked.

"Sure is," Bob replied. "Take charge, Bart," he said as he looked at Angela. *I'm going to the can.*

Bob laughed, an understanding laugh, as he walked nearer the enticing duo and their colleague. Bob smiled as Bart knew what was going on. Coy little Angela, enigmatic, sultry Amy. He wanted them both, envisioning the submission of either to his demands as somehow empowering him beyond belief, turning his whole miserable life around. Reality set in as he looked up at the menacing hulk between them. *What the hell was his role?*

CRACK! He ducked involuntarily at the sound, holding his hands to his head.

"Look out, Bob!" someone in the stands shouted.

SMACK! He heard the unmistakable sound of leather meeting skin and cringed, waiting for the gasps, the clamor to provide medical attention to the poor victim.

"Whoa!"

"Did you see that?"

He shook his head as a smattering of applause sprung forth from the stands. Looking quizzically up, he saw that the tribute was made in honor of the *hulk*. The man, now scowling at Bob, had caught the hard line drive in his bare hand!

"Gosh damn! Nice catch, sir!" he said to the man, exhibiting the ball before him.

"Amy Lou! Am I seeing double?" he winked at Angela and moved nearer. He stopped in his tracks when he saw the sudden contraction of the monster's shoulders and chest.

"What are you doing here?"

"We were returning from Queens. We saw the lights on and decided to have some fun."

"Good luck," he said playfully. "I sure ain't enjoying it. Is this Angela?"

"Yes, it is," the woman said noncommittally, brushing her hands along her backside.

"How've you been, Bob?"

"Fine. Yourself?"

"Good. Have you met my brother?" Angela responded.

"No, I can't say as I've had the pleasure. Pleased to meet you, sir," he said, extending his hand to the man.

When the man just glared, arms remaining folded, Bob quickly placed his hand in his uniform pants. What is wrong with this dude? he wondered in silence.

"You moving this weekend, Amy?" he asked, self-consciously.

"Yes, I'm going to work for Verde County on Wednesday."

CRACK! He heard the ball meet bat again, this time in a much softer tone. He turned to see the Bancroft shortstop settled under Kendall's popup.

"Game over," Bob whispered, twirling his index finger in the air as a signal for Bart to assume post-game responsibilities in his stead.

"Sorry that you're leaving us," he said, gazing at Amy's blonde curls. "Are you going to move in with Angela?"

"No, why do you ask?" she asked, guardedly.

"No reason," he replied as he watched Angela and her *bodyguard* return to the truck cab. "You taking off already?"

"Yes, we've got to find a place to crash. Can we stay with you?" she inquired sensually.

"Wow," Bob sighed, looking past her to Al, who was staring firmly at him, appearing poised to act. He stared at the open fist grasping the sill of the open window. "If you want," he said vacantly.

"I'm just teasing ya," Amy said with a grin.

"What's new?" Sellers said sarcastically as she turned slowly. "Guess this is it, then."

"For now, at least. Maybe I'll just pop in sometime, will surprise ya."

"No, you won't," he replied.

"You're bound to have me on ya again sometime," she purred. "It's fate."

He swallowed hard, searching for the mettle to confront her. The insults, the rebuff, the betrayal, the lies—all that he'd endured with her—filled his mind as he exhaled. It was time to draw it all to a close. He no longer wanted her, no longer cared. He was happy now that she came. *Take this, girl.*

"I adore you, Amy," he said as he gently reached out to touch her elbow. "I always have and always will. You're special, but...."

"Thank you," she whispered.

The simple response could not have been more soothing. The soft reply echoed in his head, rolling softly about, massaging his mind, suddenly melting his icy will.

"What you've given me," he said, then nervously cleared his throat, "with the slightest application of your angelic touch, is permanently etched in my mind. Something I can access 24/7. Something that can chase away any negativity. Something that fumigates my infested psyche." *What are you doing?* his mind shrieked.

"Damn," he whispered, spontaneously wrapping her within his arms. He braced himself for the push, the one that would knock him back into the shit in which he'd forever been wading. *Go ahead. I'm ready*, he silently asserted.

"Life at these times is really damn good. Like gentle rain on a very hot day, you bring sheer relief. I know, despite all the bad we've felt together, that you'd never hurt me, would never even think of it. You're always doing what's in my best interests, seeing things from a more proper, productive perspective. You've got such a strong, warm heart. No wonder I fell so hard, so freely. You're the only woman I'll ever feel this way toward again—the only one I'll absolutely trust, unconditionally, my guardian angel."

She patted him on the back, then moved out of his clutch. It was a soft, unforced act, one that promised return, one he was certain portended only good.

"Thank you," she whispered again.

As she turned languidly about, he felt his knees buckle. He stood, unsteady, as he watched, overawed by the misting pools of blue, which for an instant, mirrored his loving gaze before she walked slowly away toward the truck.

"Thank you. Thank you," he said gently, the words now spinning madly about his reeling head. "Wow, Amy," he said, waving adieu to her disappearing frame. "Wow," he repeated, unable now to move in either direction.

★ ★ ★ ★ ★

Amy and Angela stood behind their brother, watching intently the taut muscles of his bare, shiny back as he loaded the final box of dishes into the back portion of the crowded truck.

"You've worked really hard today, Al," Amy said approvingly.

"Yep," Al grunted. "You got anything else to load?" he asked, wiping the perspiration from his forehead.

"No, that's all," Amy replied amiably.

"I'm going to grab a drink then. You want anything?"

"No, thanks."

He walked off, then turned after a few steps. "We're taking off tonight, right?"

"Yes," Amy assured him. *No reason to stay,* she mused. *Not anymore.* "All we have left to do is vacuum."

"Good," Angela sighed. "It's already 7:30."

"Yes," Amy nodded. "We'll try to be on the road before it gets dark."

"I'll sleep good tonight," Angela said, stretching her arms above her head.

"Alone?"

"Yes, alone. Try it sometime."

Amy laughed and turned on the vacuum. She retreated to one corner, Angela to another. They both worked fervently, anxious to complete this arduous task.

Maybe you're right, Angela, she mused. But what else in life was so stimulating and engaging? So 'real'? What else was so empowering? What other setting provided such a forum for creativity?

Sure, she'd written a novel, been promoted, made money, made a nice home for herself, driven around in a new model car. But when she analyzed what had happened here, in this Rutgers, it would be the corporal matters that she'd look to first and last. *Those were the criteria she'd scrutinize to determine her degree of success herein.*

Let's see, she reflected. On the positive side, as a result of having utilized her natural advantage, were the prompt responses she'd received from attractive landlords when she called to request repairs. The embellishment of her sensual, slender form had also won her the attention of the handsome Ron, the charismatic Bart, etc. Why should she grumble? How could she, in light of having tamed some of the most gorgeous, reckless men in this town? How many of her friends here could say the same? She'd suffered virtually no cost for her hedonism, balancing abandon with her considerable intellect. *No reduction in social stature had occurred in her tenure here.*

Hell, she smiled, *they still had her on a veritable pedestal in most areas of the city.*

She shut the machine off and wrapped up the cord. Angela had stretched out now on a blanket on the floor, and Al had walked back into the house with a can of Mountain Dew.

"All through?" he asked.

"Yes, we just finished," Amy replied.

"Thank God," Angela said.

Amy laughed. "I'll check things over really quickly, and then I'll join you."

She watched them depart, then walked to the center of the room. Noting quickly that nothing remained behind, she smiled.

"I win," she grinned, then walked out.

Settling into the seat of the truck next to Angela, she instructed Al to drive to Bountiful Avenue. His listless "Okay" momentarily distracted her, making her aware that her perspective of today as transcendent and rewarding was not shared. The r manner seemed passionless, flat, forced, obligatory.

Good Lord, they were becoming as dull as Bob.

She smiled at his response to her tears in Bancroft, following his "stirring" speech. He probably thought they were real, induced automatically by his jettisoning of heavy accrued emotion. In truth, she'd merely done as an actor friend had taught her—copied the breathing pattern of the moved until the essence of the mood was ensnared. Its creation was easy, and its impact powerful.

Should've told the dumb ass that she "loved" him too, she grinned. Really thumped him...

"Where the hell are we?" Al inquired.

"We're right where we need to be," Amy replied. "There's the house right there," she stated, pointing to the brick home to her left.

Al pulled into the vacant driveway. Amy stepped quickly out and walked briskly to the door. A woman responded immediately to her ringing of the doorbell.

"Hi, Amy," the woman said coolly.

"Hi, Jan," Amy said, opening the door and stepping past the girlfriend of her landlord. She smiled in doing so, recalling the shock and anger with which the woman received the naked clinch of Amy and the landlord on the cold night her furnace malfunctioned.

She sidestepped the steel-toed work boots and gloves that lay on the man's floor and walked into his kitchen.

"All set, Amy?" she heard him ask from an adjoining room.

She touched her finger seductively to her lips as he stepped into view. She looked longingly upon his firm legs and moved to hand him the key, ensuring that her hand met his during the transfer.

"Yes, I'm all ready. Would you like to slide in behind me and inspect?" she purred.

"No, that won't be necessary," he replied, wiping his brow and nodding toward Jan.

"I'm sorry about the door. Is there any way I can make things right?"

"Nah," he whispered, in a near moan. "I'll go get the money from your deposit now."

She grinned broadly, feeling empowered, as he counted out the $200. She'd never put a deposit down on the place, she reflected, quite amused at how the last handsome man she'd encountered in this transfer had become so smitten.

She felt the expiration of breath upon her face as she drew closer, saw his expansive chest expand and contract excitedly. She leaned into him as he set the final note into her palm. She pressed her lips upon his flushed cheek. As she removed them, she grazed a hand along his stomach and thigh.

"Bye-bye," she cooed, then turned and walked out.

As she descended the steps, she turned to see if his eyes were following her. She exaggerated the oscillation of her hips with a smile as she glanced back into his stare.

"Let's go!" she shouted to Al as her hand reached the truck door.

In minutes, she realized, she'd be free of this burden and could confront the world on her terms—on the blessed, familiar land of her Queens.

She peered into the rearview mirror as Al backed from the driveway and continued looking there until the evanescent contents of town were locked away on a final right turn.

"Yes!" she exclaimed.

She turned her head slowly to the left, then looked out upon the road before them, the one carrying her and hers home.

Her town.

They could keep Rutgers. Give it to Bob, she mused.

She recalled how he'd told her he'd never again viewed the city in a positive light after the incident that occurred on a walk in the decaying northside district.

"Are you a bum?" they shouted to his twenty-one-year-old ass, an innocuous drive-by inquiry.

It was an opportunistic query, given that he was surrounded by beaten,

haggard losers on his journey.

Oh, but how it drilled his pathetic self to have his very worth questioned, to have to justify his very existence in the town in which he was born. Who else but him would take a slam by the ignorant hillbillies in such a personal manner?

The irony, he'd said, was that he, at that time, was employed as a minimum-wage garbageman, busting his ass for the town. *Should have stayed on unemployment,* he sneered.

"Screw 'em."

He said he never felt so devalued as he had in this despised place of his birth. Not in central Texas, a place fraught with potential problems inherent to strong racial and cultural diversity, and certainly not in *his* Younkers.

The utterance of the latter city's name would set his eyes to dancing—the site of his glorious resurrection, he'd tell her about those halcyon days even as he filled out the traveler's checks he'd used to pay on his odious student loans.

A dreamer, she mused, oblivious to the damage wrought by his hallucination.

For, in the final analysis, the university was inherently illusory—a place that sated the appetite of the *hope junkie* at a very prohibitive price. The most the *dealers* could ensure the customer was a five-year *trip* before these prey were returned to the beast of despair and withdrawal. These hungry, exacting demons would prod and extort violence from those they pursued. And most could not escape, could not keep the beasts at bay—not for long anyway.

That poor boy seemed incapable of understanding this. He'd made a mockery of the tacit arrangement between institution and indigent client with his endeavor to return and was rewarded with ridicule.

His 2.8 GPA, she scoffed—what was he thinking? He was through; they were through with him. It would be best for him to withdraw into his corner and try to cope as best he could—to stay ever vigilant for the stomach-wrenching symptoms of hope relapse.

Yes, the initial delirium for those most chronically smitten could not be extinguished. The best he could do was replace the relentless want with less stimulating facsimiles, to find his own *methadone*. In the end, fate tethered him to the whipping post.

Deal with it, punk! she told him now, the phrase she'd use next time he slid into despondency and contacted her with his tale of woe.

She felt restricted in the crowded cab, stifled by the silence. The liberating sensation she wanted to equate with this repatriation was somehow evading her grasp, she lamented, as she looked out upon the control tower of Liberty Airport.

Was there really any reason to hurry home tonight? It'd be nice to take a trip to anywhere.

Moving to place herself in a more comfortable position, Amy inadvertently bumped the elbow of her slumbering twin.

"Watch it," Angela said lethargically.

"Wow, is this going to be a long trip," Amy responded. She looked back at the tower. "Wish I had my car."

"I do too," Angela asserted. "Why don't we let you off somewhere so you can buy another one?"

"Good idea," Amy laughed. Lord knows she had the credit, had earned society's trust.

"It'd be easy," she said, looking upon the Republic Rental Car sign. "That's it," she asserted.

"What's it?" Angela asked.

"Al, let me off at the airport."

"Why?" he asked.

"It's too crowded in here. I'm going to rent a car," she said, then began dialing the number that was on the billboard.

"Hello," a female voice appeared on the other end.

"Yes," Amy began. "May I rent a car from you tonight?"

"If you hurry," the perplexed voice responded. "We close in five minutes."

"We'll make it. Write me up for an agreement for a small economy-size vehicle."

"Okay," the reluctant voice responded. "How many days do you need the car for?"

"I'll just need it for one day."

"How will you be paying, ma'am?"

"Visa."

"Okay, I'm writing a rental lease for a 1996 Topaz. But you've got to make it here within the next four minutes, or I have to lock the door. I'm serious."

"No problem," Amy said as the dial tone met her ears.

"What are we supposed to do about your belongings?" Al asked.

"Put them in a storage shed—that nice one on Rose Avenue. Find whomever you want to help unload. I'll give you $100."

Angela laughed. "How about the emotional trauma your abandonment will cause us?"

"It'll heal with time," Amy grinned.

Al turned right at the intersection and drove past the truck stop. As he turned left onto the interstate, he asked, "When will you be back?"

"I'm not sure. Whenever I'm ready. Maybe as early as tonight."

"Yeah, whatever," Angela scoffed.

In a minute's time, Al drove into the parking lot and pulled to a stop before the airport door. "We'll wait and make sure you can still get the car," he informed her.

"No need. I can always catch a cab to the hotel over there and come back here in the morning."

Angela rolled her eyes skyward. Amy challenged the look.

"You know I'll be back by Tuesday."

She leaned over and embraced both of them, then stepped out of the truck.

She waved at them as they drove off into the twilight, then turned on her heel and began walking toward the lobby. She was surprised by the atypical chill of the July evening, so she moved briskly.

She was relieved, despite her contingency plan, that she'd be able to rent a car—happy to see the pretty woman still attending to clerical duties beneath the *Republic* sign.

"Hello," she greeted the clerk as she stepped through the automatic doors.

The woman scanned Amy's physique intently. "Hello, how may I help you?" she asked seductively.

What the hell? Not tonight, girl, Amy mused.

"Can I still rent that sleek and powerful Topaz from you?"

"Something that's like yourself?" the clerk asked, her eyes locked on Amy's physique.

"You got it," Amy smiled as she pulled her Visa card out and set it on the counter.

"Amy," the attendant said as she scrutinized the card and finished filling out the paperwork. "That's a nice name."

"Thank you," Amy responded. "Hey, can I drop the car off at your Queens outlet?"

"Sure, but I was hoping you'd be coming back to see us. Pretty women like you are a rare phenomenon."

"I know that's a fact," Amy asserted as she read and signed the papers.

"Maybe I can come and visit you in Queens."

"Maybe," Amy smiled as she took the key from the woman. "Thank you. Bye-bye."

She walked quickly out and searched for the car.

A blue Topaz, the key informed her.

She found it within seconds. She turned the key in the lock and opened the door. The illuminated interior that was revealed as a result stood in sharp contrast to the encroaching darkness.

She stepped quickly inside and sat behind the wheel. She set the radio to *Magic 90* and leaned into the seat.

The engine barely emitted a sound as she turned the key.

"Perfect," she whispered.

Her headlights ensnared the exit, which led her to the east-west thoroughfare in minutes after her departure.

She sang along to the soft song on the radio, content now to be free to establish her own pace, to be in her own space as she wound her way to her new life.

It surprised many, she mused, to see how easy it was for her to create the good in her life. It just seemed natural in their eyes, she reflected, as she set the cruise. She liked to perceive it as a genetic advantage, albeit a benefit she'd capitalized upon and embellished. Many had let their potential lay unrealized, unrefined.

Not me, she said with a smile.

"It's all good."

That's how Kathy would have described Amy's life— the versatile manner in which she overcame the bad and placed men and women at her mercy.

"Next," she uttered giddily, envisioning yet another lost body knocking self-consciously at her door. *Kissing her ass.*

Saturday night, she smiled. *Party time.*

"Sweet, sweet city woman," the man was singing on the radio.

Singing about her, not the denizens living in the farmhouses she was rushing past.

"I'll be there soon, baby," she told the voice.

She wondered if she could still make it to the Tollbooth by closing time.

I'll give it a hell of a try, she informed herself as she changed the cruise to 65 mph.

"Move out of the way, Grandpa," she shouted to the elderly man driving the car before her.

She pressed the accelerator and passed them with ease before ascending the hill.

She laughed as she looked over at the man's elderly female passenger but became somewhat alarmed as she saw the look of concern in the woman's eyes.

She felt her hand tremble involuntarily.

"Whoa, girl, relax," Amy spoke into the mirror. "It's okay."

She descended the hill and looked down upon a trio of motorcycles.

In the darkness, she could discern that two of the motorcycles were ridden by middle-aged couples. A third bike trailed slightly behind.

What the hell is he doing?

Amy felt a sudden urge to pull into his lane, to level the unseen rider.

"Damn, girl," she muttered, scarcely recognizing her own voice.

As they pulled nearer one another, she saw the man's large frame, saw the incongruent beer can in his hand.

A smile etched his face as he lifted his fingers to wave at her.

"Crazy son of a bitch!" she yelled at the top of her lungs.

"Stupid bastard," she screamed as she crested yet another hill and began her descent again—into her private perdition.

The unfamiliar territory frightened her now and caused her to gasp for air.

She was tossed about in the small vehicle, ensnared, helpless, in the darkness.

"Where are the damn lights?" she moaned.

Why's it so damn dark out here? she shouted as the tears soaked her cheeks.

"Damn this!" she cursed. "I hope that son of a bitch is burning up in the deepest corner of that prison hellhole," she sobbed, shocked at the expletive she'd just employed.

"I was sixteen!" she shouted, as the indiscernible lyrics from the heavy metal song *serenaded* her fall.

"Shut up," she shouted, slamming her fist into the dash as she turned off the radio with her other hand.

The car weaved when she temporarily set the wheel free.

Her car tires hit the gravel before she corrected herself.

"Damn it, why?" she implored the heavens, shuddering as his wicked words met her ears—demanding, extorting, threatening the indomitable force consuming her despite her protests, smashing her will, the misogyny impaling her benevolence and faith.

Sobbing harder, she searched in the blackness for comfort, concerned that it may have become too late.

No help was in sight.

Angela and Al were miles away on a parallel highway.

Cresting yet another cursed hill, she heard him again, more clearly now, ordering her on the cool fall evening in the park.

"You want it, don't you, bitch?" he taunted her as his large fists covered her mouth.

"NO!" she would have answered on that horrible defining night had her mouth been free.

I was only out walking, enjoying the season. How did I know I'd stumble upon you, you leather jacket-wearing asshole? What kind of animal were you, out there urinating in the weeds? I wasn't looking at you...

She pulled the car to a stop.

She hung her head in defeat upon the wheel.

She again yielded to the memory, allowed herself to revisit the urine and alcohol smell, to feel the repulsive touch, her trembling stomach, to taste the bile in her throat.

She closed her eyes and watched as he walked away into the woods, his eyes shrouded by mirrored prescription glasses.

Watched him reappear in court, saw him glare and again walk away—this time in handcuffs and an orange prison jumpsuit.

Experienced her family's shouts of approval, saw her slender fist clench as he uttered the word *perfect*.

"Time for the healing to begin, girl," Amy heard Kathy assert as her head was raised from its station.

"He's gone," she reminded herself.

Let's go.

"To where?" she quietly asked.

It was then that she recalled the embrace, the warmth of the man who last sincerely and carefully held her.

He's the one for now, she assured herself, as she placed the car into drive and pressed the accelerator to the floor.

Within the span of a trio of Elton John songs, she was wiping at her blue eyes and looking down upon the illuminated town of Rice.

She crossed herself in a gesture of prayer.

"I can't go much further," she whispered. "Please have him be home."

As she slowed, she spotted his car in the drive.

The radiating, beckoning light within the shelter before the vehicle induced from her an almost involuntary deep sigh of relief.

"Thank goodness," she whispered.

It was all he could do to restrain himself.

Reclining behind the wheel of the brand-new car.

Man! It was too much, too hot.

He looked away, out upon the sight of the bishop mowing his lawn.

Probably for the thousandth time, Bob mused.

That man was a veritable prisoner of Andrews.

As for himself, he had options.

This task he'd begun that summer was near completion—one defeat away.

This, the class he'd drawn near, the cohort that had defined him as a baseball man.

He'd not be tethered to any subsequent Andrews teams.

When the counselor job lapsed into *burnout,* he'd then singe the ground with his hasty departure.

He looked back to his left, filled with gratitude by the sight.

Nothing anywhere could have compared with having her so near.

Her kiss, still not yet dry on his cheek, had left him absolutely overawed.

He leaned over and caressed her tan wrist.

"Where to?" she asked.

"Wherever you want, pretty eyes," he said softly, attempting to look into the enchanting blue orbs.

"I've got a few places to go. What if I leave you off at your house for now?" she said, looking out the driver's window.

"Okay, my love," he replied.

He was willing to accede to any of her requests.

She smiled sweetly, still without looking in his direction, then started the car and drove onto the street.

He remained silent until they'd left the city limits.

He then decided to breach the quiet—to let her know.

"I feel crushed," he said languidly.

Again, she smiled.

"You say you've got a crush on me?" she'd interjected more than once at UNEI. "Sounds like something a prep school boy would say."

He was certain that was the reason behind the grin.

Oh well, he reflected.

What she had vested him with had made him feel years younger.

She was a veritable *fountain of youth,* he mused.

He watched her as she crested the hill and drove into the hotel parking lot.

She had not spoken a word throughout the journey, a fact he found intriguing, considering the verbose manner in which she'd inexplicably pounded at his door the previous evening.

She had been stammering and shaking when he opened the door.

He was quite unsettled by the sight.

Her overwrought condition, conveyed to him through the medium of tears, had prompted him to wrap a blanket immediately around her.

"It's so dark," she said repeatedly as he guided her gently to the couch.

"So damn cold."

It frightened him, he had to admit, to see *his* powerful girl reduced to that.

He watched until a gradual calm came over her, was still watching as she apsed into a deep sleep.

He'd locked the door then and lain down on a blanket below her.

He was alternately tranquilized by her gentle breathing and unsettled by her periodic fitful, convulsive shaking.

He'd remained there for two hours, torn between his desire to immerse himself in the gentle stream and his wish to enhance the comfort of the one who somehow needed his compassion.

He was startled when he'd woken at 10:00 a.m. to discover her resting next to him.

Her breath gently ebbed and flowed, in a flawless, symmetrical tribute to her restored sanity.

She was no less beautiful, he felt, with her tousled curls and eyes covered by the prohibitive lids.

In fact, he felt she was made somehow more gorgeous as a result.

Her tan, lithe frame was adorned only with a white bra and white panties.

He'd rubbed a trembling hand over her firm belly.

The incendiary touch had seared him, blistered him, until he could no longer breathe.

Integrity scarcely intact, he rolled hurriedly away and rushed to the bathroom, daring not to look back.

"Here we are," Amy uttered softly, staring straight ahead at the hotel door.

"Yep. Do you want to come in for a second?" he asked softly.

"No," she replied, vacant eyes still staring through to nowhere.

Someone stole her passion, he lamented, *took it quick.*

He stepped out.

"Thanks, Amy," he said.

"Yep," she responded, then backed away.

He looked longingly at her, as the memory of that morning returned to him.

He walked in only after she'd left his line of vision.

If I had anything—money, time, looks, confidence—I'd empower her without end, he informed himself.

I'd let her just dive in, whenever she wants. Wouldn't ask for anything in return either.

"Yes, it would be an affront. Definitely," he affirmed as he stepped into the shower.

He rubbed shampoo onto his sparse hair, soap onto his pliant midriff.

It was she who had the might, the power here, he reflected.

It was like the strong, forlorn man he'd served beer to in The Stein—the man who had been betrayed by the steroid manufacturers, the muscle magazines, as he pursued the specter of attractiveness.

It was all ineffectual.

Chiseled physique, a wasteland—because he couldn't push or pull any of their coeds near his DMSO-sated frame in the manner like he did the weights.

"It wasn't enough," he said as he shut off the water and began drying himself.

"Who knew why?"

Why was the successful CEO brought to his knees by the minimum-wage secretary he inappropriately fondled?

Why was the U.S. wrestler inhibited from winning a certain gold medal—not by a powerful Russian opponent, but by the girl he allegedly raped in the Olympic Village?

Why the debate over whether or not an athlete should have sex the evening before competition?

You, he presumed, *could not be masculine enough to elude their impact.*

"Women, man, anyway," he said gently.

He finished toweling himself as he sauntered toward the bedroom. As he placed a tank top and shorts on his frame, his mind flashed to that morning, when he'd done the same.

It was after that morning's shower that he'd felt the urge to cook for her—to replenish whatever strength she'd lost while captured within that ominous nocturnal trap.

He duplicated that morning ritual now, again placing two eggs into a pan and adjusting the flame on the stove. Another two slices of wheat bread were placed in the toaster. He reached for the same jar of instant coffee, placed the same amount in the same cup, and began to stir.

There would be no Amy to call upon now, though.

Would be no awe-inspiring picture of her rounding the corner, dressed in a pair of his athletic shorts and an old UNEI T-shirt.

He smiled at the recollection.

The elegant angel displayed so unfashionably, rubbing at blinking eyes.

"God, she was still beautiful," he whistled.

She would have to strive impossibly hard to become anything less in his eyes.

No, he couldn't help but stare at her on that pretty summer morning.

Hell, he asked, why would he *not* have wanted to?

He was certain now that no man in that slumbering town could have considered himself as fortunate as he, at that hour.

For how many within that valley were within an arm's length of their muse?

Were addicted to someone who treated them so well?

"Damn! I can't wait until she comes back!" he said excitedly.

"Did you sleep well?" was the first question he'd asked her that day.

"I slept fine, thank you," she replied.

"I've got a practice scheduled for 1:00. Can you stay around for a while?" he'd asked, recalling having glanced at the clock to discover that the time was 11:30 a.m.

"Sure," she'd said, as his spirits soared.

"I'll drive you into town."

"Great, thanks," he said reverently.

"When is your next game?" the sweet voice had inquired.

"Tomorrow at Lare. We play Monroe Valley. It's a tournament game. If we lose, the season's over," he said nonchalantly.

"You'll win," the goddess assured him.

"I hope so. We don't hit much, especially without Pel ."

"I heard about Pell. It's a shame," she'd said sincerely.

"It certainly is," he'd affirmed, as he watched her finish her breakfast and rise from the table.

He'd followed her departure with longing in his heart as she hastened to the shower; would float behind her in the gentle breeze as they approached the car; had wrapped himself in the warmth of her conciliatory nature as she hastened to deliver him to the practice site.

Lending of herself the love that crested the banks of her tender heart to him—one who'd certainly default on repayment.

Wow!

It was all so overpowering that when she finally took leave of him after kissing his cheek, he no longer fretted over having scheduled his one and only Sunday practice session.

Yes, she was magic.

For up until her arrival, he'd been haunted by the image of the Old Dutch's lament, a half dozen years before.

The man had fielded a great team that year, and in his desire to sharpen his cat's claws for the postseason, he'd scheduled a practice on the Sunday before their first-round game versus Kent's Andrews squad.

Seems their *ace* had skipped the practice in order to attend a church-sponsored event, and so, to prove a point, Dutch had opted to withhold the pitcher from participating in the first three innings of play.

Of course, he was probably just power posturing, as he was heavily favored to upend the then outmanned, young Falcons.

But Juhl had made the decision turn into a twenty-four-hour nightmare, protecting the 3–0 cushion the Falcons had supplied him against the Cats' sophomore hurler.

By the time the Cats' ace entered the fray, the Cats' splendid season was all but over.

Poor Dutch, Bob mused.

Must've not been familiar with the commandments.

At least not that one.

Bob had no such dilemma to face with his band of overachievers.

They were all there that Sabbath afternoon, impressing him so much with their flawless defensive display that he called the session to an abrupt halt a half hour earlier than planned.

He used the extra time to commend them for the manner in which they'd come together as a unit that season.

He smiled as he placed the eggs onto the toast and sat down at the table.

It had gone so remarkably well that day.

They'd worked solely on the crossover step—the critical fundamental, as Cal Ripken had called it in Baseball Weekly.

Without the employ of this lateral movement, one would be forever backpedaling or springing erroneously forward at the sight of the ball coming in their direction, he'd told them."Try to run backward for a while," he told them.

"Feel how bad it feels, how your body is jarred with each choppy step. Observe how bad it feels to place your posterior blindly in front of impenetrable advancing teammates and unyielding wire fences.

"Touch base with the embarrassment," he continued, his eyes set upon the nodding heads of former football defensive backs, Greg and Brad, "as you move aggressively forward to try to intercept a certain short pass.

"Feel how helpless you are after the pump fake, as the ball flies over your head, beyond your line of vision. Hear your opponents mock your effort.

"Balance. Vision. Preparation, gentlemen," he reminded them as they ran, facing home, as they galloped away from him toward the centerfield fence.

He laughed at the recollection—their exaggerated arm movements belying the graceful fashion in which they soon after pursued and ensnared the fly balls he sent their way. Pivoting, pointing, crossing—as they were—they brought back long-dormant good memories to him.

His dad boasting in his now-deceased uncle's bar of how Bob had calmly run down a long fly to preserve a win in some long-forgotten Little League game; that same man hitting a ragged baseball to him in a pasture adjacent to the crowded farmhouse, uttering in awe at how well Bob played the tough ones.

"Damn!" he exclaimed reverently.

"The man really cared nothing for the game, had never been caught watching a single pitch on television. If he could become so smitten by the sight of the catch... wow!"

He finished the sandwich and stood.

His consciousness swarmed by the perpetual buzz emanating from aluminum siding as it was assailed by the softballs his kind father had tossed to his swaggering offspring.

The diabetic blackout the elder man lapsed into was the only thing that inhibited the continuation of such blissful activity—until deep into that magical night...

And then she emerged, swarming with affection on this hallowed day.

"Yes!" he exclaimed as he set the coffee cup in the microwave.

Sundays—oh, how he'd now forever cherish them—would forever equate them with his two loves.

And so, now he smiled again as the bell sounded and the cup was removed from the oven.

Because now, he said, retiring to the beckoning couch, they'd both come back to bless him—to rebuild him.

He'd wait on her, he determined, as he watched John Burkett deliver the first pitch of the game to Marquis Grissom.

Would sit right here and be made whole.

He yawned and leaned back, secure in the knowledge that no longer would she play Lucy to his Charlie Brown.

He could smell the sweet fragrance now, could taste the fresh, new air as he followed through by the sight of defeated anxiety sailing through the yielding blue.

As Kendall received the throw from Vale after retiring Monroe Valley's leadoff hitter in the bottom of the seventh, Bob had come to believe.

Two outs away.

All the breaks they'd been catching of late—he smiled.

How could he not feel this way?

"Damn! Bear down, Kendall!" he gushed.

★ ★ ★ ★ ★

This team had erased much of his pervasive self-doubt, the same doubt that had nearly destroyed him.

These boys had allowed him to rewrite his flawed past on the same Northwest Indiana field of his youth.

"Ah, redemption," he sighed.

And then, there was *her*, springing forth from the same sacred earth.

Again and again, he smiled as he looked past Greg and onto the urbane, refined Queens woman.

"Ahhh, the passion," he sighed, as his feet moved quickly in time to the up-tempo instrumental music in his head.

He looked back onto the field, to the satisfied look worn by Brad.

Consistent with the rhythm of the times, it was the unexpected, pleasant surprise—this time delivered by the normally light-hitting man—who'd placed them in this glorious position.

And not only had he doubled in Kendall for the first and only run of the game, but he'd also thrown out a runner at second *and* third.

"Good ole Brad," Bob sighed.

"Good ole defense," he whispered with a smile.

No outs and a man on third in the fourth, and Monroe still couldn't score.

He loved the excitement he felt when he saw Kendall snare the line drive and fire to Rusty for that inning's concluding double play.

And who would have thought they would escape unscathed for the fourth time that game—just an inning later?

No way, he mused, would he have believed that the tiring Kendall would turn it around after that conference.

God, he'd been aiming so bad.

He laughed softly at Bart's response to the spectacle.

"You can't catch a fish that you can see, Kendall."

That's the first thing he'd uttered to Kendall at the summit.

You can't catch a fish that you can see.

Damn, it actually worked.

With bases loaded and one out, what really could he have said?

Nobody was in the bullpen; it was Kendall's game to lose.

He was surprised at how relaxed he felt as he told Kendall, "I don't care if you give up the slam as long as you use the proper motion."

Bullshit. That's what it was.

He'd have cried like a little bitch to see this one slip away.

But it all worked.

Kendall seemed to relax after that interlude, inducing back-to-back ground outs to the box.

1-2 and 1-3.

Like there was nothing to it.

It was, he concluded, fate.

A sweet, pristine 1–0 victory was soon to be theirs.

"Ahh, sweet justice," he sighed.

He'd run onto the field to exchange Kendall's glove for the batting helmet he wore on his head.

So what if he'd just been stranded on third in the seventh, he reflected.

When they met in the coach's box, he *knew* God was a Falcon fan that night—that He had touched the hand of each of the zealous, gloved youth who stood on the dirt now before Sellers.

"Praise God!" he shouted aloud suddenly.

Bart looked languidly at him, then back onto the field.

Sellers didn't notice; his eyes were now reverently cast upon the heavens.

"Looks like rain," he mumbled as he looked upon the wall of dark clouds approaching from the west.

A smile returned to his face when he observed, juxtaposed among the clouds, the beaming, brilliant ball above him.

"Good ole sun," he whispered affectionately.

Shining down upon him and his.

"Thank you!" he shouted again.

"You alright?" Bart laughed.

"Yeah, man," Sellers sighed, gleaming, basking, watching the golden rays keep the darkness at bay.

"Falcons win," he whispered.

In an incongruent instant, his world went dark, his brilliant light nullified by a fleeting wisp of a cloud.

At the very moment the bright globe reappeared, Sellers was overwhelmed by dread.

"Forget you," he mumbled defiantly to the voice.

"Bad karma, son," it had laughed at him. "It's over."

No, I can't believe it! We've gotten this close. Why? He challenged the medium.

His eyes looked to her, sought her as a salve.

He looked upon the vacant, dazzling blue eyes, the blonde curls, the sculpted body.

He closed his eyes desperately, endeavoring to preserve the sight, to fill his consciousness with hope, to counter the damn voice...

"Goodbye, Amy Lou," the spirit whispered into his ear.

"Shit," he moaned. "You win," he spoke into the wind.

"Strike!" the umpire shouted.

He looked out at the scoreboard, past the pacing Alex at shortstop.

0 and 2, it spoke to him.

Think it through, Greg, he pleaded.

"What the hell's he doing setting up down the middle?" he asked Bart.

"Pick a corner, Greg!" Bart shouted to the backstop.

"Waste one," Bob pleaded, as Kendall lifted his hands above his head.

To his dismay, Greg remained stationary, his target centered over the heart of the plate.

Rusty had no chance to stop the line drive base hit that flew near his left shoulder seconds later.

"Damn it," Sellers cursed. "What the hell is this?" he asked the voice.

Why now? This is cruel.

He stopped mid-thought as Kendall's first pitch to the next hitter was bounced back to the mound.

"Turn two!" he shouted.

Cralt stood at second, waving his hands.

Kendall paid him no mind as he stepped and threw to Vale at first.

"Oh no," Bob moaned.

"It's over," he heard again.

"There's two outs," he countered.

"Yeah, but the winning run's at second. One mistake and—"

"Yeah, but one out and we're in. Clean-up man is up. He's 0 for 3. Damn it!" he cursed aloud.

"What's wrong?" Bart asked.

"This is anguish, man."

"What are you going to do? I say we pitch to 'em, go after the son of a bitch," Bart suggested.

"Can't we put him? Doesn't that go against *the book*?" Sellers asked vacantly.

"You know what you can do with that damn book. I didn't write it.

"Trust me on this."

Bob stood, ruing the *no-win* dilemma he felt certain he was caught upon, wishing to death that the same asshole who'd written *the book* had made a clock to regulate this game.

Football, basketball, hockey—there you could stall if you were ahead.

Run and hide, eluding time.

Time was no one's ally on the diamond, he lamented, as his feet were set into motion.

"He can get 'em. Let 'em reach deep, butt heads with the cocky bastard," he could hear Bart's advice, even as his feet hit the dirt.

"Damn time anyway," he said as his hand was raised.

"Time," the singular word was shouted—the command creating the only empowering response he'd ever had while in the dugout.

As the umpire raised his hand, a calm filled him.

The only privilege, the only thing he could do to suspend his descent, to keep the bad stuff away.

"What the hell are you doing?" he heard Bart shout above the crowd.

The force with which the question was presented induced him to snap around, to look at his scowling assistant.

His head jerked, then automatically turned toward her.

A warm smile greeted him.

He looked next toward his infielders on the hill.

He felt compelled, obligated now.

"I must defer to the messenger," he mumbled as he summoned the outfielders to the conference.

Perplexed looks locked onto him as they drew near from their original stations.

They'd never been invited to these gatherings by Sellers before—a fact of which he was well aware.

"Gentlemen," he began, "regardless of what goes down here, I just want to let all you jackasses know that I'm proud of all of you."

He waved into the dugout, motioning for his reserves to join them.

He saw them look quizzically at one another, then saw Bart disgustedly wave them away from the bench.

"Go see what the hell he wants," he heard Bart's exasperated shout.

"Vale! Hand! Roost! Welcome!" he said when the subs arrived.

"Just telling these guys that I don't give a damn what happens here.

"I just want to express my gratitude for your support and efforts this year.

"Thanks to all of you."

Stunned silence followed his words.

The nervous pacing within the circle was penetrated finally by Alex.

"Don't worry, Bob," he asserted.

"Thanks," Bob smiled in response to the reassuring words.

"Go get 'em, K.B.," he said, then walked away.

Not exactly a pep talk, he admitted, but he knew it would seem much more sincere now than later—when it all fell.

"Damn it, why'd you do that? They had momentum. That's gone now," he heard Bart's critical tirade as he looked into the stands.

She was walking away, back toward him.

"It's over, Amy," he informed her.

"It's like this," he began as his feet met the concrete dugout floor.

He then fell silent and sat down at the far edge of the cage.

He had started to explain his decision to his accomplished assistant but then thought better of it.

Bart would never understand—as he had won way too often, he mused.

It'd just piss him off, this message.

The cleanup hitter climbed into the box, one hand held in the air, as he dug his spikes forcefully into the dirt, tapped the bat onto his heel, then rubbed his uniform shirt.

Same thing every time, Bob reflected.

Superstitious son of a bitch, just like me.

Did I step over the chalk lines on my return? he asked himself.

Damn it, he lamented, *I was too busy looking for her. If I did...*

He watched, stunned, as the initial offering was hit right back to the mound.

"Must have had my wires crossed," he said aloud, rising to his feet.

Bad karma or no, the ball's rolling right to Kendall. If he just picks it up and throws it over to Vale, then it's over, he mocked the demon.

"Easiest play in baseball," he shouted giddily to Bart, repeating what Bart had always called the 1–3 putout.

Inexplicably, the ball hopped over Kendall's glove and headed out of the infield—with Bob's hopes.

At the eleventh hour, Alex somehow snared the ball as he dived to his knees.

"Wow!" Bob shouted in awe.

A midnight reprieve, a stay of execution on postseason's death row.

What a trip!

Clouds portending disaster? Fate? Emotion?

What had they to do with baseball?

Computer analysis, science, biomechanics—master them, and the game became your servant, your toy.

Research. Effort.

Certain success.

Isolate the variables and control.

Power.

"I'm crazy to buy into voices," he mused, unsettled by the temporary departure he'd taken from sanity.

Damn!

On the field, Alex struggled to set himself for the throw.

As the big Monroe Valley man raced for the bag. Alex released the ball while still on his knees.

It wasn't even close to reaching Vale.

As Vale bent at the waist, Bart's advice from the preseason came hustling toward him.

"Vale can't dig out the low ones. He's not the man for first."

"Shit!" Sellers yelled, shaken to his very core by the sight of the ball skipping off the base of the dugout screen directly at his feet.

He took a seat as the Monroe Valley runner scored standing up.

The cheers of the Monroe Valley fans nailed him, left him affixed to his seat, even as Kendall struck out the following hitter.

"What the hell?" he asked aloud.

"What in the world could the ball have hit in front of the mound?

Maybe we can plant my damn heart out there, soften it up a little."

"You joining us?" Bart asked as the eighth inning began.

"Nah. Hand, go coach first."

We ain't gonna get anybody on anyway, he lamented beneath his breath.

Three batters later, and Kendall led the reluctant Falcons back onto the field.

"This is the last inning he can pitch, Coach. Eight innings per game, that's the state rule," the umpire yelled over.

Sellers shook his head and waved in acknowledgment.

"Should've never been an eighth," he muttered.

Kendall grooved his first pitch to the number six hitter.

As the ball found the left-field gap, Bob, head bowed, rose to his feet and stepped out of the dugout.

The MV fans' cheers again accompanied him.

"Wow," he sighed as he walked toward the Monroe dugout.

"Time!"

"What the..." He looked up and saw the umpire's hands raised in the air.

Sheepishly, he noticed that the man had stopped on third.

"Nah, that's okay, blue," he asserted.

"I think I'm losing it," he said sadly, then turned away.

Should have just let it go, Johnny and Brad, he muttered.

Let that evil leather piece of crap roll on into the hell it rose from.

Should have just turned your back on it and walked silently away off this damned field.

"It's over anyway," he whispered as he opened the dugout door.

"Who cares?" he asked the blackening sky.

In a moment, he was able to officially begin mourning— to confront the loss that had stalked him all evening.

The soft, silent tap.

The perfect execution of the squeeze bunt.

Banished them all to the desert of the offseason, making sudden alums of the seniors, stealing a year of eligibility from the underclassmen.

Sellers looked out in particular dismay on the sight of Kendall, choking on the dust of the town in which he was born.

Could've been me celebrating, his perplexed countenance seemed to convey, through the residue of his former homeboy's slide across home.

Bob was sure he'd never forget this place.

This heartbreaking...

He sought for the words, sought for something to curse.

They had to use a damn bunt to beat me?

Weak, wimpy ass...

He threw the bats in the bag for the final time—the same one they'd packed some fifteen years earlier in Rice, he reflected.

He'd blamed *them*, blamed the town, their methods then also.

It was, he realized now, beyond the scope of human manipulation and understanding—these last-second defeats.

It would be more appropriate, he lamented, to direct his ire at the ephemeral presence that had so pointlessly pulled elation from his grasp.

That unforgiving spirit, he moaned, the one who'd removed the hero's crown from two brothers' heads on one misguided play.

In their former hometown.

"Damn," he sighed, then left the premises.

He heard the Monroe Valley players' ongoing celebration behind him, listened to his own players' exasperated grief as he looked upon the bus.

That yellow *coach*, he mused, was now a veritable pumpkin; it was midnight in his soul.

Blinking, he looked again to her.

He watched her speak to the umpire.

The man in blue, he scoffed. *What's he know about being blue?*

He ain't gonna lose, this voyeur of my game, he muttered as he watched the man lean closer to his new admirer.

The act, he determined now, would sentence him to a life of remembering her with bitter acrimony.

"To hell with it all," he swore.

"I should have known better, should have realized she wouldn't return to me last night."

He kicked the beer can before him and suppressed an unexpected compulsion to laugh.

"We're over," he sang sarcastically as he turned and resumed his trek to the bus.

"This sucks," he muttered.

"Welcome to *The Real World*," he heard the MTV asshole say, inviting him to view the televised antics of a selfish bunch of twenty-something fools.

No thanks.

Real world, he sang softly, in rhythm to his farewell march.

Where good is always in, Cowboys don't cry, he sang loudly now.

At the top of his voice, he continued,

Darlin', it's sad but true, but the one thing I've learned from you is that the boy don't always get the girl, here in the...

"Real world!"

He was startled to hear Bart join in the refrain, his eyes now gazing at the pretty blonde apparition, the diaphanous cloud, floating away from them.

"Yeah, *here in the Real World!"* they now sang in unison as they entered the bus.

The players glumly filled in, their frowns replaced by amused, curious looks as they observed the aberrant spectacle—the very off-key rendition of the Alan Jackson song performed by Bob and Bart.

"Let's get the hell out of here, Bart," Bob asserted after the last man, Kendall, entered.

"We'll cruise by her on the way out."

Bart pressed the horn forcefully and continued sounding the bell as she appeared in their view.

A thin smile was returned to them, the countenance visiting them for but an instant before the blue eyes turned away—looking at and through the blue-clad man before her.

"Bye-bye, baby," Bob shouted through the laughter.

A blend of envy and awe could be felt in the room by her colleagues as the secretary set the fifth set of a dozen roses on the desk, bearing the nameplate:

Amy V., County Administrative Assistant

Amy opened the card that lay in the center of the crimson bouquet, then positioned the new addition next to the flowers given to her by Tony, Dan, John, and Marty.

"What's it say, Amy?" Shelly asked.

Amy recited:

"Amy, years ago on this date, you gave me roses as a symbol of gratitude for my concern for you. I always promised myself I'd return the favor. Figure late is better than never. I hope these brighten your day, just as the memory of you has always brightened mine. Have a great Valentine's Day! Love, Bob Sellers."

"How nice!"

"That's sweet!"

Amy shuddered, despite their affirmation.

He is never going to stop, she lamented.

"Who's he?" Joann inquired.

"Oh, just some asshole from Rutgers," Amy replied, reflecting upon the possible motivation for his action.

"Hey, I'll take the flowers if you don't want them," Joann laughed.

"Oh, by the way, your fiancé called."

"Thanks," Amy said vacantly.

She threw his card beneath the pile of Valentine's cards on her desk and picked up the phone.

"You ain't foiling me, ain't disrupting my dreams," she mumbled as she dialed.

"You're going down."

"Wedding still scheduled for June?" Joann asked in parting.

"Far as I know," Amy replied with a wink, looking past her colleague at the snow falling outside the window.

Just a few things to tie up first.

"Damn it!" Bob cursed the snowflakes that clouded his vision as he drove east.

He despised winter driving, but he felt he had to set sail now—to secure whatever freedom there was left to grasp in these Indiana hills.

This, he surmised, was pure, unmitigated pain—a torturous ride he'd never get off.

One that had him reeling and wrenching during the day, screaming himself awake at night.

Up to this point, he'd felt the worst thing that had happened to him was being terminated as coach/counselor, his contract buyout.

Option exercised by Thorson.

"Shit," he sneered.

That was *pussy stuff* compared to this hell.

"You've shown an inability to properly direct the actions of those adolescents under your supervision," he heard Thorson assert, "as was evidenced in the bottle-throwing incident subsequent to the O'Ryan game and the unethical actions you took during the Wells game..."

"Screw you,' he snarled at the visage of Thorson for the hundredth-and-something time following his ouster.

The old Impala whined and bogged on as it climbed.

Bob shifted into low gear and pushed forward.

This was, he admitted, flat-out crazy.

But, he lamented, he was already screwed.

Five years.

Geez, he shuddered.

This was horrible.

No more walks, no more restaurants, getting jammed by *Bubba*—and why?

He asked the livestock to his left.

Why was such a *punitive measure* required?

What purpose would be served?

What value to society restored?

What were they trying to teach his old ass?

It'd only kill him, that's all.

Drive him completely insane.

What had Socrates asserted—that an unexamined life was not worth living?

Conversely, he stated, reflection without life was energy squandered.

That, he lamented, would be his lot—huddled in a frigid hell, analyzing his unnecessary existence, experiencing his neurotic, eroding psyche, worsening by the minute, seeing himself sink into permanent financial and spiritual ruin.

This was a real bad idea, he established as he looked to his left.

He trembled at the sight of his being captured, felt the cuffs bite into his wrist again.

He could see those self-righteous, arrogant assholes look at him like he was crazy, like he'd lost his mind—looking *through* him as they stacked up the bodies, feeling happy they were on the *right* team.

"Kjos," he uttered, looking to the north.

He could play this game.

He'd broken through every obstacle set before him, smiling smugly, defiantly.

"Alcoholism, drug addiction, assaults," Sellers began reciting.

"Surgeries, jail, arthritis, death threats."

The son of a bitch couldn't be shut down.

"That's who I should go to now," he whispered. "Get some ideas."

Ole boy was probably laying up with Cindy, his nineteen-year-old girl—that drop-dead gorgeous girl some fourteen years his junior.

The ultimate spoil of this successful battle to survive.

Maybe she had a friend for him.

She wouldn't even have to look good.

He turned on the windshield wipers and slowed his pace, struggling to decide.

Certainly, he'd not win.

But with each labored mile he drove, the compulsion to yield the dreams of polite society weakened.

If he'd learned anything from his hearty three dozen years of living, it was that it was all *bullshit*, this guise of civility.

His freedom—as the price to preserve the honor of a precocious ho?

Friggin' Andrea...

Man, but what would he do until they got 'em?

How would he preserve his dignity, his sanity?

Failure to appear.

Geez.

He used to question the mental health of those who'd flee from reality as he had today.

But now he understood.

It was a setup.

And what in heaven's name had compelled her to testify?

He didn't exactly *take* it.

"Why in the hell did I ever come home?" he lamented, as a harder rain began pelting his getaway car.

Damn baseball anyway.

None of this would've happened if he hadn't got the fever, he told himself.

What a reward I got for my efforts, he sneered.

Heartbreaking loss, termination, incarceration, death...

He felt the tears well up again as the d word triggered the painful reality of the untimely loss of Rusty.

"Damn it, shake it," he commanded himself.

He peered harder into the maelstrom.

Should've stayed down on the farm.

Should turn back—it'd impress the judge.

What are you doing?

His thoughts raced onward, recklessly, scattered by fear.

The farm, he reflected, as a gradual calm filled him.

Good ole Martens. Good ole Dan.

He was thankful for the call that had finally induced him to step down from the Rice precipice—the winter call that ended his 100-day stay in the *compound*.

"So what if it was only a pity party held in his honor?" he asked the rain.

He'd felt good carrying the numerous pails of feed to the swine, even on the bitterest cold day—happy to be *producing*, to be wakening himself from his sedentary slumber.

And so what if he'd felt typecast as the idiot savant brother-in-law, the one who mixed the wrong blend of ingredients and jammed up feed grinders?

He hadn't made any costly mistakes, hadn't done any damage that Dan couldn't easily repair.

"Just keep it slow," he reminded himself as he drove through Elphane.

"Be like these old boys in these hills," he said with a nod of his head toward the elderly man driving with his dog in the approaching pickup.

Don't overmanage or outsmart yourself.

Their methods worked, despite their lack of formal education.

They were the backbone of society—the ones who provided the jobs that sustained the white-collar professionals until they matriculated from their universities.

All would be a giant intellectual session without them.

Gridlock.

"Work, dummy," he reminded himself. "That's the answer. Don't turn your back on the culture, Mr. CEO," he scoffed in self-deprecation.

But onward he drove—away from the one who'd sired him, away from the men who taught him to survive humbly with minimal resources, and toward the arms of those who expected his addled brain to provide him with more than he'd ever be able to handle.

Indeed, even as he patted the $1,500 degrading *buyout* money Thorson had bestowed upon him, his mind sailed again toward the illusion he'd chased all the way from Martens.

That same vision conceived in the UNEI library, the one that would seemingly never expire.

The one kept alive by the boys at the clubhouse, Sir John's free lunches, Tap paychecks, Kjos' energy...

They all played a role in chasing him back here—*sober* no less—to the memory of her.

The only spark there was left within him.

The only thing that had mattered for months.

Yes, they could lock him up, beat on him, rape him...

But he *knew* he'd be back, chasing that same teenage Amy.

He had, he was certain, *no choice.*

It was his lot—the futile pursuit worthy of this Cubs and Red Sox fan, desperately chasing glory in now eroding, antiquated venues, trying to ensnare that which was once there, that which was now *not meant to be...*

"Be easier to be up there with you, Rusty," he whispered as he slowed to a crawl, searching for the exit that would propel him south.

Crazy son of a buck, he smiled, as he pointed an index finger to the sky.

"Just wasn't meant to be for ya," he told the redheaded ghost as he looked at the car upturned in the ditch to his left.

He clutched the wheel tightly and shook his head, shaken by the reminder of how Rusty had perished.

His new girl—driving his drunk ass home, doing the right thing, the safe thing—and still got stuck.

"It just ain't fair, Rusty," he said somberly.

"Two hours," he reminded himself as he started south.

Two hours and he'd be with her... *memory.*

Just *one night.*

That's all he wanted.

Then they could extradite him, kill him.

One night beneath the shadows of the UNEI campus, looking upon Holmgren.

"Damn it," he cursed.

"This is bizarre—sending her roses from 200 miles away, kissing her departed ass.

What a losing game.

Pure heartbreak.

Recreating the whole scene that began his demise— those bloody flowers sent him less than forty hours after their unlikely convergence.

"Damn, that was a long time ago," he exclaimed as he turned slowly to the right.

Nine years.

He wouldn't even recognize either of them if he saw them as they looked on that Valentine's Day.

Her in that elegant black coat, black stretch pants, heels, lipstick enhancing a smug smile.

Him in that old gray sweater and nine-dollar jeans.

He stepped on the accelerator, anxious to escape, to procure that lost portion of himself locked within the soft Indiana vessel.

It would be a challenging quest—to unearth the integral component from beneath the rubble of dozens of her flawed romantic liaisons, to search for something that was of no interest to her.

Certainly, he lamented, she'd offer no assistance in the excursion.

He was, he feared, *expendable* to her.

"Screw it," he moaned.

He had to resolve this soon.

He heard the words of the old Black gentleman in the gift shop, after lamenting his lifelong futile pursuit of troublesome women.

"I can do bad by myself."

"I heard that!" Sellers muttered.

"I *heard* that."

He turned to the left and resumed his drive to the east.

He patted the novel that lay on the seat beside him, touching his fingers yet again upon the beautiful face appearing on the glossy back cover.

"I love ya, girl," he whispered as he peered out onto the *Days Inn* billboard ad.

"Should just stop, baby. Stay in the hotel and read your whole book. Get your inspiring words etched in my head, before it all falls..."

"Damn!" he exclaimed as he missed the exit that would have delivered him to the lobby.

On he drove, barely able to read the road sign through the snow.

Harrison 100, Queens 96.

Oh well.

In less than two hours, his fugitive ass would be basking in the glow of the moon—illuminated, if only temporarily, by the brilliant, long-awaited reunion, he informed himself.

"Yeah, right," he mumbled sarcastically, as he slammed on his brakes and began his descent toward Verde County.

Amy opened the door onto her spacious porch and trudged toward her favorite chair.

She set herself gently between its inviting royal purple arms and resumed her scrutiny of the outskirts of Berlin, New Hampshire.

"Damn MCA," she mumbled, cursing the long-distance intrusion that had prompted her to take temporary leave of her post.

"Like I want to write another book," she grumbled.

"Ah," she sighed as she placed her feet on the footrest.

"It's good to be home again," she mused, reflecting now upon the past week's bus tour of the Northeast.

She was happy she had signed on with the senior citizen group that past winter.

It was simply too tiring for her to be on the road for more than an hour these days.

After all, she wasn't seventy anymore.

In the past week, they had seen the Capitol building, touched the Liberty Bell, climbed within the Statue of Liberty, and watched a baseball game in an antiquated venue they referred to as *New Fenway.*

She never would have suspected that the latter would have had the greatest impact upon her.

It was not as if she could have told anyone who the participants were, let alone who won.

No, indeed.

But as she sat in her quaint fold-down chair that day, she became transfixed by the sight of the huge green wall in the portion of the playing surface the men referred to as left field.

The *Green Monster,* they called out to it reverently—just as he had some fifty years earlier.

She recalled how he'd looked on, awestruck, as the ball ricocheted high off the upper limits of the protuberance back then.

The mighty effort—thwarted.

Rewarded by being sent again back and down into the fray...

It was the metaphor for that poor Indian boy's existence.

It was not as if she thought of Sellers often, but when these *trigger* mechanisms were engaged, the memories could reappear in startlingly vivid hue.

The trip she and Tony...

She wiped a tear from her eye as she recalled how her recently departed husband had looked on that day.

They, upon her request, had embarked upon the trip north on the interstate, in his Jeep Cherokee, in the late February snowstorm—after the call from the Pryor Police Department.

Why they had called upon her first, she never quite understood.

They did make her aware of the fact that he had died clutching what would have been the first of the twelve novels she'd published.

The back cover of which—beneath his blood-speckled fingers, they said—had contained her name and phone number.

Why would he have been out there on that wicked night, in that car? she asked herself.

What was he trying to access at such an inappropriate hour?

Why didn't he just stand trial and do his time? she sighed, recalling how all of his meager possessions were within the shambles.

It was apparent he'd been endeavoring to create a new beginning for himself.

In essence, he'd done just that.

Certainly, he had to have been concerned with the potential consequences.

She'd spent her entire advance on inducing Andrea to testify, and her and her dad's friend, the honorable Dr. Vehlen, expedited the proceedings.

If only he'd not allowed him to be released on bond, she lamented.

But he *could* have done five, she assured herself— t wouldn't have destroyed him.

Traveling south in the northbound lane...

Wow, she whispered, seeing again the incredible damage wrought by the cattle truck.

Whether it was indecision or instinct that put him in its path, he'd certainly made a poor decision, she determined.

He hadn't even died on impact...

What could have been his final thoughts?

His emotional condition as he lay dying?

She wondered once more.

Probably relieved—happy to be spared the inevitable misery that he had to know would always be his five years in prison, she scoffed.

As if he would have accomplished anything outside the walls in that period of time.

No chance, she told herself, with amusement.

Seems as if he wanted to get her attention in his final inaction, she lamented.

Those roses—which had prompted her into trying to get him institutionalized to help him—it had to have been a plan.

Then the clutching of her book at that juncture.

What a pain in the ass, she laughed.

In life and in death, she mused.

The policeman's call had inspired her into immediate movement—to arrange his final departure, to begin to *bury* him.

Permanently.

She'd called Bart within minutes of receiving the news.

A long silence had filled the airwaves after she'd calmly informed him.

He'd said only barely audible words to her then.

"I'll meet you there."

He had no clue, no direction—unlike herself.

Poised. Proficient.

That's how she was in Pryor, she reflected with a smile.

Calmly signing for his possessions, instructing Bart and Tony to place them into Bart's van.

It was easy for her—even when her professional presentation of the script was met by the obligatory wails of denial from his relatives at the other end of the phone line.

Unflappable.

That's what she was that day.

And then, three days later, she'd stood shivering, standing atop the hill framing the cemetery in Andrews.

Adorned in black, she watched him be laid to rest.

But she *looked good,* she smiled.

Breathing easy she was, despite the awkward moment, the quizzical looks.

She felt proud when the priest handed the cross to Sellers's mother and then extended the invitation for all to adjourn at the church for a *potluck* lunch.

For she had, once again, taken the proper course of action.

Lowered herself to be there for her nemesis.

She suddenly recalled standing between Bart and Tony, watching the procession of cars wind their serpentine path back into Andrews.

When only the three of them remained, she silently and fleetingly embraced Bart, then opened the passenger door of the Jeep.

Tony had followed Bart away from the cemetery, but at Amy's instruction, he turned south, away from the town.

She simply had had enough.

Had paid her dues, she'd determined.

She did not want to be slowed by more ritual, did not wish to be regaled by more tales—like the one they told her of Rusty and Sellers on the hill by the motel.

Rusty pulling Sellers over on one of his nocturnal walks, soaking him with a water pistol filled with *beer*...

Geez.

They just weren't her people.

Were not part of her world.

Never would be—

Something *the guest of honor* had been unable to accept.

Lying there in the cliché suit, surrounded by fellow *hick* farm boys, he looked lost as ever.

And that elaborate speech composed by the local priest—singing the praises of the inept, twisted man.

It was all just too contrived, too rigged for her taste.

No one—not even those who'd informed her that they'd known him from birth—got it.

She would have been the exception, in possession as she was of the whole neurotic essence of their hometown boy.

And so it was that she'd wound her own final path away from the sight of him.

"Let's go to the ballpark," she'd instructed Tony when she'd reached into the back seat.

Adjacent to the blood-tarnished book bearing her phone number—my, but she could still see it *clearly*—were the dozen roses he'd sent.

She had brought them with her for a purpose.

These symbols of death—she wished to bury them with him as well.

Bad karma, Sellers would have described them.

Just the sort of things she wished to avoid carrying into her new life with Tony.

She could see herself opening the door of Tony's Jeep next, could still hear the crunch of snow beneath her feet as she walked to the cage in which he'd stood so often that summer.

The whistles and stares of the maintenance workers in the town sewer facility behind her did not affect her journey.

She stuck the first of the roses in the wire mesh and wound its stem about until the crimson plant was firmly entrenched in the screen.

She'd walked then onto the field—to the place that had had such a powerful emotional impact upon him.

It was the same place—when touched by Cralt that June night—that had prompted him to sprint onto the field, thrusting his arms into the air.

It was the same post that—when trammeled upon by his opponent in Lare that July—had induced him to cast a forlorn look in her direction, his mouth forming the word goodbye.

She smiled now, watching her younger self scrape the snow from the odd-shaped rubber surface and place a rose at its apex.

Of the remaining ten flowers, she'd spread nine on the bench, at an equal distance apart from one another.

The remaining rose she carried to the Jeep.

"Let's go," she told Tony.

Within minutes, they were traversing the bridge that would deliver her forever from that backward town.

As they crossed, she rolled down the window and tossed the final gift he'd given her into the frigid water below.

She stood slowly now, some forty-seven years removed from that momentous day, and congratulated herself on the successful life she'd lived.

Despite him and his ilk, she'd steadily and determinedly driven through the mire that was the residue of their careless living.

She caught a glimpse of it from the corner of her tired eye—the single red tulip she had not noticed before that day.

She bent over the wooden porch and picked it from the ground.

As she stood upright, she turned her back to the southwest wind and looked toward her native land.

It was a beautiful May day—much like the one on which she'd graduated decades ago, she recalled, smiling at the memory of that ceremony.

And on this nostalgic day, she engaged in another ceremony—this one made in memory of a confused, anxious man.

"He loved me," she said with a laugh as she flipped the first petal into the wind.

"He loved me not," she said as she grasped the second petal.

She quickly discovered there was an odd number of petals on the flower, became aware that ultimately, she'd arrive at the conclusion she'd drawn long ago on a Midwestern campus.

With a smile, she set the tulip on the rail of the porch and walked to the house—unaware at that moment that she'd not make it inside.

That the next step she took would carry her instead into the afterlife—

And by the time her body had collapsed onto the oak, she'd be sitting at a banquet filled with all the sweetness befitting heaven.

She hugged the cherubic Al and Angela and Tony and her mother, felt her spirits soar in a magical, transcendent way, felt the tears of joy flow from her now-restored eyes.

"*Perfect!*" she shouted reverently, drifting among the clouds.

"*Perfect! The long, glorious journey is finally beginning,*" she shouted melodically.

One that will never end. This is gr—

The shouted inquiry was heard from afar, disconnecting her from her thoughts.

She heard it again, saw the goofy apparition float nearer.

She rolled her eyes and raised her hand in the air, preparing to slap palms with her yet unrecognizable fellow angel as her eternal redemption began.

"Amy Lou!" it shouted with glee.

"Oh, brother," Amy sighed.

Printed by Libri Plureos GmbH in Hamburg, Germany